Architects of the Russian Avant-Garde

01

arnoldsche

Boris Velikovsky

1878–1937

Elena Ovsyannikova
Nikolai Vassiliev

Authors
Elena Ovsyannikova
Nikolai Vassiliev

General coordination
Leonid Mejibovski

Arnoldsche project coordination
Matthias Becher

Project manager
Tatiana Gantser

Translator
Kenneth John MacInnes

Text editor
Wendy Brouwer

Graphic design
ABCdesign

Offset reproductions
Repromayer, Reutlingen

Printed by
Gorenjski tisk, Kranj

Paper
170 gsm, Core Silk

Bibliographic information published by the Deutsche Nationalbibliothek
The Deutsche Nationalbibliothek lists this publication in the Deutsche Nationalbibliografie; detailed bibliographic data are available on the Internet at www.dnb.de.

ISBN 978-3-89790-478-1
Made in Europe, 2017

Archive material
Schusev State Museum of Architecture, Central State Archive of Scientific-Technical Documentation of Moscow, Central Historical Archive of Moscow, Central State Historical Archive of St Petersburg, Russian State Library

Photographs
Olga Alexeyenko, Nikolai Vassiliev, Nikolai Vymorkov, Nikolai Kulebyakin, Yuri Palmin

Cover illustration
Front: House of the Book, Moscow, no. 27
Back: Gostorg Building, Moscow, no. 20
Herzenberg Tenements, Moscow, no. 14

This book has been produced with the generous support of Dmitry Velikovsky

Contents

Biographical Outline

Boris Mikhailovich Velikovsky (1878–1937) was born into a Jewish family[1] in the small town of Propoisk in the Mogilyov Province of the Russian Empire. The town was renamed Slavgorod in 1945 and is now situated in the eastern part of the modern-day Republic of Belarus.

Slavgorod (previously Propoisk) stands at the point where the River Pronya flows into the River Sozh, forty-five miles from the city of Mogilyov. In 1938, the township numbered 4,700 inhabitants and was raised to the status of an urban settlement. In 1943, Soviet troops enjoyed military successes in the area, causing the town to be renamed Slavgorod (literally "glory city") shortly afterwards.

The town is extremely old and is first mentioned in 1136 as Proposhesk (from the original name of the River Pronya, which was known back then as the Propoi, meaning "a whirlpool at the confluence of two rivers"). After the partition of the Rzeczpospolita in 1772,[2] Propoisk was awarded to Prince Alexei Golitsyn by Catherine the Great. By 1880 there were more than 2,000 inhabitants. The 1897 census lists 4,351 inhabitants, 2,304 of whom were Jewish. The township and the surrounding villages boasted many industrial enterprises – tanning, brick, tile, cable and other factories – which were largely owned by Jews. In 1986, the town suffered from the accident at the Chernobyl Nuclear Power Plant. The population is now less than 8,000 people.[3]

During the reign of Catherine the Great, a number of restrictions were placed on the Jewish inhabitants of the Russian Empire, who were confined to an area known as the Pale of Settlement.[4] These limitations, however, did not affect merchants of the first guild or Jews with a higher education. This inspired Jews to acquire a good education, so that they could rise to a better place in society. As a result, Boris Velikovsky received excellent home schooling and passed the examination for the equivalent of six classes of Realschule.[5] This allowed him to enrol at the St Petersburg Institute of Civil Engineers in 1898.

The St Petersburg Institute of Civil Engineers was the oldest college of construction in Russia. It was founded under the auspices of the Chief Directorate of Transportation in 1832 and merged with the School of Architecture in 1842. In 1877 the college was awarded the status of a higher educational establishment. Many famous Russian architects and civil engineers graduated from the institute, which provided a more wide-ranging training than the department of architecture at the Imperial Academy of Arts.

While he was a student at the St Petersburg Institute of Civil Engineers, Velikovsky was drawn into the revolutionary movement and suspended for a year.[6] But he was allowed to continue his education and graduated from the institute in 1904. He then found employment at the architectural bureau of Sergei Solovyov in Moscow.

Sergei Ustinovich Solovyov (1859–1912) was one of the most authoritative architects in Moscow.

Like his teacher, Konstantin Bykovsky, he worked in the style known as Historicism.[7] *He engaged in a series of restoration projects with his brother-in-law, Dmitry Sukhov, who was a well-known restorer. Solovyov taught at the Imperial Stroganov Central School of Art and Industry, where he was the director for several years. He was an academician with an outstanding knowledge of European and Russian architectural history.*

Velikovsky joined Sergei Solovyov's studio at a time when it was designing two important buildings in Moscow – the Tretyakov Care Home[8] at 27 Bolshaya Serpukhovskaya Street and the Moscow Higher Courses for Women at 1 Malaya Pirogovskaya Street on the Devichye pole ("Maidens' Field"). The latter was Solovyov's most famous creation and the design team included the young architect Ilya Golosov, who later became one of the leaders of the avant-garde movement in Russian architecture. The engineering calculations were made by Vladimir Shukhov.[9] Velikovsky possibly had creative contacts with this fascinating individual and the chance to observe the construction of the paned vault, the reinforced-concrete ceilings and other modern elements which perfectly co-existed with the Neoclassical decor of the building.

In 1906, Velikovsky began working on private commissions as the partner of an experienced architect from Moscow called Alexei Milyukov.

Alexei Nikolaevich Milyukov (c. 1869–1914) was the son of the architect Nikolai Milyukov, the brother of the politician Pavel Milyukov and a cousin of the architect Nikolai Sultanov. Alexei Milyukov graduated from the Imperial Technical College in Moscow in 1884. He designed a series of buildings for the Tryokhgornaya Manufactory[10] *in 1896 and a number of townhouses in Moscow in collaboration with Boris Velikovsky.*

It is widely believed that Neoclassical Revival architecture was a purely Russian phenomenon and that Art Nouveau (known as Style Moderne in Russia) represented the Western influence. In fact, it was the exact opposite, as seen by the fact that foreign customers living in Russia mainly preferred the Neoclassical Revival style. Many of them lived in the areas of Moscow where Velikovsky designed tenements – the districts near Myasnitskaya, Maroseika and Pokrovka

Streets and the Basmanny Lanes. Such property investors wanted to both avoid risk and correspond to fashion, and this Neoclassical version of Art Nouveau offered the best option, particularly as it seemed so close to the common European heritage.

In his autobiography Velikovsky names his most important commissions. This list is headed by the Gribov Mansion on Khlebny Lane in Moscow. In parallel he independently designed the Gryaznov Textile Mill in the city of Ivanovo-Voznesensk in Vladimir Province. He then built a

whole series of tenements[11] in Moscow (partly in collaboration with Alexei Milyukov) and one in St Petersburg for Ivan Kuznetsov.

Ivan Yemelyanovich Kuznetsov became Velikovsky's most important and prestigious customer. He came from a large family of Old Believers[12] who owned many factories throughout Russia.

The most famous member of the family of factory owners was Matvei Sidorovich Kuznetsov (1846–1911), whose name is synonymous with the concept of Kuznetsov porcelain, Russian crockery created in the style of national traditions and widely exported to Europe and Asia. Velikovsky worked for his cousin, Ivan Yemelyanovich Kuznetsov, who owned several factories near Novgorod, including the Chudovo Crystal Glass and Lamp Factory in Volkov and the Porcelain and Faience Factory in Gruzino. Ivan Kuznetsov was also the owner of a porcelain factory in the district of Gzhel outside Moscow.

The Second World War and the numerous reconstructions of the industrial buildings mean that it is now virtually impossible to see Velikovsky's original creations in those locations. The only survivor is the factory complex in Gruzino, which was known as the Red Porcelainist Factory during the Soviet period. The Church of St George in Novo-Kharitonovo near Gzhel, which was commissioned by Ivan Kuznetsov, is also intact. One of Ivan Kuznetsov's descendants is now the family biographer and is an expert on the buildings commissioned by the famous industrialist.

Between 1907 and 1912 Velikovsky designed a workers' settlement for Ivan Kuznetsov near Gzhel, including a church and a care home. All this was part of the factory complex in the village of Novo-Kharitonovo, where the famous Gzhel ceramics were produced.[13]

The early 1910s were one of the most successful periods in Velikovsky's career, when he became an acknowledged leader of Neoclassical Revival architecture (a version of Art Nouveau which borrowed extensively from the classical heritage). Even after the revolution, when private property was abolished, Velikovsky's pre-revolutionary constructions continued to enjoy a high status. They are particularly prestigious today, now that it is again possible to acquire property in Russia and sign long-term leases. The main reasons are the well-planned inner layouts and spatial designs and the high quality of construction of all his buildings.

Velikovsky's list of pre-revolutionary constructions includes a series of industrial buildings. They were created for some of the country's most important enterprises, such as the Podolsk Cement Factory, which still operates to this day. Although Velikovsky's buildings were lost in the course of the recent modernisation of the cement factory, local historians have published information on them and the site has been listed as a place of historical interest. The Chudovo Crystal Glass and Lamp Factory and the Porcelain and Faience Factory near Novgorod, like the Kuznetsov Porcelain Factory in Gzhel, remained important centres of production both before and after the revolution. The Kovrov Armaments Factory is the largest industrial enterprise in Vladimir Region. The factory's administrative headquarters and oldest industrial blocks, which were designed by Velikovsky a hundred years ago, dictated the consequent development of the entire complex and, to this day, still occupy a dominant position among all the other buildings.

Family

Unfortunately, Velikovsky's industrial buildings tend not to be fully appreciated by their modern occupants and mostly attract the attention of local historians. Although the architect created extremely important factory designs and developed his own version of the red-brick style, [14] his civilian architecture is much better known – and has also better survived. One of the main reasons was the tendency in the Soviet period to gloss over the initial capitalist contribution to the country's industrial transformation in the twentieth century. More recently, the transfers from public to private ownership in the decades following the collapse of Communism have led to the deterioration of many state enterprises.

Velikovsky is better known for his leading role in the creation of the Druzhba ("Friendship") settlement near the Perlovskaya station of the Yaroslavl Railway Line outside Moscow. This was a classical fan-shaped garden city with a park, public buildings in the centre and no long or straight roads. While the layout of the settlement echoes European analogues, the houses themselves were clearly adapted to local conditions. Velikovsky designed practical duplexes intended for two families – wooden log huts with corner verandas and a shared attic. The houses were heated by stoves and had kitchens with direct access to a plot of land. These snug wooden dwellings were as attractive as brick cottages and had convenient, modern layouts. Everything was planned and arranged with the same love and care that one would expect from an architect creating his own home.

In Soviet cities, Velikovsky was an advocate of multistorey blocks of flats constructed by housing cooperatives: "When building a house, the state does not take into account the tastes of the people. It builds on a grand scale, tailoring everything to one form. The result is the same as with clothes – no matter how fine a ready-made suit is, the one which is stitched to order is always the more comfortable."[15] A cooperative, on the other hand, listened to the opinions of all its members while accomplishing tasks which could never be done by someone on their own: "A private individual can build a separate house, but he is incapable of installing the water supply, the sewage system or planting the vegetation. And, most importantly, this house will become dear to his heart".[16]

Blocks of flats belonging to housing cooperatives were extremely popular in the 1920s. Their construction was often based on standardised designs called "Mossovet sections".[17] Architects could only add a personal touch by applying such additional elements as unconventional corners, balconies, loggias or canopies over the entrances. But Velikovsky differed from the rest and rejected the standard sections recommended by Moscow City Council. He designed every house individually, from scratch, resulting in more interesting and convenient interiors and a wider range of housing units. The architect was assisted by his vast experience of constructing pre-revolutionary tenements – a "bourgeois" phenomenon now ostensibly consigned to the past – when creating residential blocks in Moscow for such housing cooperatives as Koopstroi, Lnotorg Worker and the employees of Gosstrakh.[18]

Velikovsky worked in an age of great experimentation, when the old way of life was being swept away and new visions were taking over. In the 1920s, the Iron Curtain[19] had not yet descended and Soviet architects were still able to communicate with their foreign colleagues. Many of the latter idealised the USSR and believed that freedom of creativity was only possible in the

At the office

new Russia. Soviet architects, meanwhile, were convinced that they could change the way people lived just as much as politics could. They discussed the future development of the country and the widely expected collective forms of living. To this end, Russian architects started dreaming up new types of buildings, such as communal homes, factory kitchens and enormous public bathhouses.

Velikovsky managed to strike the correct balance by constructing modern buildings without rejecting traditional architecture. He interpreted the new style in his own unique way. Paradoxically, he rejected the order system of Neoclassical architecture, the very movement in which he had previously been such a leader. This same path was followed by

With his wife

other pre-revolutionary masters of the Neoclassical Revival style, such as two famous sets of brothers – Leonid, Victor and Alexander Vesnin and Ilya and Panteleimon Golosov. They headed a new movement in Soviet architecture in which the leading theorist was Moisei Ginzburg (a close friend of Velikovsky).

A very important role in this period was played by the civil engineers. Boris Velikovsky and two of the three Vesnin brothers (Victor and Alexander) had received a practical education in construction and engineering at the St Petersburg Institute of Civil Engineers. Along with the graduates of the Imperial Technical College in Moscow (now known as the Nikolai Bauman Technical University), they competed with the less practically trained graduates of the Imperial Academy of Arts in St Petersburg and the Moscow School of Painting, Sculpture and Architecture.

As a measure of comparison, the St Petersburg Institute of Civil Engineers trained around one hundred engineers every year in such specialities as civil architecture, road-and-bridge construction and industrial architecture, while no more than a dozen or so architects graduated annually from the Imperial Academy of Arts. There was a similar correlation between the number of students at the Imperial Technical College and the Moscow School of Painting, Sculpture and Architecture. As a result, civil engineers constituted the overwhelming majority in design and construction work. And it was the quality of their training – as well as their professional efforts – which contributed to the high volumes of building work both in the final years of the Russian Empire and in the first decades after the revolution.

In the light of this information, Boris Velikovsky clearly occupies an important place in the history of Russian architecture in the first third of the twentieth century. Recently, architectural historians have come to better understand the importance of such figures as Velikovsky, who designed and constructed real works of architecture rather than just engaging in radical experiments on paper. At the same time, Velikovsky's most famous projects of the 1920s and early 1930s – the buildings of Gostorg, Tsentrosoyuz and the House of the Book – fully reflect his masterful command of the progressive ideas advocated by his innovative colleagues, often evoking their professional jealousy.

From the 1910s onwards, many of the architects working in Moscow were graduates of foreign schools and colleges. A large number of them were Russian Jews, who had been forced to study abroad due to the aforementioned national restrictions – El Lissitzky in Darmstadt, Arkady Langman in Vienna, Moisei Ginzburg in Milan and Boris Jofan in Rome. They then returned to Russia, where they verified their degrees and competed with their non-Jewish colleagues. Such professional activities reflected their general aspiration towards self-expression during those years. This was a time when Russian Jews were finally able to study and collect their own national art. The Jewish State Theatre was opened in Moscow and books were published in Yiddish. Although these tendencies were later crushed as the country moved towards totalitarianism under Stalin, almost none of the architects emigrated. They continued to work professionally, attempting to find their own place in this new and very complicated world.

Boris Velikovsky's wife – Rosa Atlas

The creative atmosphere in the Soviet Union, at that time, was even extolled by Le Corbusier. The famous European architect visited the country and wrote on his way back to Paris in 1930 that "Moscow is a *factory for making plans*, the Promised Land of technicians (without a Klondike). The country is being equipped! A striking flood of plans: plans of factories, of dams, of mills, of dwellings, of entire cities. All of them under one sign: whatever brings progress. Architecture swells, moves, bestirs itself, and gives birth, breathed on and fertilized by those who know something, and those who make believe they do"[20]. Interestingly, when Le Corbusier first visited Moscow in 1928 and examined the site of the building he later designed for Tsentrosoyuz on Myasnitskaya Street, the only modern construction he could see there was by Velikovsky (Gostorg).

The early designs of Le Corbusier's Soviet colleagues were often either purely "paper" dreams of the architecture of the future or works distinguished mainly for their external attributes – radio masts and linear volumes. The practical implementation of their projects resulted in "striped" facades – brick walls divided horizontally in imitation of ribbon windows. Pilasters and artful paintwork were used to create images of the frame on the walls of buildings. Imitations of flat roofs – attics concealing actual sloped surfaces – were also typical of this period. That is why there was such great interest in Velikovsky's Gostorg building, which was genuinely created in frame constructions, despite the difficult conditions, virtually becoming a manifesto for modern architecture at that time (1925–27).

Reinforced-concrete frames had been applied before the revolution by Alexander Kuznetsov, an authoritative civil engineer who designed a series of townhouses, factory buildings and the studios of the Imperial Stroganov Central School of Art and Industry in Moscow (1912–14). But he did not go so far as to reject a simplified order system, of which there is not even as much as a hint in the Gostorg building. From that time onwards, Russian architects aspired to be at the very forefront of the radical changes taking place in Europe. Such architecture is commonly known as "avant-garde", although the term "Constructivism" is often employed as a synonym in Soviet architecture, even though, strictly speaking, Constructivism only applies to the activities of one creative group, the OSA (Organisation of Contemporary Architects).

Velikovsky's Gostorg building is classified among works of Constructivism, although this term has a double meaning. Abroad, it usually refers to all Russian avant-garde architecture, while in the Soviet Union the word was actually first put into circulation by artists. In 1923, Moisei Ginzburg applied the term to the functional style – buildings in a reinforced-concrete frame lacking any decoration. Many masters of the avant-garde were not members of OSA (which was created with the active participation of Ginzburg and the Vesnin brothers) and did not consider themselves Constructivists.

Velikovsky was not a member of the Constructivists. He worked on his own, attracting other talented architects to his studio. The latter included Vasily Voinov, a graduate of the Moscow School of Painting, Sculpture and Architecture; Alexander-Isaac Grinberg, a graduate of the Imperial Academy of Arts in St Petersburg; Arkady Langman, who had studied at the Technische Hochschule in Vienna; and Georgy Wegmann and Maria Gaken, who had trained, respectively, at the Moscow Institute of Civil Engineers and the Moscow Polytechnic Institute.[21] Working under Velikovsky, these young masters successfully assimilated and applied the new construction and sculptural devices in Soviet architecture.

1 Boris Mikhailovich was the Russian version of the architect's original Jewish name, which was "Boruch, son of Echil". The surname Velikovsky is derived from the shtetl in which he lived.

2 Between 1772 and 1795 the territory of the Rzeczpospolita (Polish-Lithuanian Commonwealth) was divided up between Prussia, Austria and Russia. The first partition took place in 1772 and gave Russia parts of the eastern lands of modern-day Latvia and Belarus. The border of the Russian Empire moved westwards as far as the Rivers Dvina, Drut and Dnieper, including the major towns of Vitebsk, Polotsk and Mstislavl.

3 *See: http://shtetle.co.il/shtetls_mog/slavgorod/slavgorod_hist.html*

4 The Pale of Settlement was a region of the Russian Empire outside of which Jews were not allowed to live, with the exception of a limited category of individuals. This rule was established by Catherine the Great in 1791 and existed right up until the 1917 revolution. As a result, Jews could not study in St Petersburg or Moscow, forcing many to go abroad to receive a higher education.

5 A secondary school in pre-revolutionary Russia and several other European countries which concentrated on the teaching of practical (mathematical, scientific and technical) subjects.

6 The students were the most radical social group and the main mass-protest movement in Russia at the turn of the century. This movement reached the peak of its importance and intensity in the years between the nationwide student strike of 1899 and the 1905 revolution. Students held strikes, joined revolutionary groups

and spread anti-government propaganda, despite the threat of suspension or expulsion from university, prison sentences or exile to Siberia.

7 Historicism (also known as Eclecticism) was a movement which combined new architectural elements with former styles to create a wide variety of possible designs. Historicism was particularly widespread across Europe in the second half of the nineteenth century and included the Gothic Revival, Baroque Revival, Napoleon III, Queen Anne and Neo-Russian styles.

8 The Tretyakov Care Home was established by the wealthy industrialist, art collector and philanthropist Pavel Tretyakov as a shelter for the mentally handicapped after his eldest son, Mikhail, was found to be mentally ill. Pavel Tretyakov donated 400,000 roubles to the institution, which was housed in a building designed by Sergei Solovyov in the style of traditional Pskov architecture (it is now home to the Alexander Vishnevsky Institute of Surgery).

9 Vladimir Grigoryevich Shukhov (1853–1939) was a Russian engineer, scientist, inventor and architect. He studied at the Imperial Technical College in Moscow (1871–76) and visited the Centennial International Exhibition in Philadelphia (1876). Shukhov made many important scientific breakthroughs, such as the thermal cracking process, while working for the Russian oil and chemistry industries before the revolution. He was also famous as the first in the world to use steel gridshells for the construction of buildings and towers (1896).

10 The Tryokhgornaya ("Three Hills") Manufactory was a textile enterprise founded by the merchant Vasily Prokhorov in Moscow in 1799. The company won many awards for its produce and remained in the hands of the Prokhorov family right up until the 1917 revolution. The Tryokhgornaya Manufactory was nationalised in 1918 but privatised in 1992 and still exists to this day.

11 A tenement is a multi-occupancy residential block in which the individual apartments are rented out to tenants. Tenements were particularly popular in European cities in the late nineteenth and early twentieth centuries, when they were built to provide both an income for the owner of the house and high-density housing for the large number of people moving from the countryside to the towns.

12 The Old Believers were a breakaway sect of the Russian Orthodox Church which rejected the reforms introduced by Patriarch Nikon in 1652 to correct errors he believed had crept into Russian Orthodoxy during the reign of Ivan the Terrible. Nikon was convinced that the Russian prayer books, rituals and icons had diverged from the original Greek sources, but many believers regarded his changes as a direct attack on true Orthodoxy. The result was a schism in the Russian Orthodox Church. The opponents of Nikon's reforms were officially condemned by the Church Council in 1661 and generally persecuted by the Russian state until Tsar Nicholas II granted freedom of religion in 1905.

13 Gzhel ceramics are a traditional style of Russian pottery centred around the village of Gzhel to the south-east of Moscow. The classical Gzhel works of crockery, toys and figurines are painted solid white with distinctive blue designs.

14 The red-brick style refers to a trend in the Historical (Eclectic) period of Russian architecture in the second half of the nineteenth century, when the facades of buildings were left unplastered and the bare brickwork was considered the main decorative element. The style is closely related to the Brick Gothic Revival movement popular in northern Europe in the same period.

15 B. M. Velikovsky, *Zhilischnaya nuzhda i kooperatsiya*, Moscow, 1924, p. 3.

16 Le Corbusier (1887–1965) was born as Charles-Édouard Jeanneret-Gris in the town of La Chaux-de-Fonds near the French border in north-west Switzerland. After studying at the École des Arts Décoratifs at La Chaux-de-Fonds he travelled across Europe and settled in Paris in 1917. Le Corbusier was a pioneer of the International Style in modern architecture and his designs combined Functionalism with a strong sense of Expressionism.

17 In 1925, Mossovet (the Moscow City Council) attempted to tackle the housing crisis by developing standardised designs called "sections" – blocks of municipal flats based on an economic use of space. The first model of 1925 consisted of four apartments on one floor. Each apartment had two or three rooms (one room for one family) but no bathroom, only a sink in a communal kitchen. The initial designs were criticised for a lack of ventilation and sanitation, leading to improved models in 1926 and 1928.

18 The name of the state agency which handled domestic insurance in Soviet Russia after all private companies were nationalised following the 1917 revolution. Gosstrakh existed from 1921 until 1992, when it was transformed into a state-owned joint stock company (Rosgosstrakh) and later privatised.

19 A phrase first introduced by Winston Churchill in a speech made in Fulton on 5 March 1946 to describe the geographical barrier running "from Stettin in the Baltic to Trieste in the Adriatic", dividing the Western Allies from the lands occupied by the Soviet Union. The Iron Curtain also referred to the ideological, political and communication barriers imposed by the USSR during the Cold War.

20 Le Corbusier, *Precisions on the Present State of Architecture and City Planning*, Chicago, 2015.

21 The Moscow Institute of Civil Engineers was created in 1921 on the basis of the Moscow Polytechnic Institute (previously a college for women). In 1924, the Moscow Institute of Civil Engineers became part of the Faculty of Engineering and Construction of the Moscow Higher Technical College, which had been called the Imperial Technical College (until 1918) and is now known as the Nikolai Bauman Technical University (since 1989).

Вседержитель

01

Church of St George
Novo-Kharitonovo, Gzhel District, Moscow Region
1907–1912
Architect: Boris Velikovsky

The Church of St George was built in the settlement for workers of the Kuznetsov Porcelain Factory in the village of Novo-Kharitonovo near Gzhel in Moscow Province. The church belonged to the Old Believers, a breakaway sect of the Russian Orthodox Church which rejected the liturgical reforms undertaken by Patriarch Nikon and Tsar Alexis Mikhailovich in the middle of the seventeenth century.

The church is crowned with a tented roof, recalling analogues from the reigns of Ivan the Terrible and Boris Godunov in the second half of the sixteenth century. Churches with tented roofs were built back then as a symbol of the growing power of the Russian state. This was before the Time of Troubles[1] in the early seventeenth century and the aforementioned schism in the Russian Orthodox Church.

While adhering to traditions in liturgical matters, the Old Believers were certainly not retrogrades in other matters in the early twentieth century. Many of them were rich industrialists and bankers whose deep religious feelings compelled them to privately fund hospitals and other charitable institutions for the poor. Until the proclamation of the October Manifesto,[2] the Old Believers were not allowed to build places of worship, only small roadside chapels. But after religious freedom was introduced in 1905, there was a boom in the construction of their churches, and the architects applied the latest technological advances, such as monolithic reinforced concrete. The Old Believers supported architectural innovations and did not aspire to follow the canonic forms of the official orthodoxy in their new buildings. The church designed by Boris Velikovsky in Novo-Kharitonovo is a perfect example.

Velikovsky constructed a reinforced-concrete cupola above the brick walls and arches of the church. A magnificent tented roof was then placed over the cupola. The base of the tented roof was surrounded by pointed kokoshniks.[3] Their unusual Gothic forms harmonise well with the elongated form of the tented roof.

Church of St George
Novo-Kharitonovo, Gzhel District,
Moscow Region
1907–1912
View of dome, 2016

The roof conjures up associations with a famous work of Old Russian architecture created in the sixteenth century – the Church of the Ascension in Kolomenskoe. The first stone church to be built with a tented roof in Russia, it was designed by an Italian architect and remained unsurpassed in its grandeur.

All the other forms of the Church of St George in Novo-Kharitonovo recall Old Russian architecture. The general asymmetric configuration of the interior space and the keel-shaped outlines around the windows on the northern facade, however, are typical features of Art Nouveau architecture. Other examples of this style are the keel-shaped silhouette of the barrel roof of the entrance porch and such decorative details as the ornamental frieze directly above the entrance.

The church is two-pillared and has an asymmetric inner space. The two squat pillars support the wall arches of the vault near the entrance on the western side. This is also an example of the use of pre-Petrine architectural forms. On the altar side, the arches lean against the walls, limiting the apses. The surfaces of the inside walls, vaults and cupola still retain vestiges of the original frescoes. The floor of the church is paved with tiles – grey and white hexagons, which form a simple geometric pattern.

The socle floor was employed as the winter church and was initially intended to be the Kuznetsov family tomb. This explains the burial niche under the altar on the eastern side, which has now been filled in. The Baroque-style iconostasis was made of porcelain (it has not survived). Although the iconostasis was created in Europe, Ivan Kuznetsov clearly wanted something which would echo the decorative paintwork of his own Gzhel produce.

Church of St George
Novo-Kharitonovo, Gzhel District,
Moscow Region
1907–1912
Plan of the church

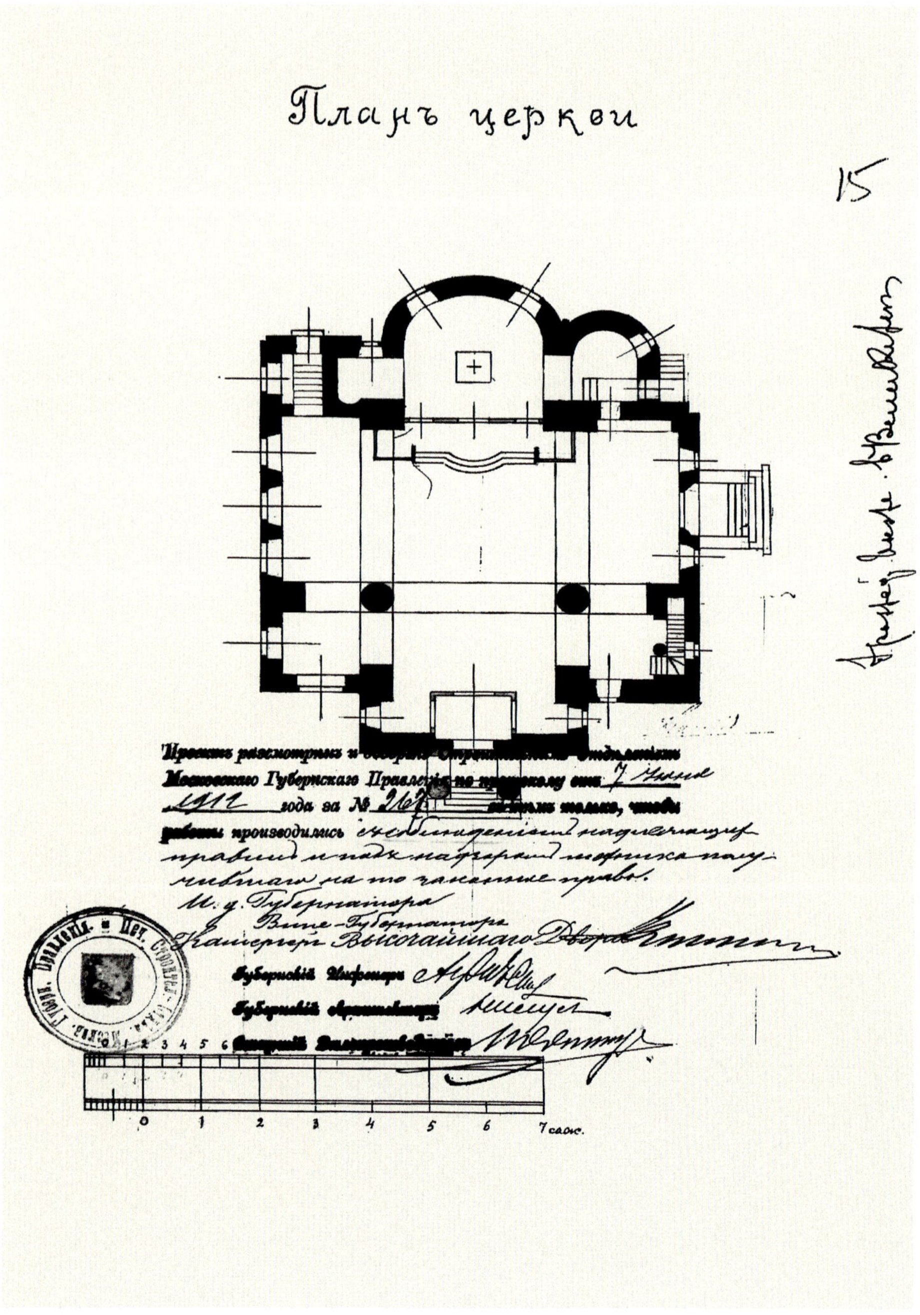

Church of St George
Novo-Kharitonovo, Gzhel District,
Moscow Region
1907–1912
View from the east, 2002

Such pioneers of the Neo-Russian style[4] as Sergei Malyutin and Victor Vasnetsov employed similar architectural devices in the 1900s. Alexei Schusyev,[5] who was employed at that time as an architect of the Holy Synod, also designed places of worship in the Neo-Russian style. But Velikovsky's creation is most like the churches of Ilya Bondarenko,[6] who innovatively interpreted historical prototypes when designing a whole series of buildings for the Old Believers. As the leading architect of the Old Believer community, he personally endorsed Velikovsky's project in Novo-Kharitonovo.

Velikovsky also designed several wooden buildings alongside the Church of St George. The most prominent of these structures was probably the care home, which represented a long timber frame with high pyramidal gable roofs. The general silhouette of the care home repeated the images of the terems[7] popular at the turn of the century. Unfortunately, this building has not survived.

1 The Time of Troubles was a fifteen-year period of national strife between the death of the last tsar of the Rurikid dynasty in 1598 and the accession of the first tsar of the Romanov dynasty in 1613. A three-year famine during the reign of Boris Godunov led to a wave of popular discontent and mass protests. Polish and Swedish armies invaded the weakened country and captured several towns, including Moscow. The Time of Troubles only ended when the Russians finally expelled the foreign invaders in 1612 and elected Michael Romanov as the new tsar in 1613.

2 Manifesto drawn up by Count Sergei Witte and signed by Tsar Nicholas II on 17 (30 N.S.) October 1905 with the aim of ending the mass strikes, uprisings, mutinies and political assassinations which had engulfed the country following the events of Bloody Sunday and the defeat in the Russo-Japanese War. The October Manifesto granted broad civil rights, including freedom of conscience, and promised elections to a parliament or Duma.

3 A kokoshnik is a rounded or pointed arch used to decorate Russian churches, particularly in the sixteenth and seventeenth centuries. Kokoshniks are usually arranged in receding tiers at the base of a tented roof. The word is derived from the Old Slavonic *kokosh* ("hen") and also refers to the similarly-shaped headdress worn by married Russian women from the sixteenth century onwards.

4 The Neo-Russian style flourished in the late nineteenth and early twentieth centuries and widely applied the motifs of Old Russian architecture in the general context of Art Nouveau. The best examples of the Neo-Russian style in Moscow are Victor Vasnetsov's facade of the Tretyakov Gallery (1900–05), Sergei Malyutin's Zinaida Pertsova Tenement (1905–07) and Alexei Schusyev's Convent of St Martha and St Mary (1908–12).

5 Alexei Victorovich Schusyev (1873–1949) was a Russian architect who was born in Kishinyov (Chişinău). He studied at the Imperial Academy of Arts in St Petersburg (1891–97) and followed the Neo-Russian style before the 1917 revolution. After the revolution Schusyev worked on the "New Moscow" plan for the redevelopment of the city (1918–23) and designed the Lenin Mausoleum (1924–30). In the 1930s, he headed an architectural bureau which created new buildings in Moscow and many other Soviet cities.

6 Ilya Yevgrafovich Bondarenko (1870–1947) was a Russian architect who is primarily known for designing churches for the Old Believers before the 1917 revolution. He studied architecture at the Moscow School of Painting, Sculpture and Architecture (1887–91) and the Eidgenössische Polytechnische Schule in Zurich (1894). A member of the Abramtsevo circle in the 1890s, Bondarenko combined his knowledge of traditional Russian architecture with the Art Nouveau style when designing many Old Believer churches between 1906 and 1917. He continued to work as an architect in the Soviet period and died in Moscow in 1947.

7 A terem was an attic or chamber at the top of a house, often set apart for the womenfolk before the eighteenth century. The word is derived from the Greek *teremnon*, meaning "shelter" or "abode", and has the wider meaning of the upper story of a palace or residential building, often with a pitched roof.

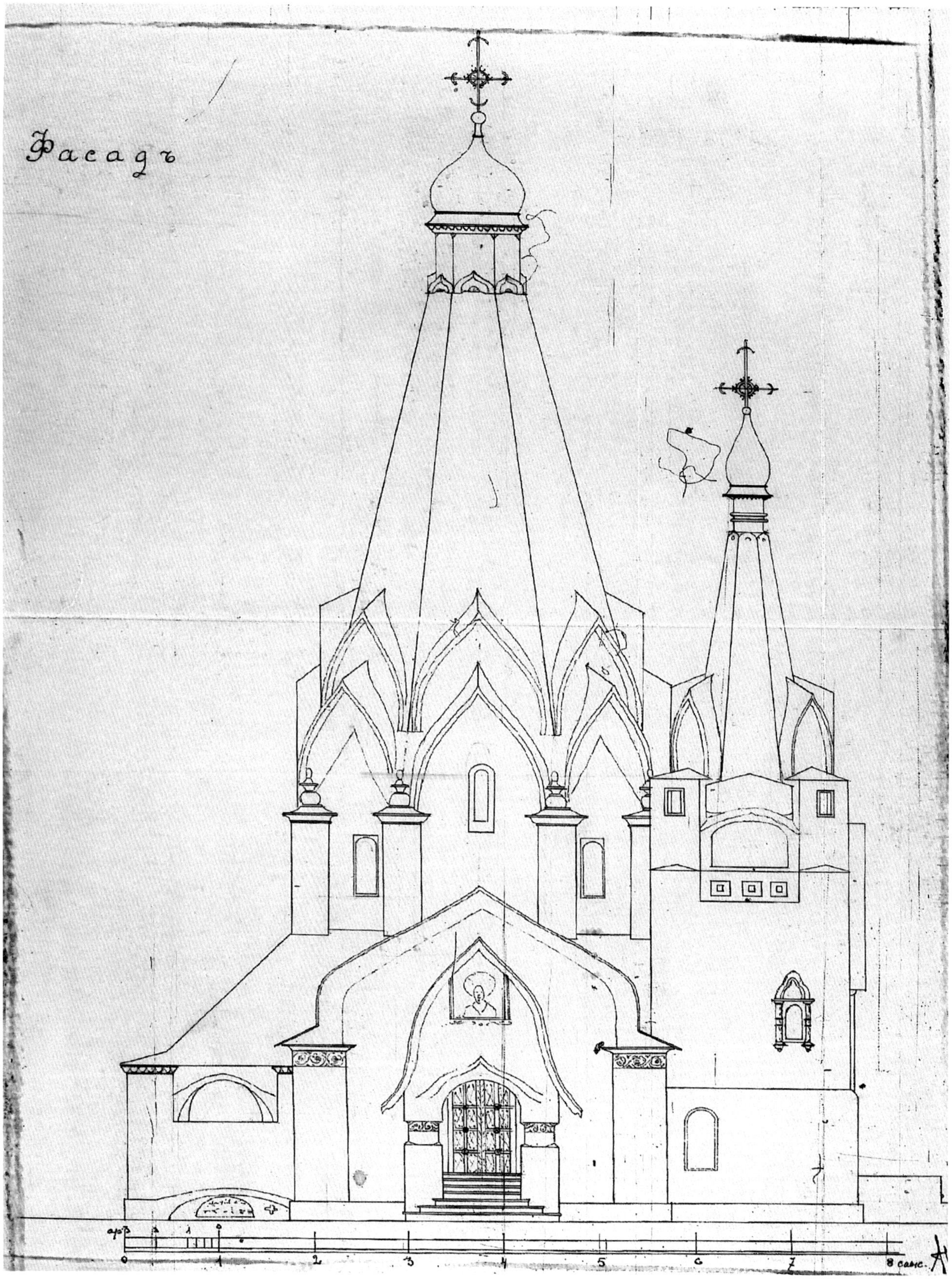

Church of St George
Novo-Kharitonovo, Gzhel District, Moscow Region
1907–1912
Main (western) facade design

Church of St George
Novo-Kharitonovo, Gzhel District,
Moscow Region
1907–1912
Southern facade and entrance detail, 2015

Church of St George
Novo-Kharitonovo, Gzhel District,
Moscow Region
1907–1912
Interior view from the choir, 2015

02

Gryaznov Textile Mill
Ivanovo
1906–1908
Architect: Boris Velikovsky

The Gryaznov (later Fyodor Samoilov) Textile Mill was built on the lower bank of the River Uvod in the city of Ivanovo-Voznesensk in Vladimir Province (now the city of Ivanovo in Ivanovo Region). The main facade was symmetric and looked towards a number of small-storey buildings. Residential houses (many of them wooden) were located on an elevation, higher than the textile mill. In order to make the main factory block more visible, Boris Velikovsky artificially increased the height of the building by adding an attic to the central section. The attic was divided by pilaster strips, crowned with a cornice and decorated with a round window. This made the silhouette of the factory more dominant in the architectural context. The architect placed a large water tower directly behind the main factory block with the similar aim of making the general silhouette more attractive.

In Velikovsky's interpretation the textile mill recalls the image of a medieval European town. Other industrial buildings were constructed on either side of the main block, which still remains the architectural dominant to this day. The view onto these constructions, however, is obstructed by the fences, huts and garages now surrounding the historical buildings.

Gryaznov Textile Mill
Ivanovo
1906–1908
Main facade detail, 2015

Gryaznov Textile Mill
Ivanovo
1906–1908
Facade

03

Kuznetsov Porcelain and Faience Factory Complex Gruzino, Chudovo District, Novgorod Region 1911–1912 Architect: Boris Velikovsky

The Kuznetsov Porcelain and Faience Factory was constructed in the village of Gruzino on the River Volkhov near the town of Chudovo in Novgorod Province. Like other industrial enterprises owned by the Old Believers, this complex included buildings with a social purpose intended to improve the quality of life of the workers.

The workshops, administrative buildings and other blocks were designed in the red-brick style, which still retains its romantic charm today, even in a ruined state. All across Europe, many former factory buildings now enjoy a second life as fashionable offices, museums, hotels, shops and restaurants. Velikovsky's creation slots perfectly into this group of historical architectural monuments.

Three industrial buildings, the management wing and a couple of minor structures still survive from the original constructions designed by Velikovsky in Gruzino. There is also the building of a club or theatre and the nearby care home.

The elongated factory blocks are divided into sections by avant-corps, the silhouettes of which are embellished by elevated volumes. The numerous windows of the workshops have arched lintels. The cornices beneath the high roofs recall Old Russian analogues.

The main factory block was a long three-storey building with large windows. There was also a large and imposing water tower. The round chimneys of the furnaces used to bake the ceramics rise above the inclined roof, imparting an air of monumentality to the building, and the mansard windows on the pediments are decorated with elaborate casing.

Kuznetsov Porcelain and Faience Factory Complex Gruzino, Chudovo District, Novgorod Region 1911–1912
Facade detail of the main production facility, 2015

Kuznetsov Porcelain and Faience Factory Complex Gruzino, Chudovo District, Novgorod Region 1911–1912
Production facility central section, 2015

The management wing was located outside the factory yard and recalled a town-hall building with a tower and a clock (which possibly existed but have not survived). The facades were decorated with architectural details in the spirit of Neoclassicism.

The care home was designed in the Neo-Russian style popular among many Old Believers, including the Kuznetsovs. After the main factory block, this was the largest three-storey structure in the entire complex. Although the building has now been abandoned, it was once the home of indigent female workers. The roof and attic have been reconstructed, but some of the decorative details on the facades – the casing and the arched portals – still survive. The residential rooms were accessed from a wide corridor, while the gable ends contained the nurses' premises.

There is a large faceted avant-corps in the centre of the northern facade of the care home. The ground-floor premises clearly had a public function and recall the configuration of the Mansbach German Gymnasium later designed by Velikovsky in Moscow (1913–14). The southern facade is grander and has three arched windows with elegant casing. A magnificent view opens up from there onto the floodland of the River Volkhov. This architectural touch can be compared to the ornate decoration on the river facades of churches built in Yaroslavl in the seventeenth century.

The overall style of the Kuznetsov Factory Complex in Gruzino recalls Velikovsky's earliest industrial construction – the Gryaznov Textile Mill in Ivanovo-Voznesensk (1906–08). In both cases, all the buildings had red-brick walls and decorative details in the spirit of Historicism (Eclecticism).

A workers' settlement was built alongside the Kuznetsov Porcelain and Faience Factory, which was renamed the Red Porcelainist Factory during the Soviet period. The original houses in this settlement, however, have not survived.

Kuznetsov Porcelain and Faience Factory Complex
Gruzino, Chudovo District, Novgorod Region
1911–1912
pp. 30–31. Poorhouse facade detail, 2015

04

Gribov Mansion
15 Khlebny Lane, Moscow
1909–1911
Architect: Alexei Milyukov
with contributions from Boris Velikovsky

On 14 April 1909 the hereditary honorary citizen Vladimir Nazarovich Gribov submitted a planning application for the construction of a mansion at 15 Khlebny ("Bread") Lane in Moscow. The documents were accompanied by a project signed by the civil engineer Alexei Milyukov. The list of works compiled by Boris Velikovsky at the end of his life, however, records the Gribov Mansion as his first construction. The documentation suggests that the young Velikovsky, who was awarded the degree of civil engineer in 1904, was invited to assist Milyukov, although his surname was not included in the project materials.

The Gribov Mansion was completed in 1911 and recalls the finest buildings created in Moscow during the Neoclassical period a hundred years earlier. These include the Prince Lev Gagarin Mansion on Novinsky Boulevard (designed by Joseph Bové in 1817 and destroyed following a German air raid in 1941) and the surviving Prince Alexander Lobanov-Rostovsky Mansion at 43 Myasnitskaya Street. There are major differences, however, between the Gribov Mansion and such historical analogues. This house is more modest in scale and is comprised of several blocks, while all the architectural details are hypertrophied, rather like in a theatrical set. This approach was typical of the Neoclassical Revival of the 1900s and 1910s, which was not so much a continuation of the traditional classical style but more a version – the most retrospective version – of Art Nouveau in Russia.

Another important difference is the positioning of the front porch right on the frontage line of Khlebny Lane. In Neoclassical urban estates, the main house was placed deep inside the courtyard – only auxiliary buildings would have stood on the street. The horse-driven carriages which drove into courtyards back in

Gribov Mansion
15 Khlebny Lane, Moscow
1909–1911
Portico detail, 2016

the early nineteenth century required large spaces for turning around. But automobiles had already appeared on the roads of Moscow when the Gribov Mansion was being constructed a hundred years later. This new form of transport was more manoeuvrable and allowed the large open courtyards to be replaced by gardens with flowerbeds. The interiors of the new mansions also differed from their Neoclassical precedents. There was less emphasis on symmetry, and the architects rejected the obligatory principle of formally aligning rooms in enfilades.

The Gribov Mansion is a two-storey building with a high hall in the centre of the composition, which is crowned by a cupola (its key position can be clearly seen on the sectional drawing). The asymmetric configuration of the interiors is reflected in the exterior forms. The front porch is framed by pendant Ionic columns. At the top is a triangular pediment with a large semicircular window set deep inside the wall. A rounded avant-corps faces the garden on the left, providing a link to the drawing room on the ground floor. In the Neoclassical period, this avant-corps would probably have been matched by a symmetrically placed avant-corps on the opposite side. The asymmetric layout was clearly inspired by the other famous mansions created at that time for the wealthy bourgeoisie by such masters as Fyodor (Franz Albert) Schechtel, Lev Kekushev and Illarion Ivanov-Schits.

The moulded decor consists of bas-reliefs in the ancient spirit and is exaggeratedly large. This serves to both underline the small scale of the mansion and to draw attention to these Neoclassical elements. The same applies to the two lions guarding the entrance to the house and even the ornamentation on the iron railings.

The interior decor is particularly well preserved and includes oval medallions with female figures, garlands and coffers in the cupola. While these are all features of Neoclassicism, the asymmetry of the general composition and the haphazard combination of various rooms are much closer to Art Nouveau. The supple lines of the window casing, which recall stylised tree

Gribov Mansion
15 Khlebny Lane, Moscow
1909–1911
1910s

branches, also correspond to the new stylistics. Even the large semicircular window is interpreted in the spirit of Art Nouveau (Neoclassical masters would have employed more austere and fan-shaped casing). The same applies to the modern forms of the columns inside the house and the winding details of the wooden staircase bannister, which transform the classical-order system in the style of Art Nouveau.

Vladimir Nazarovich Gribov and his brothers owned paper, silk and cloth factories and the Nazar Gribov with Sons trading concern. They also possessed tenements at Chistye Prudy in the Ogorodnaya Sloboda in Moscow. The Gribov family emigrated after the 1917 revolution. Their mansion on Khlebny Lane was nationalised and awarded to a secondary school, a Party school and the Institute of Military Cartography. After the Second World War, it housed the Belgian embassy and is now the official residence of the Belgian ambassador to Russia.

Gribov Mansion
15 Khlebny Lane, Moscow
1909–1911
Interior design

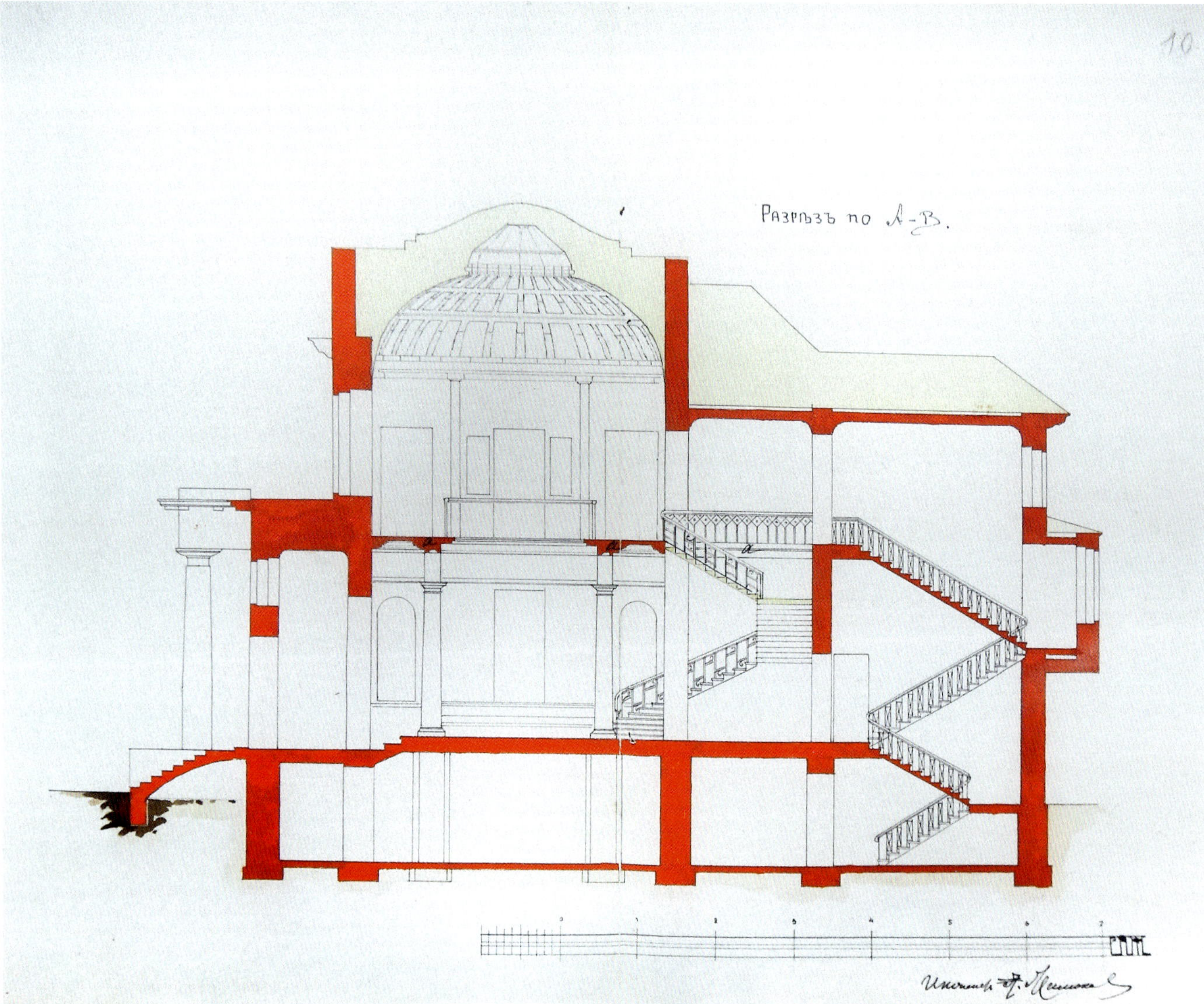

Gribov Mansion
15 Khlebny Lane, Moscow
1909–1911
Cross section

Gribov Mansion
15 Khlebny Lane, Moscow
1909–1911
Main facade design

Gribov Mansion
15 Khlebny Lane, Moscow
1909–1911
pp. 38–39. Main facade, 2016

Gribov Mansion
15 Khlebny Lane, Moscow
1909–1911
View from the east, 2016

Gribov Mansion
15 Khlebny Lane, Moscow
1909–1911
Entrance and stairs, 2016

Gribov Mansion
15 Khlebny Lane, Moscow
1909–1911
Stairwell, 2002

Gribov Mansion
15 Khlebny Lane, Moscow
1909–1911
Main enfilade view, 2002

Tenements are as popular today as they were over a hundred years ago. Apartments in tenements cost the same (if not more) than flats in prestigious houses built after the 1920s. The reasons for this are their practical inner layouts, imposing exteriors and prime locations in fashionable districts.

Neoclassical Revival architecture was the most desirable style for the owners of Russian tenement blocks, as it appealed to a broad range of wealthy investors, renters and buyers. This style allowed the nouveaux riches to feel just like the previous aristocratic owners of country and urban estates, which had also been built in a Neoclassical style a century earlier. There were, however, important differences between the Neoclassical Revival of the 1910s and the pure Neoclassicism of the late eighteenth and early nineteenth centuries.

Firstly, the ancient-order system was not copied literally. On the contrary, it grew less tectonic and less regular during the Art Nouveau period. Architects freely interpreted not only the columns, pilasters, architrave beams, friezes and cornices but even the stucco moulding. A textbook example is the oeuvre of Boris Velikovsky, who approached the order system analytically, detached from ancient analogues. Pilasters appeared on the upper floors of six-storey houses or on reinforced-concrete bay windows. Such decorative elements as wreaths and garlands, which had previously been confined to friezes on single-storey buildings, were now encountered on the attics of six-storey buildings (meaning at a height of over twenty metres). Intertwined or extending along the vertical or horizontal, such wreaths and garlands were transformed as much as the columns and pilasters. All this dynamism contrasted with the use of such decor by the Ancient Greeks and Romans to, on the contrary, underscore the stability and staticness of their buildings.

Secondly, the configuration of the different components of the buildings was now much freer and more inventive. Entire apartments or individual rooms were gathered together in separate blocks and positioned with a slight shift in relation to one another. The axis of symmetry was disrupted and the dynamism of all the components grew clearly discernible, particularly on the level of the plans and partially on the facades, which still retained their symmetric structure. Staircases were no longer placed strictly in line with the axes or in the corners, but in any convenient spot. This was a result of both the development of new construction systems (such as the use of reinforced concrete, which allowed high houses to be built) and the desire of customers to utilise the plot of land as efficiently as possible. So Neoclassical Revival architects working in the Art Nouveau period filled almost the entire territory under construction with one or several multistorey blocks, rounding any protruding corners to create a convenient passageway for cars or to improve the lighting in the premises located in any inverted sections of the building.

The often haphazard layout of these tenements was a direct result of the attempt to squeeze as many residential premises as possible onto each floor. The street facades and arched entranceways concealed "well-courtyards" which had, rather than the austere geometric forms of the Neoclassical period, complex configurations far removed from the possibilities provided by the rectangular elements of post-and-beam constructions.

In general, Russian – and, in particular, Moscow – Neoclassical Revival architecture did not contain any exact "quotations". Rather, it was a free interpretation of the classical heritage, combined with the use of relatively innovative structural elements. The architectural details were not the overriding factor. The spatial designs of the apartments were far more important than what was happening on the facades (beyond which many historians are unable to see).

What made Boris Velikovsky the undisputed king of this style? On the one hand, he was an expert on construction systems and a practical builder who had graduated from the country's leading college of engineering. On the other, he was a subtle connoisseur of Neoclassical architecture, which he developed within the bounds of Art Nouveau. Velikovsky did not copy antiquity as such; he merely designed refined facades with elegant sculptural elements. But, in many ways, he was responsible for the popularity of the Neoclassical Revival style in Russia. For example, after he constructed the Mikhail Lunts Tenement at 9 Krivokolenny Lane (1910–11), Ivan Kondratenko designed a tenement for Yevgeny Skalsky in a similar style directly opposite at 14 Krivokolenny Lane (1913–14).

In 1912, Karl Greinert built a four-storey brick tenement for Hugo Eberling in a style very reminiscent of Boris Velikovsky. The linear configuration of the facades with the symmetric framework of the courtyard and the strict symmetric arrangement of the decor, which was openly taken from definite analogues (ancient sarcophaguses), were all familiar devices which Velikovsky would have reinterpreted rather than directly borrowed. The presence of this house at 6 First Basmanny Lane probably explains why Velikovsky departed from the Neoclassical Revival style in favour of a Neo-Gothic version of Art Nouveau when building a nearby tenement for the Myasnitskaya Housing Association at 12 First Basmanny Lane (1913–14).

So, in many cases, it was the context which determined the actual architectural design in the Art Nouveau period, unlike the previous age of Historicism (Eclecticism), when the role of the customer had been much more prominent. Architects were now less constrained by their wealthy clients – surgeons, factory owners and bankers – although there were exceptions, such as the Mansbach German Gymnasium at 10 First Basmanny Lane (1913–14), which Velikovsky built next to the two aforementioned tenements.

In general, Boris Velikovsky's tenements had their own individual faces with recognisable features of the Neoclassical Revival style of the 1910s, a phenomenon in which the social roots are very often overlooked. The archive materials on Velikovsky's tenements reveal that his customers were members of the middle classes who wanted to make a return on their investments while avoiding the risks taken by such larger financiers as the Ryabushinsky family. Neoclassical Revival architecture was the most obvious choice for both the investor and a broad range of potential tenants – a happy medium and a win-win situation for everybody. This explains the appearance of this particular style on the historical arena in the age of the mass development of towns and cities.

05
Kuznetsov Tenement
15 Myasnitskaya Street, Moscow
1909–1912
Architect: Boris Velikovsky with contributions from Alexei Milyukov, Victor Vesnin and Alexander Vesnin

This tenement building represents an entire complex of residential blocks. They were constructed one by one on a comparatively small piece of land, which stretched back into the surrounding territory. The narrowest portion on Myasnitskaya Street has the most striking architecture and was created later than the other buildings further back inside the plot.

The first block to be constructed was the building on the left-hand side of the territory (when looking from the street). This project was approved in 1909. The new house replaced several old structures and had a spacious three-storey basement. The following projects concerned the most distant section on the right-hand side of the courtyard. The block extending out onto Myasnitskaya Street was designed in parallel. As a result, all three sides of the plot of land were developed. By this stage, the entire area beneath the courtyard had already been occupied by basements. Unlike the first rectangular building, the following blocks had complex configurations with rounded avant-corps and bay windows.

The section facing the street had the most striking architecture. The main facade was designed as symmetrically as possible, something which was not possible to achieve on the courtyard side. The central section of the building slightly protrudes and has a large arched entranceway flanked by two rounded sets of bay windows with balconies on top. The main decorative elements are grouped around the archway. The top of this section is crowned by a triangular gable with a semicircular window in the mansard. The ground floor is lined with natural stone and

Kuznetsov Tenement
15 Myasnitskaya Street, Moscow
1909–1912
Sculpture near the courtyard entrance from the street, 2016

Kuznetsov Tenement
15 Myasnitskaya Street, Moscow
1909–1912
Main facade views, 2016

Бабетта

the first floor is lavishly decorated with sculptures. The traditional contrast between a heavy lower part and a lighter upper part, dating from as far back as the Renaissance, is abandoned here. The Ionic order is employed only to decorate the bay windows, the volumes of which are more expressive than the engaged columns themselves.

The most fascinating features of this complex of buildings are actually concealed behind the main facade. The desire for a practical spatial organisation led to the asymmetry of many inner elements of the various blocks. This can be clearly seen on the plans, particularly in the diverse locations of the staircases. The architect nevertheless sought to place the main accent on the symmetric details of the most visible sections of the facades – the stucco moulding and the "windoors".

The apartments at 15 Myasnitskaya Street were mainly five-room flats, which were entered from the back staircases. The large rooms in the two bottom floors looking out onto the street, to the left and right of the arched entranceway, had enormous windows and could be used either for commercial purposes or for entertaining guests. Traditional apartments were created on the second, third and fourth floors. Their inhabitants could use the balconies or bay windows, while the central balcony was accessible from the mansard.

Alexei Milyukov, along with Victor and Alexander Vesnin, contributed to the project. The Vesnin brothers, the future leaders of the Constructivist movement in the 1920s, also worked successfully before the revolution. Like Velikovsky, they applied Neoclassical Revival devices when designing either townhouses or factory buildings.

Although the main facade on Myasnitskaya Street is very expressive, the layout of the apartments was extremely mechanical. The building had all the outward attributes of a Neoclassical enfilade. But, in this particular case, there was not a series of halls interconnected by hinged doors, only combined pairs of large rooms. The apartments in the blocks inside the courtyard were more modest and had adjoining communicating rooms.

The inner structures of Velikovsky's following tenements are more interesting. Having gained experience in his work on the Ivan

Kuznetsov Tenement
15 Myasnitskaya Street, Moscow
1909–1912
Floor plans

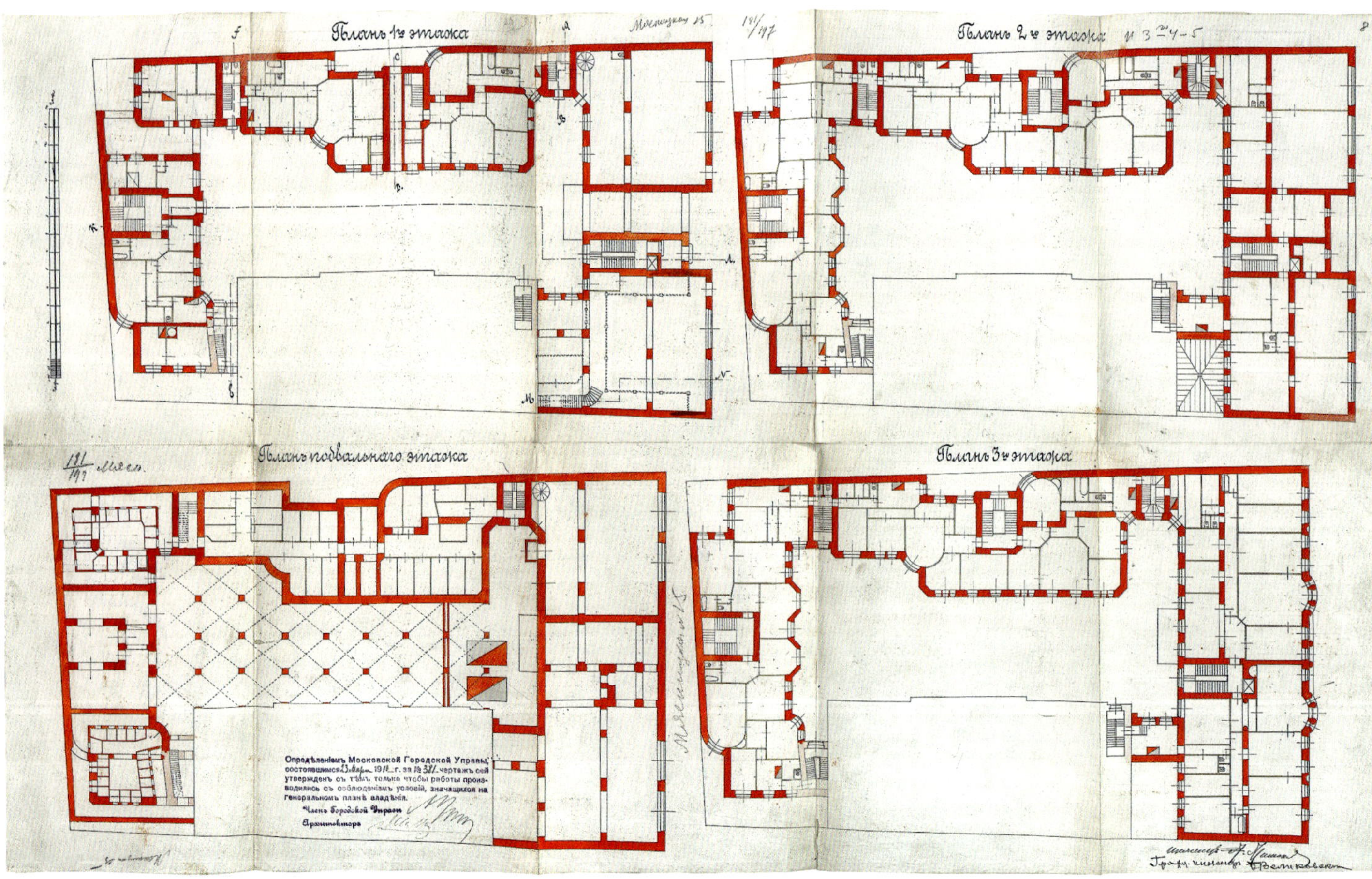

Kuznetsov Tenement, he came up with interesting new ways to configure the functional zones in the Mikhail Lunts Tenement (1910–11) and the Arkady Merkel Tenement (1911–14). Right up until the Soviet period, Velikovsky's trademark was a masterful quotation of the classics combined with features of Art Nouveau. His favourite devices were a complex inner composition, a recognisable general silhouette not aligned with the single cornice, an increased scale of the architectural and functionally important elements, rounded bay windows, entrance portals in niches, arched windows in mansards with inclined roofs, and contrasts between moulding and smooth walls.

The aforementioned forms and features in the design of the main facade went on to become model specimens in the eyes of many of Velikovsky's contemporaries. His colleagues paid extremely close attention to his work, adopting similar symmetric, upward-extending facades with light decor, which did not conceal the main constructive forms (in contrast to the simplified street facades, the courtyard sides clearly reflected the functions of the various premises).

Boris Velikovsky greatly enhanced the image of the owners of the Kuznetsov factories. Their plants manufactured widely-known products, which they marketed with the help of eye-catching artistic designs (often verging on kitsch). Kuznetsov porcelain is still an established concept, even today, albeit only among collectors. The Kuznetsov family implicitly trusted Velikovsky to create a broad range of functional buildings for them, ranging from the Old Believers' church in Gzhel and the nearby settlement for factory workers and employees to the industrial workshops, administrative blocks and hostel in Novgorod Province and the commercial and residential buildings on Myasnitskaya Street in Moscow.

Kuznetsov Tenement
15 Myasnitskaya Street, Moscow
1909–1912
Courtyard (southern) facade design

Kuznetsov Tenement
15 Myasnitskaya Street, Moscow
1909–1912
Main facade design

Фасадъ
181
197
7

06

Lunts Tenement
9 Krivokolenny Lane, Moscow
1910–1911
Architects: Boris Velikovsky and Alexei Milyukov with contributions from Victor Vesnin

The old chambers still survive in the courtyard of 9 Krivokolenny Lane. One part of them dates from the seventeenth century, while the other dates from the eighteenth century. The historical part of the vaulted chambers was later extended upwards for housing. The plot of land was owned by Doctor Mikhail Arkadyevich Lunts, a neuropathologist who worked at the First City Hospital. The doctor's surgery and the Kirchner and Co. chemist's were located in this and in another building. Mikhail Lunts also lived there with his wife, Sofia, and daughter, Lyubov. The wing extending into the lane was rented out as a state wine shop. A six-storey tenement was built in its place in 1910.

On 2 June 1910 the doctor of medicine and state councillor Mikhail Arkadyevich Lunts, along with his wife, Sofia Grigorievna Lunts, submitted an application to build a six-storey tenement in Moscow. The house was designed by Boris Velikovsky and Alexei Milyukov and the documents were accompanied by a general plan of the proposed plot of land at 9 Krivokolenny Lane. The plan showed that the new house would take the place of a series of small constructions at the curve of the lane, from where there was a good view of the Menshikov Tower. The house partially bordered the courtyard formed by the tenement of the Imperial Stroganov Central School of Art and Industry, designed by Fyodor Schechtel on Myasnitskaya Street (1904–06). This imposing building was faced with brown "subway tiles" typical of Art Nouveau architecture. The outer walls of the Lunts Tenement were also faced with tiles, albeit in a lighter tone.

The Mikhail Lunts Tenement represents an excellent example of the adaptation of the sculptural and decorative advances of the Art Nouveau style within the bounds of the Neoclassical

Lunts Tenement
9 Krivokolenny Lane, Moscow
1910–1911
View from the south-east, 2016

Revival in Russian architecture. The exterior elements are only partially similar to the forms of the Ivan Kuznetsov Tenement (the symmetric main facade is crowned by a triangular pediment). The central axis of the facade is established by the two semicircular windows – one above the entrance and one on the top floor. The upper window is decorated with a relief of an archivolt, while the capstone over the lower window is transformed into a heraldic element – a coat of arms with a shield. Two semicircular bay windows run from the second to the fourth floors. While their surfaces lack Ionic engaged columns – clearly expressed elements of an order system – many of their details recall ancient analogues. For example, the interfenestration above the second floor is decorated with reliefs depicting figures in ancient dress inside oval medallions, followed by wreaths and garlands in the interfenestration over the third floor.

The vertical windows of the staircase running up the main facade were a characteristic feature of Moscow Art Nouveau architecture. The principle of the division of the facade into three horizontal tiers with different ornamentation also emerged in the 1900s. The first two floors are smoothly plastered with large rustication. The windows on the ground floor are crowned by massive arches imitating large capstones. From the second to the fourth floors, the walls of the main and one of the side facades are decorated with beige ceramic tiles. The fifth (top) floor is divided from the other floors by a massive cornice with dentils. As in Baroque architecture, the cornice is interrupted at the point where the vertical window of the staircase passes through it.

The plan of the Mikhail Lunts Tenement reflects the flexible thinking of the two architects, who approached the historical analogues with a sense of detachment. For practical reasons, owing to the irregular form of the plot of land, they cropped off one of the sides of the house and the

corner on the courtyard side. The main and back staircases were positioned with a slight shift away from the central axis in order to accommodate two large six-roomed apartments on each floor. The windows of these apartments look out onto the lane, the side facades and the courtyard. Looking at the building from the street, the left-hand side of the house is curved. A faceted avant-corps extends on this facade, making the interiors of these apartments more spacious and interesting. Their corner rooms occupy 42–45 square metres and are larger by 5–7 square metres than the corresponding rooms in the apartments on the right-hand side (which occupy 35–40 square metres).

It was equally important that the Lunts Tenement should form a single ensemble with the tenement of the Imperial Stroganov Central School of Art and Industry on Myasnitskaya Street. This explains the presence of glazed tiles on the side (left) and main facades.

A free inner layout was particularly highly valued in Art Nouveau architecture, with each room accorded a special form and regarded as an independent section. This allowed architects to clearly highlight the main functional groups of premises, not only on the inside but also on the outside. So, in this case, both the external sculptural forms and the inner layout of the house reflect the advantages of the Art Nouveau style in the eyes of Boris Velikovsky.

The Mikhail Lunts Tenement was located opposite the Yevgeny Skalsky Tenement at 14 Krivokolenny Lane. The latter house was designed by Ivan Kondratenko (1913–14) in a similar style, with three sets of bay windows on the main facade. In this way, both the Ivan Kuznetsov Tenement and the Mikhail Lunts Tenement can be seen to have influenced other Moscow customers and architects.

Lunts Tenement
9 Krivokolenny Lane, Moscow
1910–1911
Bay window detail, 2016

Lunts Tenement
9 Krivokolenny Lane, Moscow
1910–1911
Main facade, 2016

07

Davydova (Spiridonova) Tenement
13 Myasnitskaya Street, Moscow
1898 and 1913 (extended upwards in 1934)
Architects: Semeon Eibuschitz and Boris Velikovsky

The house was originally built in the second half of the nineteenth century for honorary citizen Spiridonov, based on a project by Vladimir Sokolov. In the 1870s the Claudia Ivanovna Korotkova Library was located in the house. The famous chemist Dmitry Mendeleyev and the writer Gleb Uspensky stayed at the Hotel Royale, which opened there in the 1880s. The house was later rebuilt based on a design by architect Karl Treiman.

A three-storey brick residential building with three entranceways.

Built circa 1865.

Numbering of the apartments: 1–7.

No. 13, structure 2 – tenement of Serafima Vladimirovna Davydova, widow of a privy councillor, 1913, Boris Velikovsky (extended upwards in 1934).

The building renovated by Velikovsky (structure 2), as noted by local historians, was used until 1918 by various technical firms and offices, one of which belonged to engineer Leonhard Knipper, father of the famous Russian actress Olga Knipper.[1]

In 1898, at the request of Serafima Spiridonova-Davydova, the daughter of the first owner, Semeon Eibuschitz designed a two-storey house with a portico (13 Myasnitskaya Street, structure 1). The new owner wished to expand the premises and make the main facade look more imposing. She later commissioned Boris Velikovsky to reconstruct the main building and also asked the architect Alexander Kaminsky to design several storerooms on the same territory.

The plans show that all three floors of the building renovated by Velikovsky had universal spaces. There was a main hall in the centre and two side rooms, to which the staircase blocks were attached. Such spacious premises with large windows looking out onto the street could easily be used as either shops or offices.

Davydova (Spiridonova) Tenement
13 Myasnitskaya Street, Moscow
1898 and 1913 (extended upwards in 1934)
Columns and arch order, 2016

Velikovsky does not appear to have been very enthusiastic about the commission to reconstruct an existing building because he came up with a project which was not typical of his creative persona. He designed a traditional Renaissance arcade, employing a composite-order system much favoured by the Ancient Romans and the masters of the Renaissance. Both the stucco rustication on the ground floor and the smooth interfenestration on the top floor correspond to this particular architectural theme. The building was extended upwards and turned into a three-storey construction in 1934.

The archive materials include an unrealised version of the main facade of the neighbouring building, which has a small inflection echoing the curve of the street. This facade was designed by Velikovsky in 1914 and was intended to form a single ensemble with structure 2. This explains the similar decor – the facade has rectangular openings in the rusticated wall, while the first floor is decorated with composite pilasters.

1 Olga Leonhardovna Knipper (1868–1959) was a Russian stage actress who was born to German parents in the town of Glazov in Vyatka Province. She studied at the Moscow Philharmonic College of Music and Drama under Vladimir Nemirovich-Danchenko (1898), who invited her to join the Moscow Art Theatre (1898), where she met and married Anton Chekhov (1901).

Davydova (Spiridonova) Tenement
13 Myasnitskaya Street, Moscow
1898 and 1913 (extended upwards in 1934)
Main facade, 2016

Davydova (Spiridonova) Tenement
13 Myasnitskaya Street, Moscow
1898 and 1913 (extended upwards in 1934)
Capital, 2016

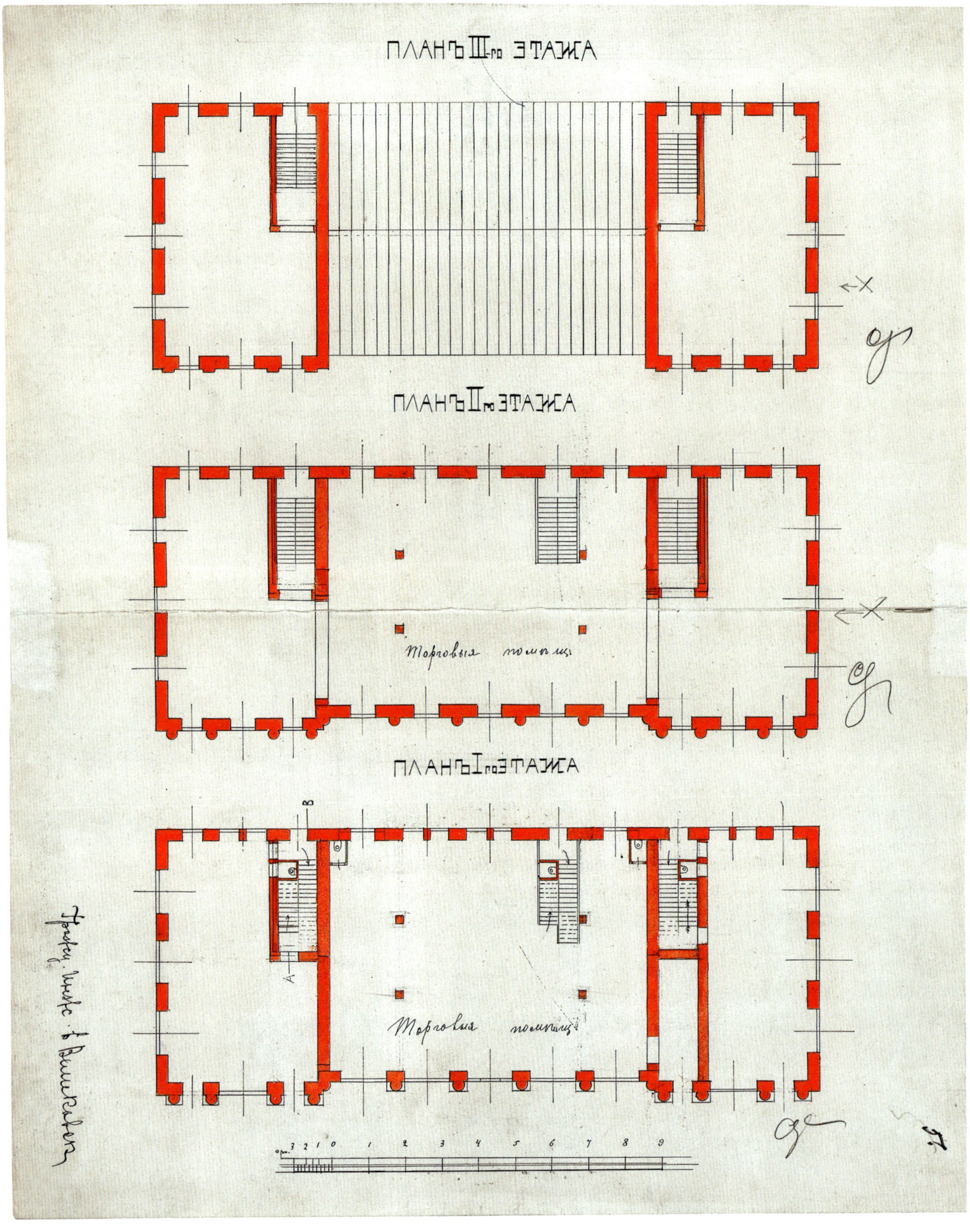

Davydova (Spiridonova) Tenement
13 Myasnitskaya Street, Moscow
1898 and 1913 (extended upwards in 1934)
Floor plans

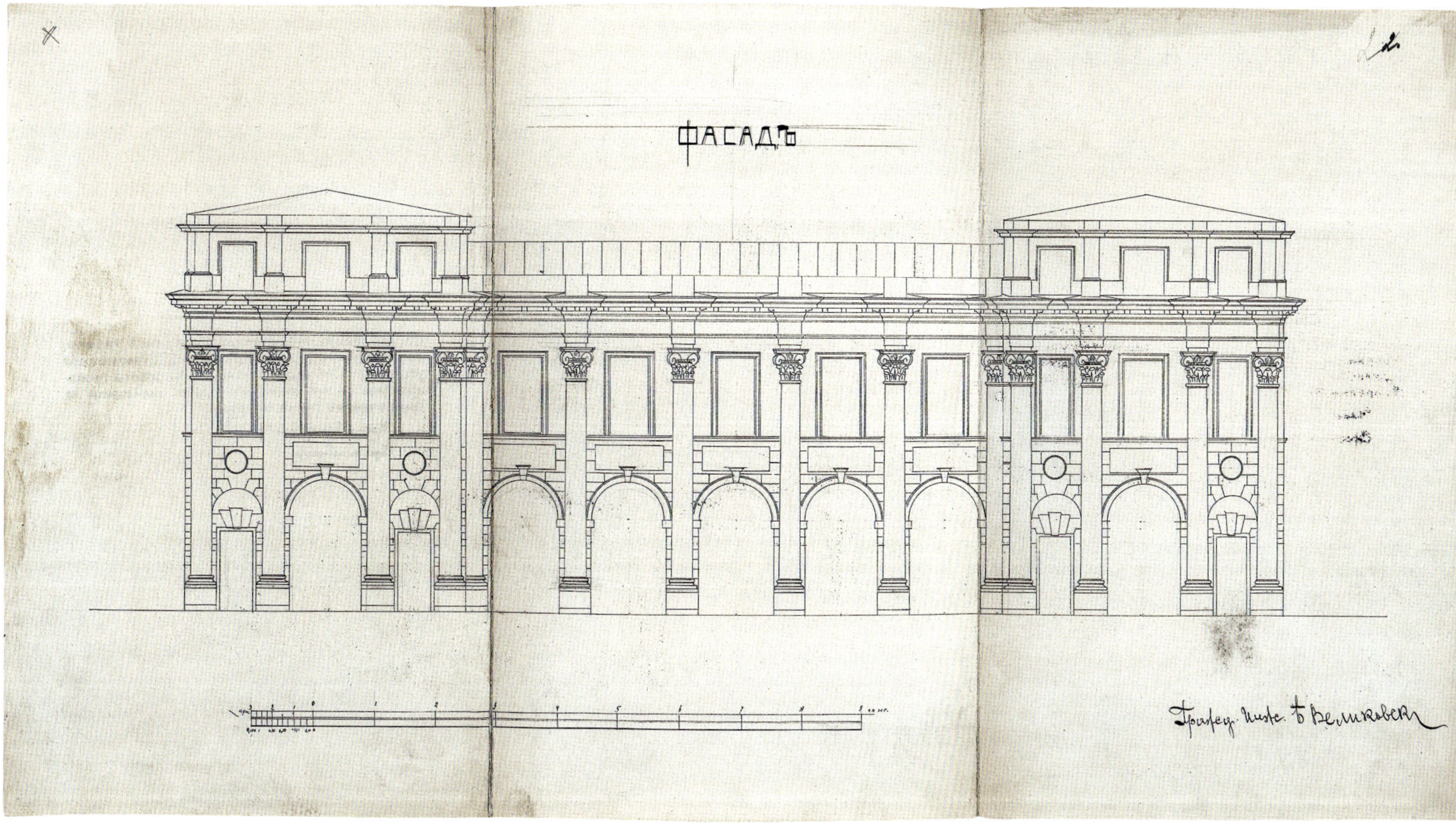

Davydova (Spiridonova) Tenement
13 Myasnitskaya Street, Moscow
1898 and 1913 (extended upwards in 1934)
Main facade designs

Davydova (Spiridonova) Tenement
13 Myasnitskaya Street, Moscow
1898 and 1913 (extended upwards in 1934)
pp. 64–65. Sidewall, 2016

08

Merkel Tenement
7 Arkhangelsky Lane, Moscow
1911–1914
Architect: Boris Velikovsky

On 7 February 1911 hereditary honorary citizen Arkady Yakovlevich Merkel, "a resident of the house of the Stroganov School", submitted a request to the Moscow Municipal Council. The request was addressed to the district architect of Moscow and concerned the Second Myasnitskaya Plot. Merkel wrote: "I herewith attach the blueprints of the plans, sections and facades and kindly ask to be allowed to construct a six-storey stone building." On 9 February 1911 the general plan for the plot of land was scrutinised and approved. Arkady Merkel died on 1 July 1912 and all his property, money and shares were divided among his wife and four children.

Boris Velikovsky designed a T-shaped house for Arkady Merkel at 7 Arkhangelsky Lane in Moscow. The plot of land was surrounded by the Armenian Church of the Exaltation of the Holy Cross (on the left), a tenement belonging to state councillor Ivan Grinberg (on the right) and the Verrein Factory (at the back). Although Merkel's territory had an irregular form, the architect decided to construct a building which looked symmetric. This was a deliberate device intended to make the house look more solid and imposing in order to attract wealthy tenants.

Velikovsky employed the same system of Neoclassical tiered decor that he had developed when designing the Ivan Kuznetsov Tenement. The ground floor had narrow pendant windows, while a moulded frieze stretched above the first floor. The entrance section above the ground floor was flanked by elliptical bay windows and decorated by simple engaged columns. The triangular pediment at the top was embellished by a semicircular frieze. The actual entrance was flanked by two pylons, which supported relief images of two women in ancient dress holding a discus entwined with ribbons.

The main entrance and vestibule were positioned in the very centre of the house. The vestibule had a wide main staircase, followed by a lesser staircase with a lift running between

Merkel Tenement
7 Arkhangelsky Lane, Moscow
1911–1914
Main facade, 2016

the flights of stairs. The house also had two back staircases.

In the original design of the house, the sole decorative elements on the central facade were the two semicircular bay windows, which were indeed striking spatial forms but not actual decor as such. Over the course of the work on the project, a bas-relief appeared on the rounded attic in the central section of the main facade – three wreaths of the kind often employed by the masters of the Empire (Regency) style in the early nineteenth century.

The tenement had both “a non-residential semi-basement and a non-residential basement”. The original version of the project included a rectangular driveway for entering the courtyard from the truncated corner of the territory.

Each floor of the house had three apartments – two on either side of the main staircase and one in the avant-corps. The latter apartments protruded right into the courtyard, were more modest in size and were well isolated from the first two apartments by the main and back staircases. The outside walls of the avant-corps had skewed corners. This was a typical device in Art Nouveau architecture and had several purposes: to make the rooms better lit, create the impression of less cramped space in the courtyard and facilitate the ease of driving by in a car.

The apartments above the ground floor looking out onto the main facade had elegant drawing rooms with bay windows. All residences had from five to seven rooms, including one near the washing facilities which could be used by servants. The bathrooms, toilets and kitchens adjoined the back staircases, which ran down to the courtyard. The house maintained the strictest standards of hygiene and all the apartments had cross ventilation and pull-out cupboards in the kitchen. The architect created a classical and functional tenement in which all the apartments were complete isolated from each other yet still enjoyed access to both a main and a back staircase.

Interestingly, the exact same scheme was chosen by architect Arkady Langman when designing the OGPU[1] house in nearby Milyutin Lane during the Soviet period. As Langman collaborated with Velikovsky on the project to design the Gostorg building in the mid-1920s, this is clearly a case of the more experienced architect conveying his professional skills to a younger colleague.

The project of the Arkady Merkel Tenement was reworked in 1913. The two back staircases were relocated and one of them now adjoined the main staircase. The lift was moved into a separate shaft. A single-storey auxiliary building appeared in the right-hand corner

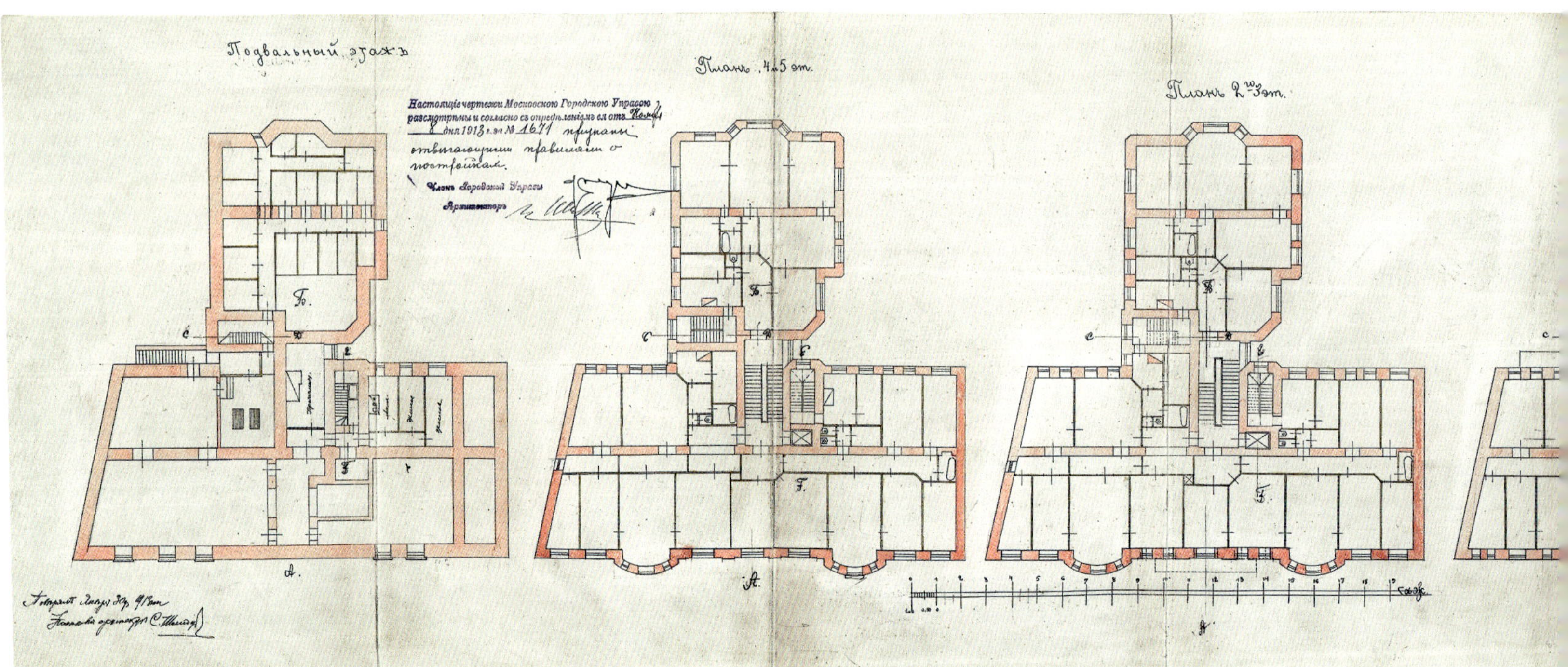

of the courtyard, directly opposite the arched entranceway. Storage rooms were created in the basement. The main facade was now decorated with semicircular windows and classical-order elements (Ionic pilasters and moulding). A round balcony appeared in the centre of the main facade, on the top (fifth) floor. The attic crowning the building grew more impressive. A small garage with storage space was planned in the courtyard (the garage was built but no longer exists).

The archive documents reveal the rents paid for the apartments, which ranged from 1,500 to 2,500 roubles.[2] The papers concerning the division of the late Arkady Merkel's property describe the structures of the facades, inner walls and ceilings – as well as details of the interior decor of the apartments.

The house is "made of stone, six-storey, roofed with iron, with a vaulted basement. There is one longitudinal wall and two cross walls [...]. The floors are of oak parquet in the rooms, wooden boards in those for the servants, ceramic tiles on reinforced concrete in the kitchens, bathrooms and closets. The ceilings are wooden, on iron beams, plastered, with moulded rosettes and cornices. The walls are plastered and wallpapered. The walls in the bathrooms are partially faced with tiles. There is central heating (hot water) and electric lighting. An elevator. One staircase is made of Italian marble and two are made of Tarusa stone. The window ledges are of marble. The windows and doors are of pine carpentry and are painted in imitation oak. The facade of the house is decorated with protruding lamps and balconies with cement plaster and stucco moulding. There are two iron fire escapes in the courtyard. The house is occupied by residential apartments, while the basement is occupied by servants' premises with wooden floors, a laundry, a place for storing firewood with asphalt floors, a boiler room, transformers and storerooms. Approximately 2,240 cubic sazhens.[3] The shed, the stables and the garage are made of stone, single-storey and roofed with iron. The ceiling is wooden, while the floors are made of boards, cement and asphalt."

The house was valued at 300,000 roubles and the garage was valued at 4,200 roubles. All the inhabitants of the apartments, the back wing and the basement were also listed. They included rich merchants, foreigners, doctors, engineers, the widows of eminent citizens and the members of Merkel's own family. The ground floor was occupied by the Evangelical Poor Fund.

The list of tenants included the family of a Latvian dentist called Pauls Dauge. Before the revolution, Dauge had been a supporter of the Social Democrats and met with Vladimir Lenin in Switzerland in 1904. For some time, the Bolsheviks even used the dentist's apartment block as a safe house. After the revolution, Lenin came to the house as a patient of Dauge, who also treated other Soviet officials.

1 OGPU (Ob'edinyonnoe gosudarstvennoe politicheskoe upravlenie, or Unified State Political Directorate) was the name for the Soviet secret police from 1923 to 1934. The OGPU was later replaced by the NKVD (1934–46), MGB (1946–53) and KGB (1954–91).

2 One golden rouble in 1913 was roughly equivalent to €33 in today's money, so rents ranging from 1,500 to 2,500 roubles were the equivalent of €45 to €75 a month. The average rent in the Merkel Tenement works out as 2,000 roubles a month or 24,000 roubles a year. The average annual salary of a worker in the Russian Empire in 1913 was 32,300 roubles (€1,000), although a well-qualified teacher or civil servant could earn around 100,000 roubles a year (€3,000).

3 The sazhen was a measurement used in pre-revolutionary Russia and equivalent to exactly three Russian arshins, or seven British feet (2.1336 metres). An area measuring 2,240 cubic sazhens would be approximately 28,456 cubic yards, or 21,755 cubic metres.

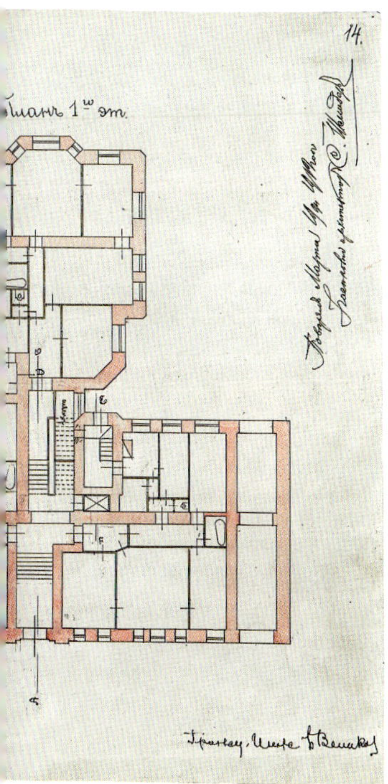

Merkel Tenement
7 Arkhangelsky Lane, Moscow
1911–1914
Floor plans

Merkel Tenement
7 Arkhangelsky Lane, Moscow
1911–1914
pp. 70–71. Main facade and entrance detail, 2016

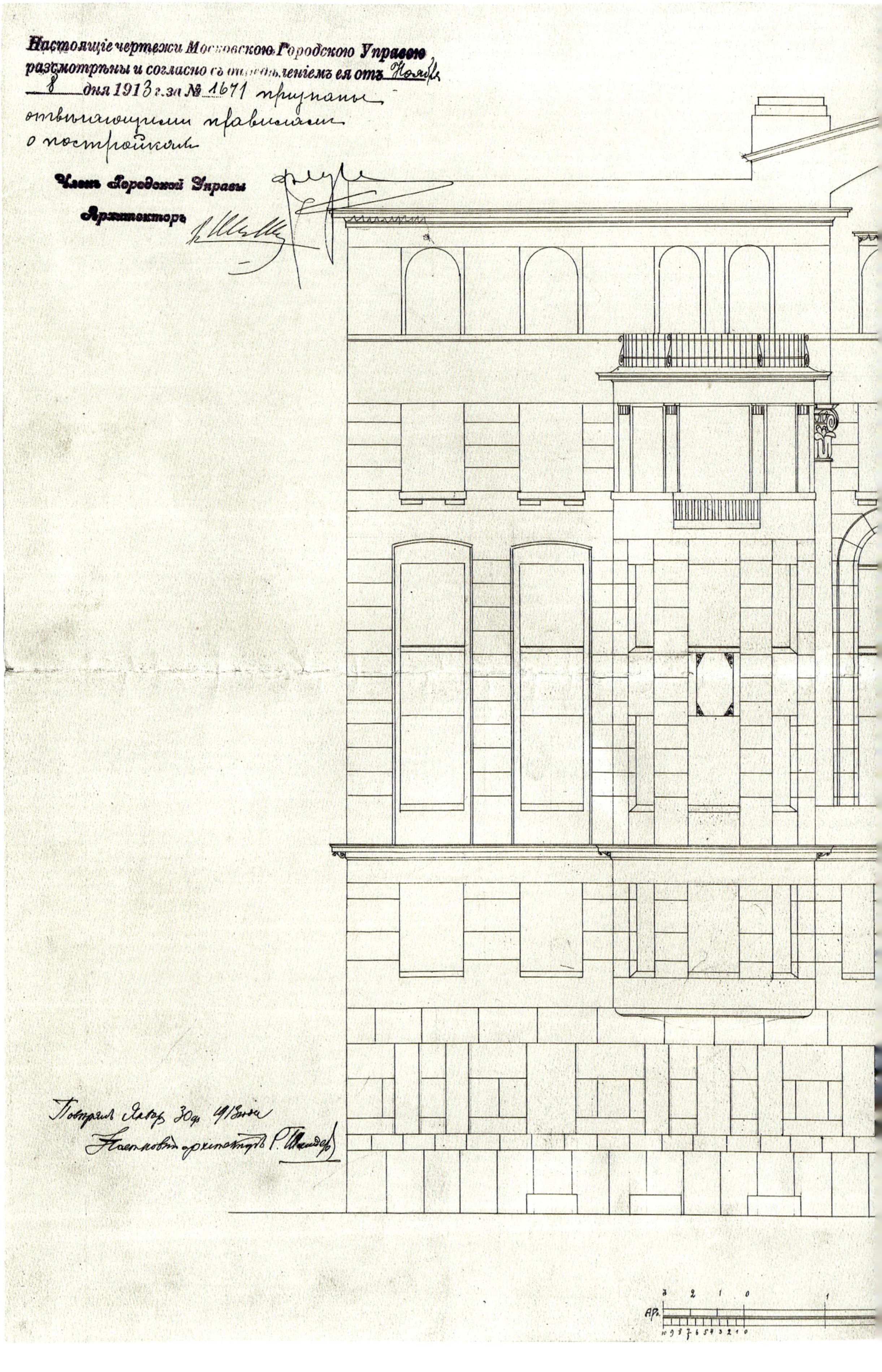

Merkel Tenement
7 Arkhangelsky Lane, Moscow
1911–1914
Main facade design

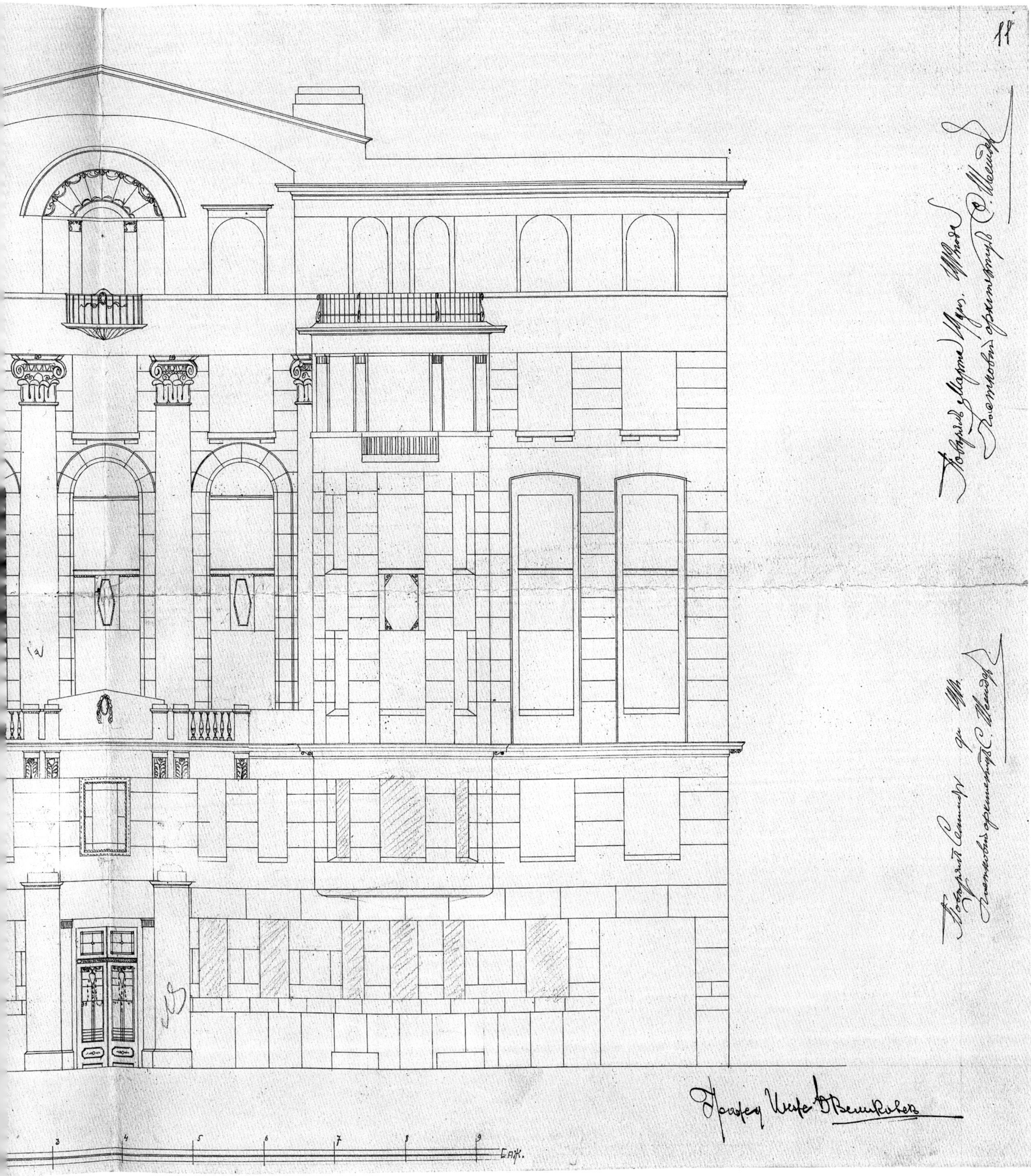

09

Prowe Tenement
16 Novaya Basmannaya Street, Moscow
1912–1913, late 1920s (attached block)
Architect: Boris Velikovsky

On 24 April 1912, permission to build a house at 16 Novaya Basmannaya Street in Moscow was granted to hereditary honorary citizen Ivan Karlovich Prowe, along with Roman (Rudolf) Ivanovich Prowe, Karl Ivanovich Prowe, Fyodor Ivanovich Prowe and Adele Ivanovna Prowe. Boris Velikovsky originally intended to construct a large residential house, but only part of the general composition of his project was actually implemented – less than half of the entire complex. In the original design, the house consisted of alternating longitudinal and cross blocks, forming courtyards on two sides – on the main side and on the auxiliary side.

The Prowe Tenement has an unusual outward shape, which is a result of the complex plan and the very original configuration of the apartments. The exterior decor is quite restrained and the composition of the building reflects the architect's masterful command of planning devices. Placed perpendicular to one another, the blocks form a short square (*carré*). The main facade is flanked by two avant-corps. Both the main and the back staircases are located at the conjunctions of the principal blocks and serve the apartments of the two different sections.

The original project was grandiose. Despite their similar dimensions, the two extended blocks were planned in different ways. The main and the back staircases changed places, which provided different ways of attaching the perpendicular blocks to them. All the apartment sections had truncated corners, a deliberate device to improve the lighting of the premises at the conjunctions. The plan of the general composition recalled a complex ornamental design.

The most prestigious apartments occupied the gable ends of the two perpendicular blocks. The largest rooms formed a grand enfilade, while the windows let in light on three sides. These blocks flanked the cour d'honneur facing the nearby park (now the Nikolai Bauman Park). The opposite side also had a courtyard, which is now hidden by the surrounding buildings. In the late

Prowe Tenement
16 Novaya Basmannaya Street, Moscow
1912–1913, late 1920s (attached block)
View from the south, 2016

1920s, a block of flats was attached to the Prowe Tenement on the left-hand side (looking from the garden). Fortunately, its austere architecture does not spoil the overall effect of Velikovsky's building.

The numerous truncated corners of the Prowe Tenement are decorated with vertical rods underscoring the fractured form. The interfenestration is accentuated by hexagonal and tetrahedral raised panels. The high crooked pediments concealing the pitched roof are embellished with a cornice, which is supported in the central section of the facade by five atlantes. Although the forms of their tensed bodies date back to classical models, their general silhouette is much simpler. The figures are stylised as warriors protecting the home (the scabbards of their swords are entwined with ribbons). The main facade is distinguished for its faceted bay windows, while the opposite facade has a protruding staircase with a stepped form underlining the central axis.

The implemented part of Velikovsky's project is famous for the original decor on the facades. The atlantes and the vertical rods are typical features of the Northern Art Nouveau style encountered in countries bordering the Baltic Sea.

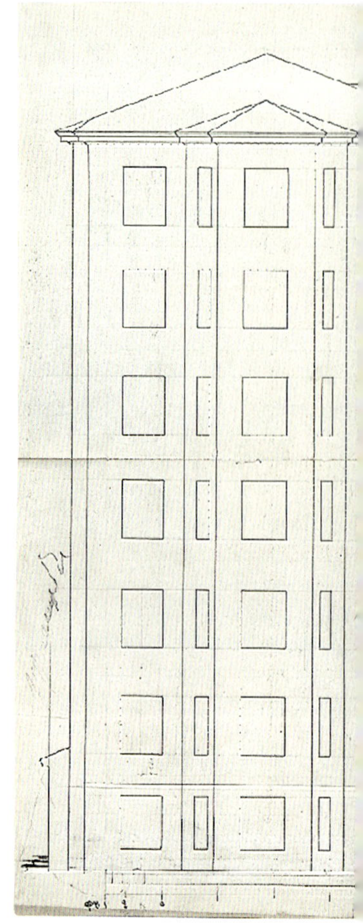

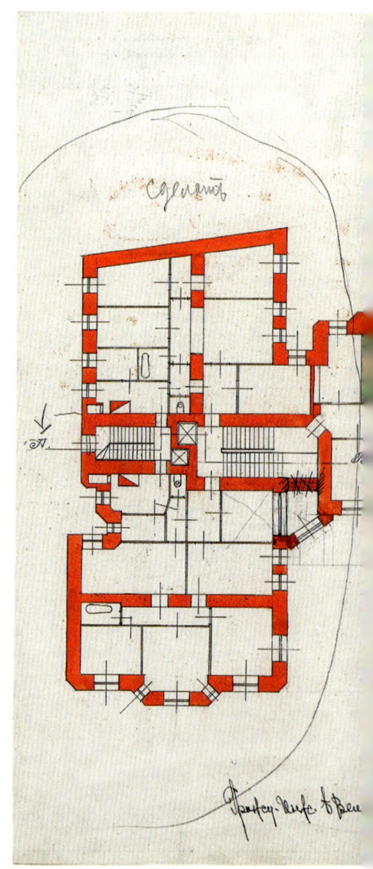

Prowe Tenement
16 Novaya Basmannaya Street, Moscow
1912–1913, late 1920s (attached block)
Park facade design and ground-floor plan

Дворовый фасадъ стр. № 4.

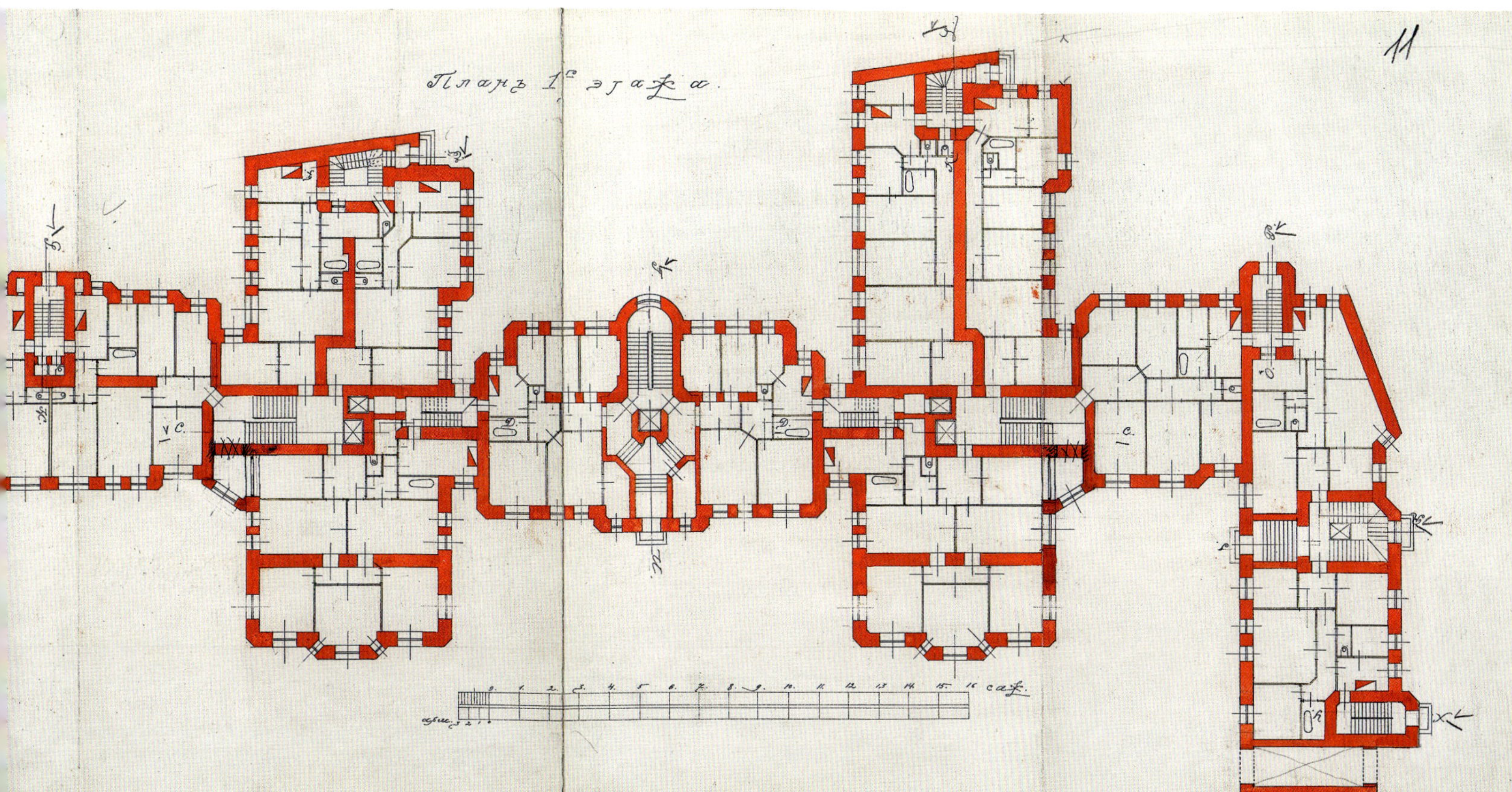
Планъ 1го этажа.
11

Prowe Tenement
16 Novaya Basmannaya Street, Moscow
1912–1913, late 1920s (attached block)
Entrance and lobby view, 1913–1914

Prowe Tenement
16 Novaya Basmannaya Street,
Moscow
1912–1913, late 1920s
(attached block)

НОВАЯ БАСМАННАЯ
16

Prowe Tenement
16 Novaya Basmannaya Street, Moscow
1912–1913, late 1920s
pp. 80–81. Main facade attic detail, 2016

Prowe Tenement
16 Novaya Basmannaya Street, Moscow
1912–1913, late 1920s
(attached block)
Southern wing views, 2016

10

Myasnitskaya Housing Association Tenement 12 First Basmanny Lane, Moscow 1913–1914 Architect: Boris Velikovsky

The plan of the house – T-shaped and not quite symmetric – is typical of the Art Nouveau style. This had the benefit of allowing courtyards to be created in conjunction with the nearby buildings. The house contained apartments with four or five rooms and different forms of bay windows. External protuberances existed not only on the street facades but also on the walls facing the courtyards. This was also typical of the Art Nouveau period, when customers sought to make the enclosed "well-courtyards" equally attractive to renters. In this particular case, many of the surrounding buildings have now been pulled down, so there is less need for such "compensation" at the present moment.

Unlike Velikovsky's other houses, the main facade of this building includes Neo-Gothic elements, which were as popular as Neoclassical features in the Art Nouveau period. The exterior decor partially repeats the neighbouring tram depot and the other industrial constructions in the surrounding area, which included the famous "square of the three railway stations".[1] The essential difference is that these were red-brick buildings, while Velikovsky's tenement was roughcast.

Two balconies have been placed above the arched entrance, while the central section ends in a triangular gable. Bay windows are located on either side of the entrance with slender vertical pilasters reminiscent of Gothic bundles of columns. The pilasters are crowned on the level of the top floor with capitals resembling fortress towers. These delicate decorative details contrast with the brutal walls of the two lower floors, which appear to be composed of large stones and boast ponderous Roman-style semicircular arches.

In the original blueprint of the main facade, the decor is arranged in the form of scattered groups. In the course of construction work, however, this plan was only partially realised. Only the blank parapets of the balconies with their square, rectangular and rhomboid

Myasnitskaya Housing Association Tenement
12 First Basmanny Lane, Moscow
1913–1914
Entrance detail, 2016

raised panels were actually created. The right-hand corner of the main facade is accentuated by an elevated tower section. The wall there was intended to be decorated with paintwork and high turrets, while the niche set in the wall was probably designed to include a statue.

The house does not have a fully-fledged cornice. The silhouette of the building is deliberately fractionary, and the contours are interrupted by the numerous finials, chimney pipes and gables. The courtyard facade is also fractionary and equally imposing, despite the absence of roughcasting and rustication.

The presence of a nearby tenement in the Neoclassical Revival tradition – the Hugo Eberling House at 6 First Basmanny Lane (1911–12) – may have influenced Velikovsky's decision not to repeat this same style. The Hugo Eberling House was designed by Karl Greinert, a graduate of the Imperial Academy of Arts in St Petersburg. At that time Greinert was a lecturer at the Imperial Stroganov Central School of Art and Industry in Moscow, where he had already designed a series of buildings.

1 Komsomolskaya Square in Moscow is informally known as the "square of the three railway stations" because it is home to the Yaroslavl, Kazan and Leningrad railway stations. The location was initially known as Kalanchyovskaya Square after the Palace of Tsar Alexis Mikhailovich, which had a wooden viewing tower (*kalancha*). It was renamed Komsomolskaya Square in 1933, in honour of the fifteenth anniversary of the founding of the Komsomol (Communist Youth League).

Myasnitskaya Housing Association Tenement
12 First Basmanny Lane, Moscow
1913–1914
Floor plans

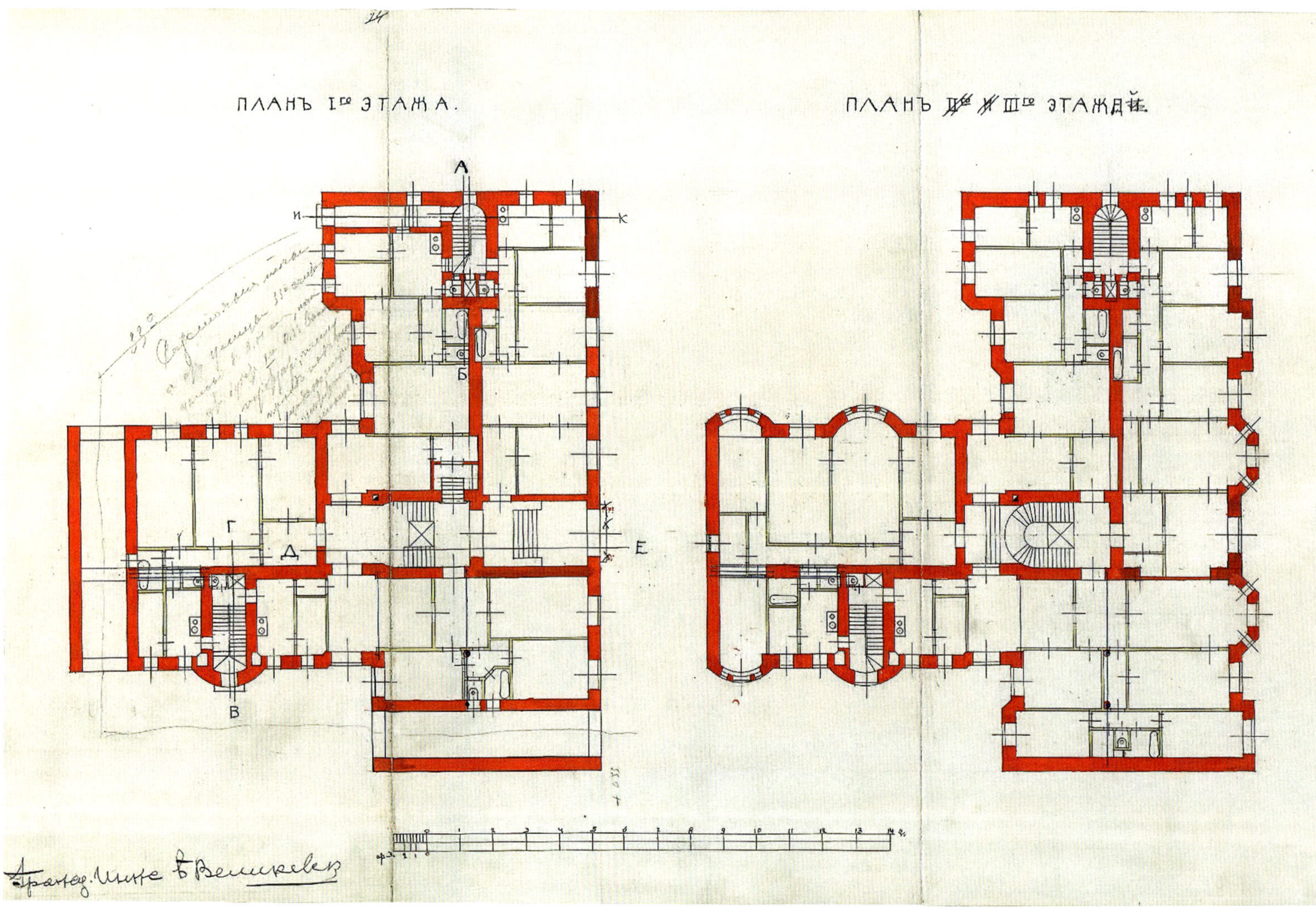

Myasnitskaya Housing Association Tenement
12 First Basmanny Lane, Moscow
1913–1914
Main facade design

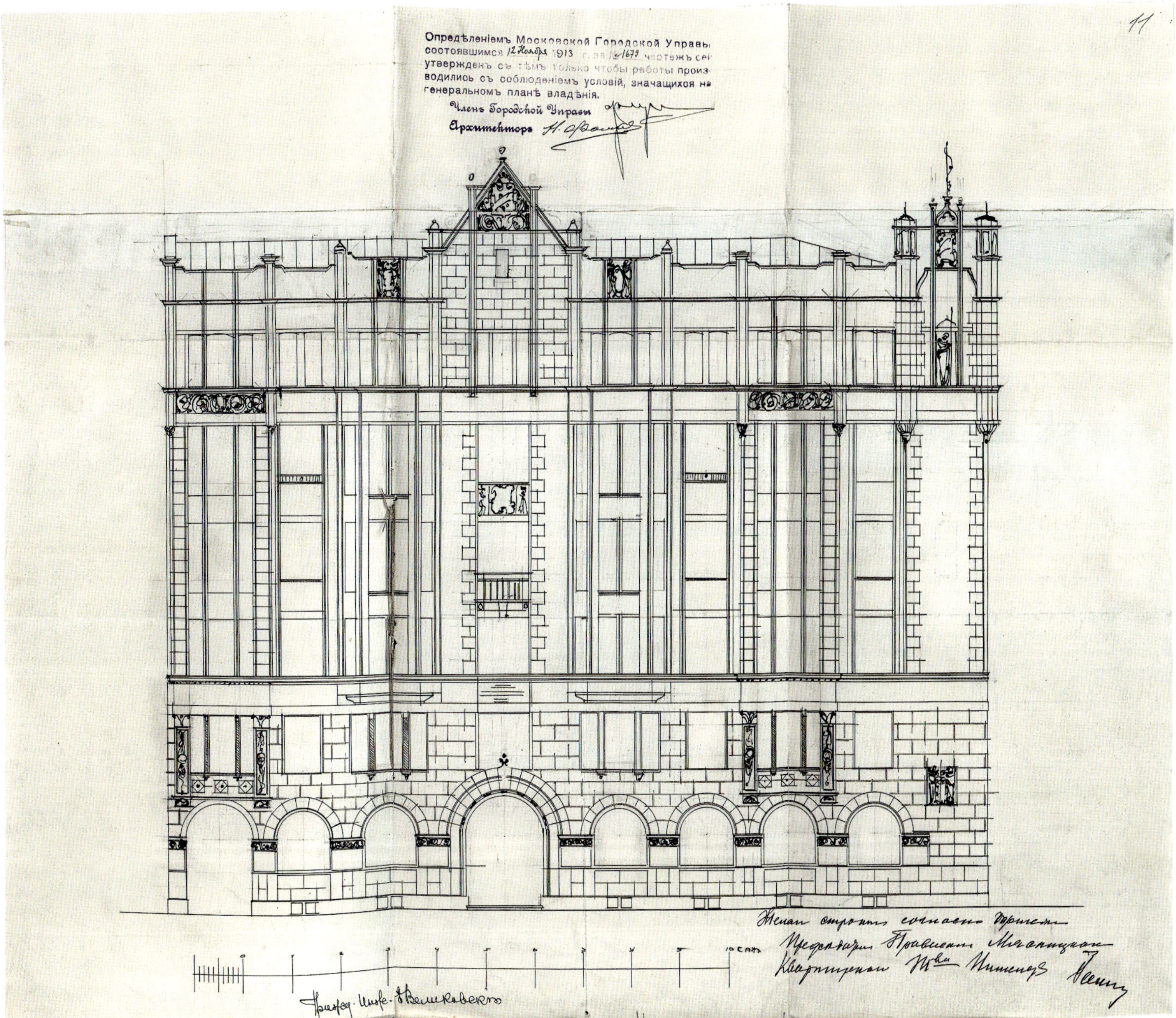

Myasnitskaya Housing Association Tenement
12 First Basmanny Lane, Moscow
1913–1914
Courtyard facade and false attic, 2016

Myasnitskaya Housing Association Tenement
12 First Basmanny Lane, Moscow
1913–1914
Attic detail, 2016

II

Doctor Eberlin House
9/1 Klimentovsky Lane, Moscow
1912–1913
Architect: Boris Velikovsky

On 28 June 1912 a medical doctor called Afanasy (Afroim) Moiseyevich Eberlin submitted a request to be allowed to construct a five-storey house from stone with a two-storey residential section. Permission was granted and Boris Velikovsky designed an L-shaped house with bay windows facing three streets. The three main facades were all different and looked onto the Church of Pope Clement I, Klimentovsky Lane and Malaya Ordynka Street.

The most imposing side stands on Malaya Ordynka Street. This facade is symmetric and has a typical axial composition with three vertical segmentations. Two sets of bay windows are flanked by composite pilasters. The pediment is rectangular rather than triangular, while the semicircular attic window – a virtually obligatory feature of tenements in the Neoclassical Revival style – is created with the help of a relief depicting a wreath.

The corner of the house is accentuated by rounded bay windows, which are repeated by even more prominent bay windows located to the right-hand side – rather than the centre – of the facade looking onto Klimentovsky Lane. The third facade on Golikovsky Lane has a rectangular avant-corps. There is another bay window on the courtyard facade.

Such detailing of the facades represents an original reflection of the principles of a dynamic composition. Yet while this system was very typical of Art Nouveau architecture, the approach was employed very circumspectly by Velikovsky in this particular case. The facades of this building do not reflect the inner arrangement of the premises to the same extent as they do in his other constructions.

The large-scale rustication on the ground floor gives way to more refined rustication on the first, second and third floors. The interfenestration on the second floor is embellished with imitation balustrades, while the third floor is decorated with small medallions and shallow niches with reliefs of wreaths and garlands. The cornices above the ground and third floors are small in scale. The

Doctor Eberlin House
9/1 Klimentovsky Lane, Moscow
1912–1913
Main facade plasterwork details, 2016

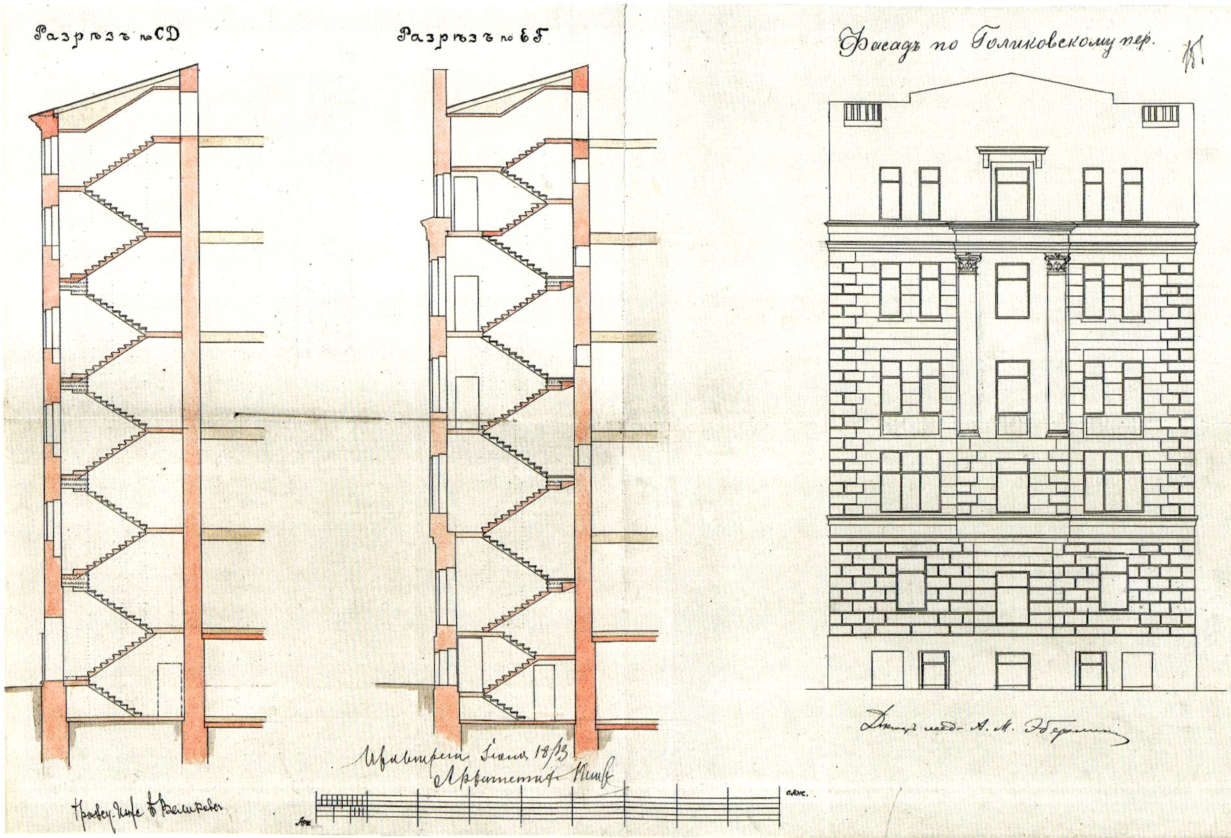
Разрѣзъ по CD
Фасадъ по Голиковскому пер.

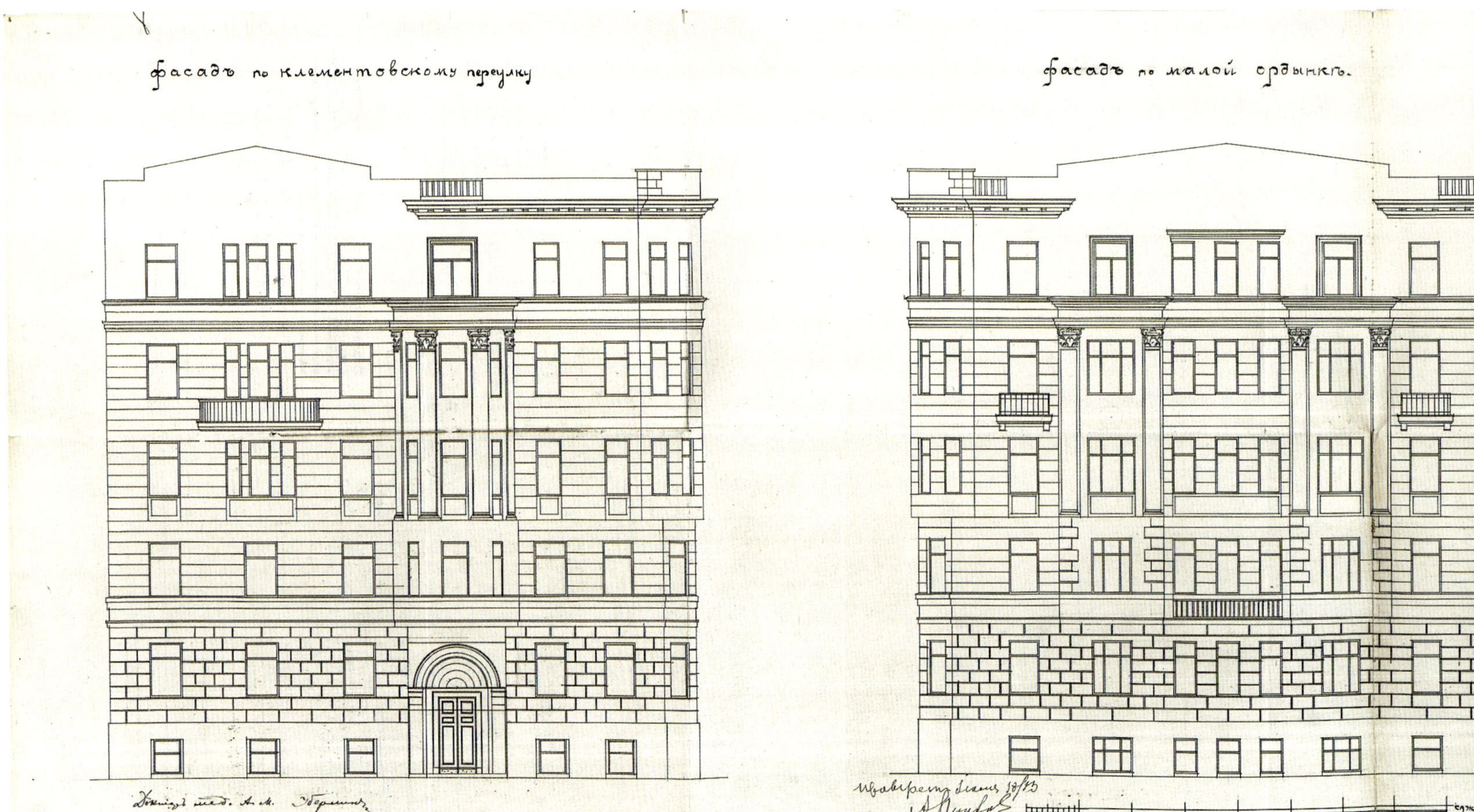
фасадъ по клементовскому переулку
фасадъ по малой ордынкѣ.

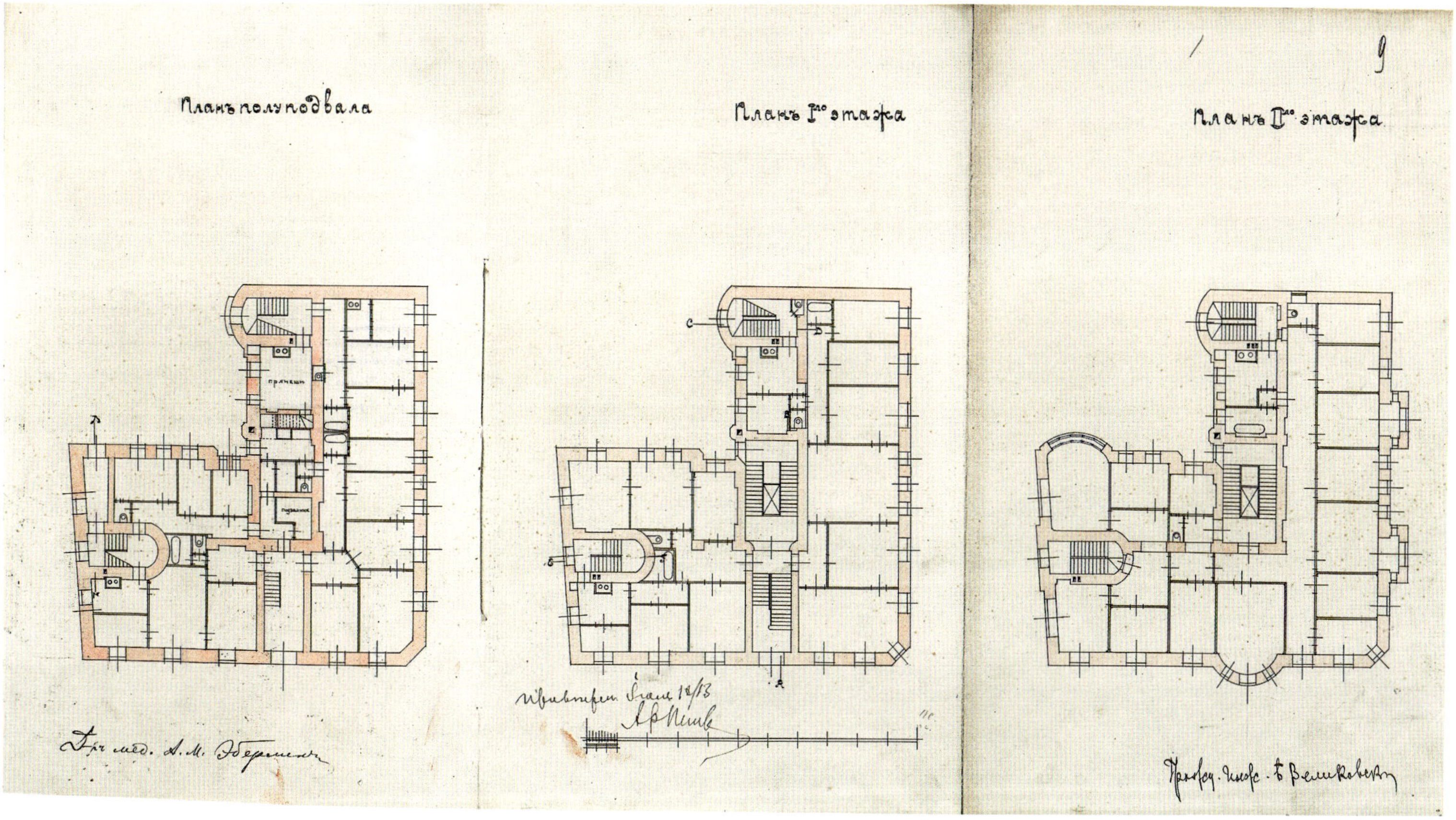

Doctor Eberlin House
9/1 Klimentovsky Lane, Moscow
1912–1913
Semi-basement
Plan of the 1st floor
Plan of the 2nd floor

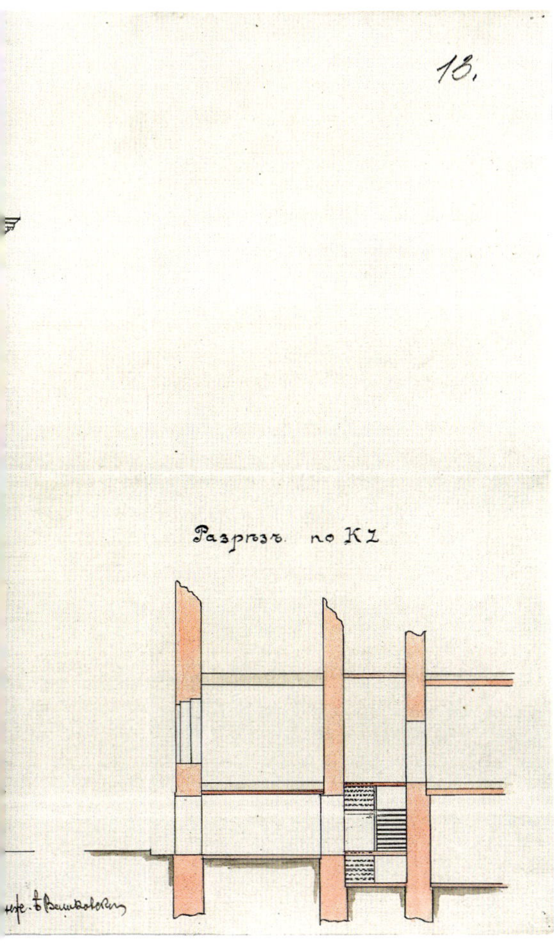

Doctor Eberlin House
9/1 Klimentovsky Lane, Moscow
1912–1913
Sections
Facade

Doctor Eberlin House
9/1 Klimentovsky Lane, Moscow
1912–1913
Main facade design
On the side of Klementovsky Lane
On the side of Malaya Ordinka St.

upper cornice has the largest overhang and the most detailed brackets. All these modest details contrast perfectly with the blank surfaces of the walls.

The rooms looking out onto the streets were used as the premises of Doctor Eberlin's gynaecological clinic and as private apartments. They were linked by corridors in the semi-basement and on the first and second floors. The ground floor housed a large reception room for visitors to the clinic, while the second floor contained the more spacious premises of the owner's private apartments. The third and fourth floors had smaller and more compact apartments, which were rented out.

A grey five-storey building known as the Doctor Eberlin House stands on the corner of 9 Klimentovsky Lane and 1 Golikovsky Lane in Zamoskvorechye.[1]

The state councillor Afanasy (Afroim) Moiseyevich Eberlin was a medical doctor who specialised in female illnesses. By the time he moved to Klimentovsky Lane, he had already lectured for ten years at Moscow University and was working at the Golitsyn Hospital. In 1917, he became a professor of the department of operative gynaecology and obstetrics.

Doctor Eberlin made careful plans to fully utilise each part of this enormous house, the size of which would have been envied by his literary colleague, Professor Preobrazhensky from Mikhail Bulgakov's novel The Heart of a Dog.[2]

The doctor's private gynaecological clinic was located on the first floor of the building. Besides comfortable wards and what was, for those days, a modern operating theatre, there was even a maternity hospital. Only well-off women could afford to be treated by Eberlin – the same class of people who inhabited the ground floor [...].

Neither was the attic at 9/1 Klimentovsky Lane left unused. There the professor created a winter garden, which was protected from bad weather by a glass roof shaped like a marquee (it is currently covered by tin sheets).[3]

1 Zamoskvorechye is the land on the right or southern bank of the River Moskva. The name literally means "beyond the Moskva river" and referred to the territory directly on the other side of the river from the Kremlin.

2 Mikhail Bulgakov (1891–1940) was a Russian novelist and playwright best known for the satirical story *The Heart of a Dog* (1925) and the novel *The Master and Margarita* (1928–39). He was born and grew up in Kiev but moved to Moscow in 1921 with the aim of becoming a writer. After working as a newspaper reporter from 1921 to 1926, Bulgakov mainly staged plays at the Moscow Art Theatre. He died of hypertensive nephropathy in Moscow in 1940.

3 See: http://progulkipomoskve.ru/publ/doma/klimentovskij_pereulok_9_1_golikovskij_pereulok_dom_ehberlina/39-1-0-1354

Doctor Eberlin House
9/1 Klimentovsky Lane, Moscow
1912–1913
View from north-west, 2016

СВЯЗНОЙ
СВЯЗНОЙ

12

Alexeyev Tenement
42/2 Bolshaya Polyanka Street, Moscow
1912–1913
Architects: Boris Velikovsky, Alexei Milyukov and Vyacheslav Korchagin

The tenement on the corner of 42 Bolshaya Polyanka Street and 2 First Spasonalivkovsky Lane in Moscow stands on the very edge of a pointed piece of land. The configuration of the building is extremely practical, ensuring that every single square metre is utilised to the maximum. The five-storey multi-sectional house is asymmetric, and the main accent falls on the rounded corner section jutting out onto the street, where the entrance is located.

The entrance is set inside a niche and framed by two thick pylons decorated with vases and Doric columns. Two pairs of Corinthian columns support the arches of a loggia. This loggia is located directly above the entrance, drawing attention to the most important apartments on the first and second floors. The two floors located above them had more standardised apartments, and this part of the house, which is also rounded, was designed in a simpler fashion. The corner section of the building ends in a rotunda with a cupola.

While the presence of such details as the vases and the coffers above the entrance indicate the Neoclassical Revival style, the dynamic forms of the building reflect the influence of Art Nouveau. Even similar elements, such as the numerous bay windows, alternate with variations. For example, the bay windows closest to the corner have a more complicated configuration. Moving away from the corner, they are semicircular and then, even further away, they become three-sided. Moreover, on the facade on First Spasonalivkovsky Lane the bay windows have been slightly shifted in relation to the compositional axes of the corresponding sections of the building. In addition, the ones furthest from the corner are crowned with elliptical and triangular gables, contrasting with the simple attic girdling the rest of the house like a ribbon.

Alexeyev Tenement
42/2 Bolshaya Polyanka Street, Moscow
1912–1913
Rotunda, 2016

The cornice crowning the facades is interrupted in places, contributing to the overall dynamic effect. While the simple shapes of the windows lack the diversity typical of Art Nouveau, some of the vertical windows end in a semicircular arch. In several places the interfenestration is embellished with raised panels or decorated with cartouches. The walls of the socle and ground floors have virtually indiscernible rustication.

The courtyard facades also contain many features of Art Nouveau – protuberances, avant-corps and truncated corners. Although such forms were dictated by the practical need for insolation, their configuration reflects the creative hand of an architect working in close correspondence with the predominant style of that period.

Alexeyev Tenement
42/2 Bolshaya Polyanka Street, Moscow
1912–1913
Rotunda detail, 2016

Alexeyev Tenement
42/2 Bolshaya Polyanka Street,
Moscow
1912–1913
Rotunda, 2016

Alexeyev Tenement
42/2 Bolshaya Polyanka Street, Moscow
1912–1913
View from the south, 2016

Alexeyev Tenement
42/2 Bolshaya Polyanka Street, Moscow
1912–1913
Eastern facade, 2016

13
Kuznetsov Tenement
27/21 Zagorodny Prospekt, St Petersburg
1915–1916
Architects: Boris Velikovsky, Alexander Rosenberg and David Buryshkin

The building included the house previously existing on the plot of land, which had belonged to the Eristova princesses, daughters of a full state councillor. The new tenement belonged to Ivan Kuznetsov, "St Petersburg merchant of the first guild" and owner of major "porcelain-faience and crystal-glass" factories, which were famous across the whole of Russia and won numerous awards at national and international exhibitions. These factories constituted the capital of the Ivan Kuznetsov Co-Partnership in 1913 and were nationalised in 1918. During the Soviet period the Kuznetsov Porcelain and Faience Factory in Gruzino was known as the Red Porcelainist Factory but was renamed the Kuznetsov Factory in 2003. The famous Russian writer Kornei Chukovsky[1] lived in this house from 1917 to 1919.

The Ivan Kuznetsov Tenement was built in Petrograd (St Petersburg) during the First World War. Despite these circumstances, the architecture of this house is even more commanding and imposing than the equivalent tenement which Boris Velikovsky designed for Ivan Kuznetsov in Moscow (1909–12).

The building occupies a large plot of land. The rounded corner emerging onto the crossroads is decorated by a coat of arms with the date 1916 inside a cartouche with floral garlands, which are supported by two putti.[2] The extended facade running along 27 Zagorodny Prospekt is designed in a deliberately traditionalist style. The central section is made slightly higher by the creation of an attic with open arches. This arcade recalls the park structures in Italian gardens during the Baroque period.

The ground, first and second floors are embellished by two massive porticos with engaged columns and pilasters. The architect chose the most imposing composite-order system, widely applied by both Ancient Roman and Baroque

Kuznetsov Tenement
27/21 Zagorodny Prospekt,
St Petersburg
1915–1916
Main facade plasterwork detail, 2016

Kuznetsov Tenement
27/21 Zagorodny Prospekt,
St Petersburg
1915–1916
pp. 104–105. Entablature detail, 2016
pp. 106–107. Main facade, 2015

Kuznetsov Tenement
27/21 Zagorodny Prospekt,
St Petersburg
1915–1916
View from the east, 2015

Kuznetsov Tenement
27/21 Zagorodny Prospekt,
St Petersburg
1915–1916
Entrance niche, 2016

Kuznetsov Tenement
27/21 Zagorodny Prospekt,
St Petersburg
1915–1916
Lobby stairs, 2016

Kuznetsov Tenement
27/21 Zagorodny Prospekt,
St Petersburg
1915–1916
Banister, 2016

Kuznetsov Tenement
27/21 Zagorodny Prospekt,
St Petersburg
1915–1916
pp. 112–113. Main stairwell, 2016

masters. The cornice above the columns is broken, creating a play of light and shade. The porticos emphasise the two front entrances and the three balconies with coats of arms on the parapets. Two pairs of windows on the third floor, positioned directly above the porticos, are decorated with large keystones and pediments. The vestibules still retain the decorative forms of the vaults, the forged railings of the staircases, the moulding on the ceilings and the stone paving. A similar portico with a vestibule was also created on the side facade running along 21 L'Estocq (now Jambyl) Lane.

The Ivan Kuznetsov Tenement in St Petersburg is probably Boris Velikovsky's most classical creation. The return to academicism was, in this particular case, dictated by the desire of the customer to reflect the solidity of his factories, even during wartime. The final design was possibly influenced by Alexander Rosenberg (1877–1935), who graduated from the St Petersburg Institute of Civil Engineers the same year as Velikovsky and mostly worked in a retrospective style. The other co-author, David Buryshkin (1890–1959), was younger, less experienced and did not create anything significant until the Soviet period.

1 Kornei Chukovsky (1882–1969) was the pseudonym of Nikolai Korneichukov, a Russian-Jewish writer who was born in St Petersburg, grew up in Odessa and worked as a newspaper correspondent in London (1903–04). Returning to Russia, Chukovsky translated English poetry, compiled biographies of Russian writers and wrote nonsensical poems for children. He was the father of the writer Lydia Chukovskaya (1907–1996).

2 Putti is the plural of *putto*, the Italian word for a chubby male child in art, usually depicted as winged and nude. They first appeared in ancient art as physical forms of the *genii* (spiritual beings) believed to influence people's lives. Putti reappeared during the Renaissance and became increasingly confused with cherubim from the Baroque period onwards.

Kuznetsov Tenement
27/21 Zagorodny Prospekt,
St Petersburg
1915–1916
Main facade design

Kuznetsov Tenement
27/21 Zagorodny Prospekt,
St Petersburg
1915–1916
Portico, 2016

14
Herzenberg Tenements
22 Tsvetnoi Boulevard, Moscow
1912–1914
Architect: Boris Velikovsky

The owner of the plot of land at 22 Tsvetnoi Boulevard in Moscow was a hereditary honorary citizen called Alexander Robertovich Herzenberg. In the years before the First World War, he applied for permission to construct two tenements at that address, far back from the road. The project of the first tenement was submitted for approval on 8 March 1912, and the second was submitted a year later, on 7 May 1913.

The two houses were designed without any visible connection to one another, besides the fact of their common ownership. The first tenement was located furthest of all from Tsvetnoi Boulevard, and its main facade looked onto the passageway formed between the other buildings. This house was a one-section building with a symmetric main facade and very simple decor, which can be described as Neoclassical Revival, albeit with virtually no elements of an order system except for such minor details as cornices. The archive materials include the blueprint of the courtyard facade and the plans of the residential semi-basement and the four storeys above ground.

The plans of the house show that it was built for customers of a very high status. Besides the main staircase, providing access to four apartments, there were also two back staircases. The best apartments looked onto the main facade, where four rooms were arranged in an enfilade. They were connected to a narrow corridor intended for the cook and servants, which, along with the kitchen and the toilet facilities, looked onto the courtyard. The three residential rooms of the apartments facing the courtyard are located in the protruding avant-corps. Remarkably, even the semi-basement was occupied by similar apartments, which were extremely comfortable by the standards of the 1910s. Their facade section is simplified and so does not reflect the high quality of the inner space to quite the same extent.

The second and more fashionable tenement was also built deep inside the plot of land. The facades had distinct lines and professionally drawn decor. The architecture of this building conjures up associations with

Herzenberg Tenements
22 Tsvetnoi Boulevard, Moscow
1912–1914
Order detail, 2016

the Soviet version of Neoclassicism in the late 1940s and 1950s. In both houses the corner cylindrical volume acted as a "knuckle joint" at the conjunction of the two perpendicular sections. The right angles and the edges of the facades in the second house are enhanced by rustication. However, many details reflect the architecture of the 1910s. These include the elongated proportions of the vertical windows and the artistically executed iron railings of the balconies. The oval (rather than circular) forms of the outside walls of the bay windows were also typical of the Art Nouveau style, which was still fashionable on the eve of the First World War.

Alexander Herzenberg intended to construct another block in direct proximity to Tsvetnoi Boulevard. The intricate form of this house may have recalled the dynamic and complex composition of the Prowe Tenement (which was not fully realised). However, there is no information in the archives on the construction of this final building on Tsvetnoi Boulevard.

Herzenberg Tenements
22 Tsvetnoi Boulevard, Moscow
1912–1914
View from the north, 2016

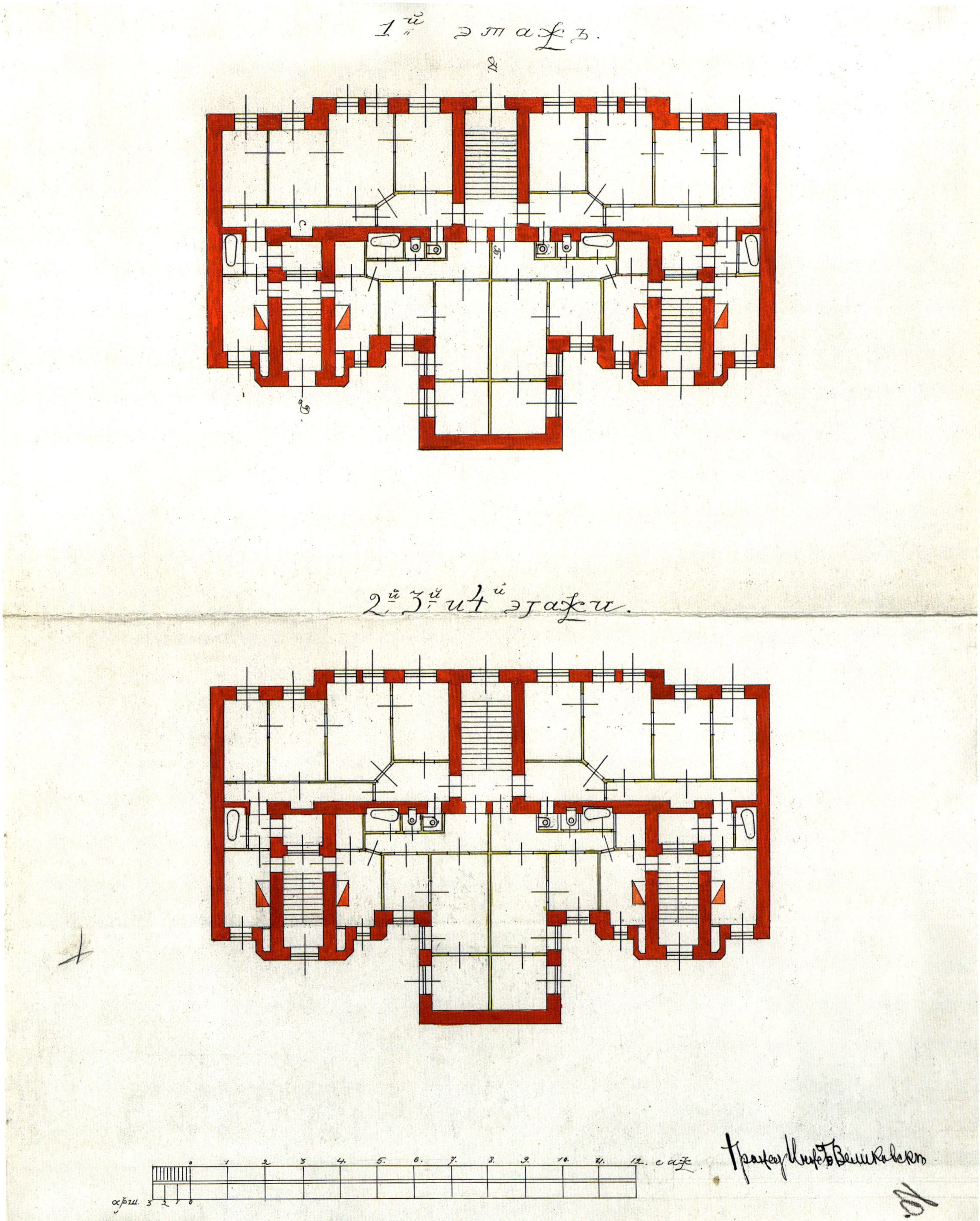
1й этажъ.
2й, 3й и 4й этажи.
0 1 2 3 4 5 6 7 8 9 10 11 12 саж.
арш. 3 2 1 0

Herzenberg Tenements
22 Tsvetnoi Boulevard, Moscow
1912–1914
Left (eastern) wing floor plans

Herzenberg Tenements
22 Tsvetnoi Boulevard, Moscow
1912–1914
Left (eastern) wing main facade, 2016

Н079ЕВ 777

15

Mansbach German Gymnasium
10 First Basmanny Lane, Moscow
1913–1914
Architect: Boris Velikovsky

The Mansbach Gymnasium was a German grammar school which stood well back inside the courtyard of 10 First Basmanny Lane in Moscow (the back wall now looks onto Novoryazanskaya Street). On 27 August 1913 Felizia Franzevna Mansbach received permission to construct a four-storey stone building on that plot of land for use as a grammar school. The original plans included an open veranda at the top, creating a five-storey structure. Although this scheme was not implemented, the four-storey building with a basement still stands to this day.

The archive documents show the usual array of different premises found in any boarding school – a science laboratory, a gym, classrooms for drawing and other subjects, dormitories for the children and the apartments of the headmistress. The entrance to the building is from the courtyard between structures 8 and 12. The basement contained a boiler house, an ironing room and other auxiliary services. The ground floor had a vestibule with a staircase and a large dining room with a semicircular avant-corps.

The assembly room, which also had an avant-corps, was located on the first floor above the dining room. The classrooms on the first and second floors were arranged in a single row. Their windows were set in the main facade, while their doors exited onto a common corridor running along the entire block. The corridor on the first floor provided access to the residential rooms of the attendants, the seamstress and the housekeeper. The second floor consisted solely of classrooms, with the drawing room and the science laboratory located in the avant-corps above the assembly room. The third floor contained the toilet facilities, dormitories, lounges, monitors' rooms and the apartments of the headmistress. The original plans envisaged premises for a doctor above these rooms and a small hospital with an exit onto the open veranda.

The configuration of all these diverse and functional interiors explains the striking architectural composition with widths of different

Mansbach German Gymnasium
10 First Basmanny Lane, Moscow
1913–1914
Main facade, 2016

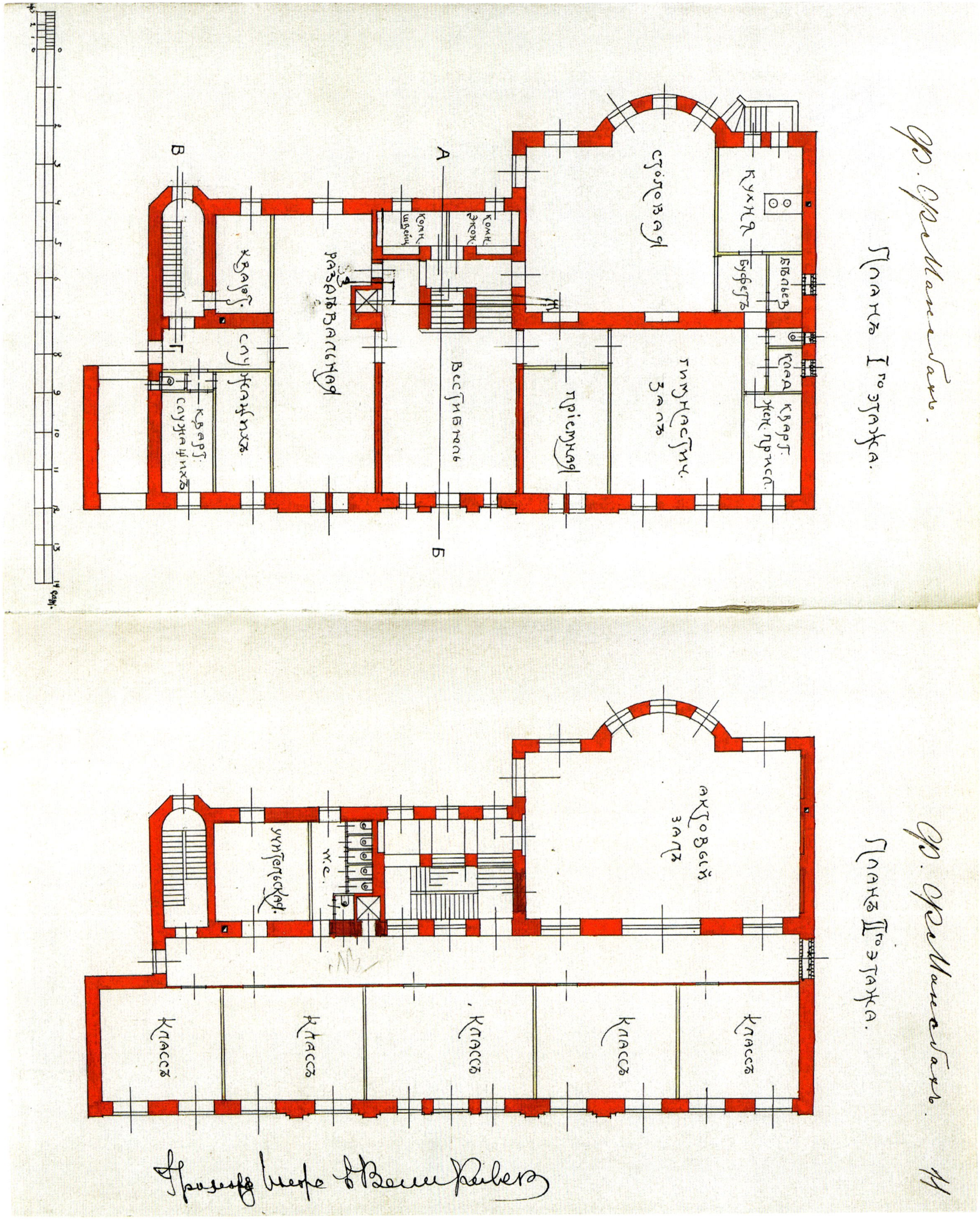
Планъ I^го этажа.
столовая
кухня
буфетъ
гимнастич. залъ
пріемная
вестибюль
раздевальная
служащихъ
кварт. служащихъ
Планъ II^го этажа.
актовый залъ
учительская
классъ
классъ
классъ
классъ
классъ

sizes. Remarkably, this asymmetry in the plan of the grammar school is not reflected in the symmetric facade. To this day, the building looks the same from the courtyard – the central section is decorated with four composite pilasters on the first and second floors and is crowned by an attic with a gable.

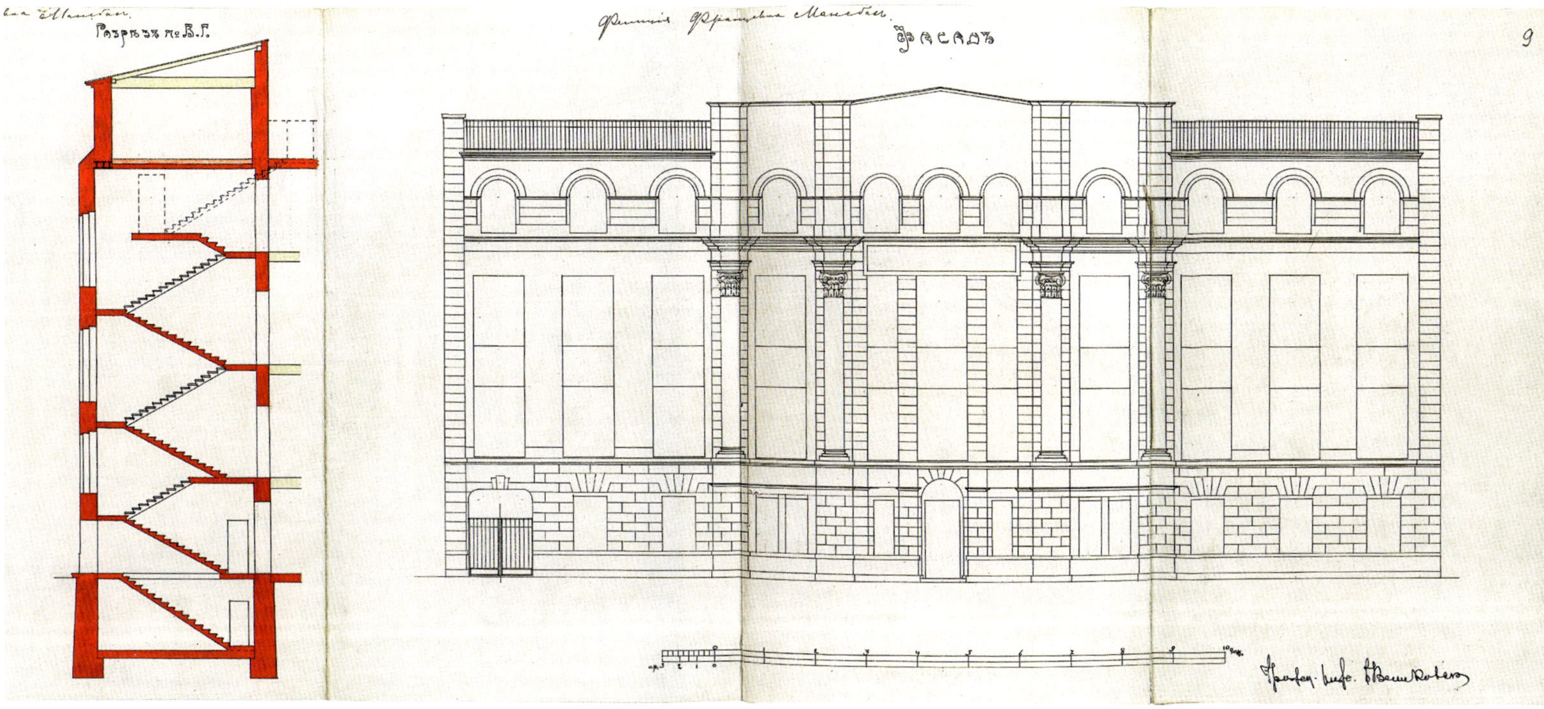

Mansbach German Gymnasium
10 First Basmanny Lane, Moscow
1913–1914
Floor plans

Mansbach German Gymnasium
10 First Basmanny Lane, Moscow
1913–1914
Stairwell section and main facade elevation design

17

Kovrov Armaments Factory (Block A, Block B, boiler house) Kovrov, Vladimir Region 1916–1921 Architect: Boris Velikovsky

Velikovsky's factory buildings stand on an elevation and can be well seen from the centre of Kovrov, as well as from the Moscow-Nizhny Novgorod Railway Line, beyond which they are located. This explains the logic behind the large proportions of their simple forms and the hypertrophied scale of all the architectural details. The diverse forms of the blocks echoed the specific purpose of each building, while their exteriors reflected the perfected cycle of production.

The "directors' block" (Block A) was conceived and created in the form of a monumental, symmetric, three-part building. The smaller production block stands between the two taller side sections. The administrative premises face north, in the direction of the railway line and the old town centre. This section recalls many of the industrial edifices designed by the Vesnin brothers in the late 1910s, which had the exact same strategic importance. It is also similar to the earliest section of the AMO Factory (1916–20s, later renamed first the ZiS and then the ZiL Factory), which was designed by Alexander Kuznetsov with contributions from Konstantin Melnikov.

The architecture of Block A anticipates the monumental forms of Soviet Neoclassicism in the 1930s. This small construction has exaggeratedly large details, such as the smooth archaic columns with massive rustication, the cornices and the keystones of the arches. They recall Ancient Roman analogues and the works created in a similar spirit by the Italian Neo-Renaissance and Neo-Baroque master Armando Brasini.[1] The two double-storey wings of Block A have arched windows and are decorated with porticos of two columns. The central section is flanked by porticos with two pendant columns, which support the massive entablature with the broken cornice above the first floor. A large

Kovrov Armaments Factory
(Block A, Block B, boiler house)
Kovrov, Vladimir Region
1916–1921
Block A central section
view, 2016

semicircular window with a keystone marks the centre of the facade. Beneath this window is the small porch of the entrance, which is framed by columns of a smaller scale. Unlike the windows of the side wings, this one has complex stone detailing. The second floor of the central section is interpreted as the support for a high rotunda with pilasters, eight round windows and a cupola. The square windows are in casing frames, which likewise only became typical of Soviet architecture in the mid-1930s.

The administrative section was adjoined by two workshops of different heights. The smaller workshop originally had unplastered walls and large semicircular apertures (now filled in), which recalled a Roman aqueduct. The main light came from above, through the triangular section on the roof. The taller workshop had striking vertical windows echoing the double-height space.

Kovrov Armaments Factory
(Block A, Block B, boiler house)
Kovrov, Vladimir Region
1916–1921
Block B view from the south, 2016

Block B was placed in the same position as Block A, facing the railway line. This cubic frontal two-storey building was completely paned with glass and was interpreted as the support for the water tower (an invariable feature of all factories at that time). Pilasters divided the main facade into three equal parts. The central section ended in a semicircular attic with a roof window and a large capstone. The building is adjoined by a one-storey workshop. Its walls are made of brick and are unplastered. The small porches with brick columns of a simplified order system have survived on one side.

Blocks A and B and several technical buildings (including the surviving boiler house) were completed towards the end of the Civil War. The settlement of one- and two-storey log houses for the factory workers has partially survived to the west of the factory. The architect could never have imagined the subsequent transformation of his creation into an enormous multifunctional complex, where his original constructions are now lost amid the general conglomeration of buildings.

1 Armando Brasini (1879–1965) was a self-taught Italian architect who worked in the style of Historicism (Eclecticism). He was born in Rome and studied restoration and theatrical decoration at the Istituto di Belle Arti. Brasini designed buildings in the Neo-Baroque, Neo-Renaissance and Neoclassical styles, attempting to capture and resurrect the former splendour of Rome. He caught the attention of Mussolini, who awarded him many commissions during the Fascist period.

Kovrov Armaments Factory
(Block A, Block B, boiler house)
Kovrov, Vladimir Region
1916–1921
Block A column detail, 2016

Kovrov Armaments Factory
(Block A, Block B, boiler house)
Kovrov, Vladimir Region
1916–1921
Block B after completion, 1921

Kovrov Armaments Factory
(Block A, Block B, boiler house)
Kovrov, Vladimir Region
1916–1921
View from Block A towards
Block B, 2016

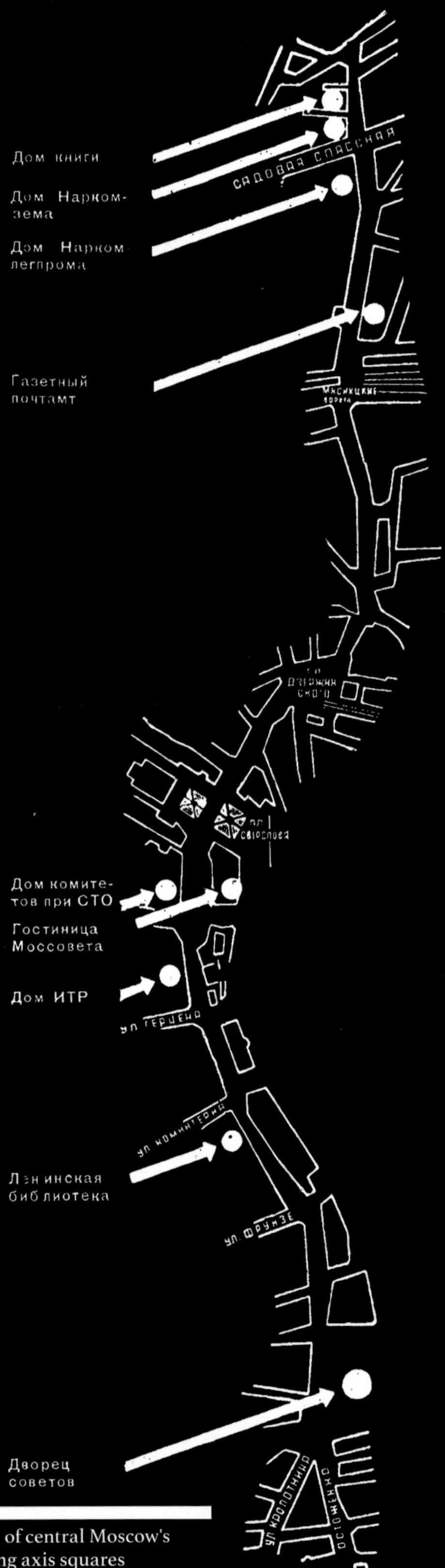

System of central Moscow's planning axis squares and streets, with principal buildings of the late 1920s and 1930s indicated

Velikovsky's great experience ensured that there was continued demand for his talents after the revolution. Among his creations of the 1920s, the Gostorg[1] administrative building is particularly well known. The customer was a powerful Soviet organisation with ministerial ambitions. The new Gostorg headquarters on Myasnitskaya Street became the first innovative office block in Moscow. Along with such new buildings as the Central Telegraph Office (architect Ivan Roehrberg), the Lenin Institute (architect Sergei Chernyshov) and the *Izvestiya* editorial offices (architect Grigory Barkhin), it signalled the start of a construction boom in the city centre. Among all these names Velikovsky was the most consistent in implementing the ideas of modern architecture, from the organisation of the inner space to the appropriate use of new construction materials and engineering systems.

From the celebrations marking the tenth anniversary of the revolution in 1927 right up to the Nazi invasion in 1941, Moscow was actively transformed into a prestigious government centre. Top architects like Velikovsky were awarded extremely important and highly responsible commissions. The master was employed by Tsentrosoyuz, a sprawling Soviet organisation with responsibility for agriculture and the handicraft industry. Velikovsky designed one of the two Tsentrosoyuz pavilions at the All-Russian Agricultural and Handicraft-Industrial Exhibition of 1923. He also took part in the competition to design the new headquarters of Tsentrosoyuz in 1928, taking the first and third prizes in the initial round – the ultimate winner was none other than the world-famous architect Le Corbusier![2]

Working in Moscow, Velikovsky built a series of residential blocks for the employees of Soviet organisations, which today are virtually forgotten. The same applies to his attempts to improve the quality of public housing in the countryside. The architect was fascinated by the new idea of a garden city, which he believed to be the perfect solution to the problem of urban sprawl in Soviet towns: "In the matter of urban improvement, we have started limiting the heights of houses and the density of construction. While invigorating the city, this makes it grow outwards, if not upwards. Buildings which are too cramped and too high do not permit enough light and air to enter some apartments. For example, in the basements and lower floors there is a lack of lighting caused by the high density of construction [...] the sun's rays do not penetrate down there at all and, as they say, 'the doctor often goes to the places where the sun rarely shines'"[3].

Velikovsky was convinced that garden cities offered the perfect alternative to "the monstrosities that so abound in today's towns, which in many places represent a forlorn stone desert filled with dust and bad air – a heap of stone teeming with diseases"[4]. The ideal city should "be transformed into something healthy and convenient, combining culture and technology with all the advantages of the countryside – fresh, clean air and the proximity of nature"[5]. The architect noted that "the municipalisation of all urban land in Soviet Russia creates extremely favourable conditions for the construction of housing cooperatives and, in particular, for the building of cooperative

But such high hopes were not justified. Even after the revolution, the tradition continued of tying man to production, just like in the early days of the first factory towns, where the serfs had lived and worked. The Soviet principle of limiting the movement of people adopted equally oppressive measures. Peasants were not issued with internal passports and workers were forced to live wherever they were settled by the state, usually directly at their place of labour. They were not allowed to leave and could not buy their own private property, which had been abolished. Anyone wishing to live outside a town had to rely on public or their own personal transport.

As criticism of government policies was not allowed, Soviet architects could only adapt as best they could to the existing system. In his collaborations with Victor Vesnin, Nikolai Markovnikov and several other colleagues, Velikovsky was nevertheless able to develop his vision of a garden city. One successful project was the Sokol settlement in the north-east of Moscow. The architect created the first version of the general plan for Sokol along with the engineer Pavel Nakhman. But their layout was subsequently redeveloped and Velikovsky is now overlooked as the initial designer of this revolutionary project.

1 Gostorg was a state-run agency which carried out all foreign trade in the early years of the Soviet Union. The institution was formed in 1922 as a subdivision of the People's Commissariat of Foreign Trade.

2 B. M. Velikovsky, *Zhilischnaya nuzhda i kooperatsiya*, Moscow, 1924, pp. 10–11.

3 Ibid., pp. 16–17.

4 Ibid., p. 12.

5 Ibid., p. 13.

6 Ibid., p. 4.

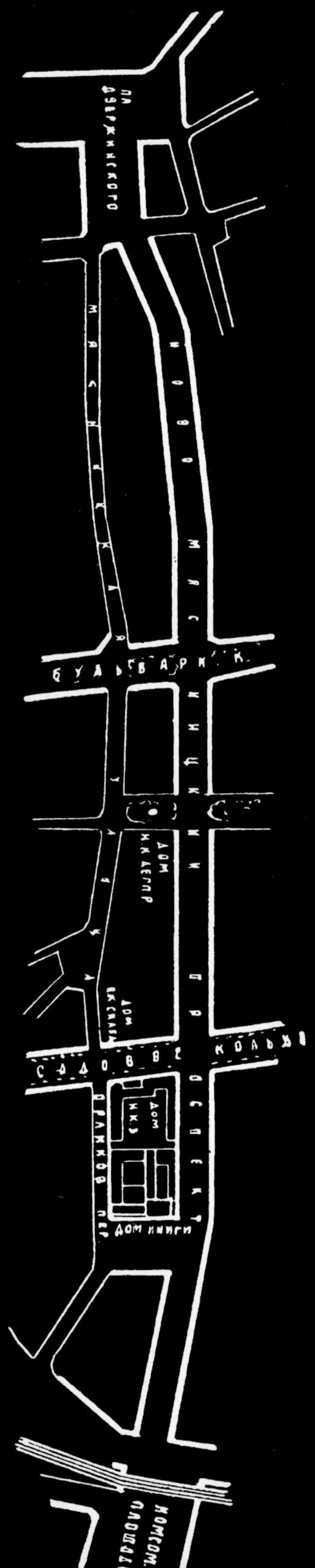

Novo-Myasnitskaya street proposal drawing

Sokol garden-city settlement master plan

18

Tsentrosoyuz Pavilion
All-Russian Agricultural and Handicraft-Industrial Exhibition, Moscow (unsurviving)
1923
Architect: Boris Velikovsky (engineer: Mikhail Maslennikov)

Tsentrosoyuz (Central Union of Consumer Societies) was the most influential Soviet organisation in the NEP[1] period, and so its pavilion at the largest post-revolutionary fair in Moscow was expected to be vast and imposing. Like the other buildings at the All-Russian Agricultural and Handicraft-Industrial Exhibition of 1923, it was made from wood. All of the pavilions were built from timber frames, logs and boards and decorated with colourful emblems, painted panels, flags and garlands.

The U-shaped pavilion was similar in size to enclosed markets, railway stations, musical halls and other such contemporary structures. Two large double-height exhibition halls with galleries inside surrounded an inner courtyard. The enormous pitched roofs of the two main wings evoked associations with rural granaries, while the three pediments in the centre of the main facade suggested a row of wooden huts. The pavilion was entered through a large, semicircular, glazed veranda. Two other rounded verandas adjoined the exhibition halls on the opposite side.

Such absolute symmetry lent an air of monumentality to the pavilion, while the large glass surfaces underlined its modernity. Velikovsky managed to achieve expressiveness using very simple resources, employing unusual proportions in everyday forms – the long and steep slopes of the roofs, the high pediments and the large square windows, which were two floors in height on the main facade. These major elements contrasted with such minor architectural details as the fine mesh on the windows. This approach reflected Velikovsky's experience of work in the Art Nouveau period, although the pavilion itself

Tsentrosoyuz Pavilion
All-Russian Agricultural and Handicraft-Industrial Exhibition, Moscow (unsurviving)
1923
Facade detail

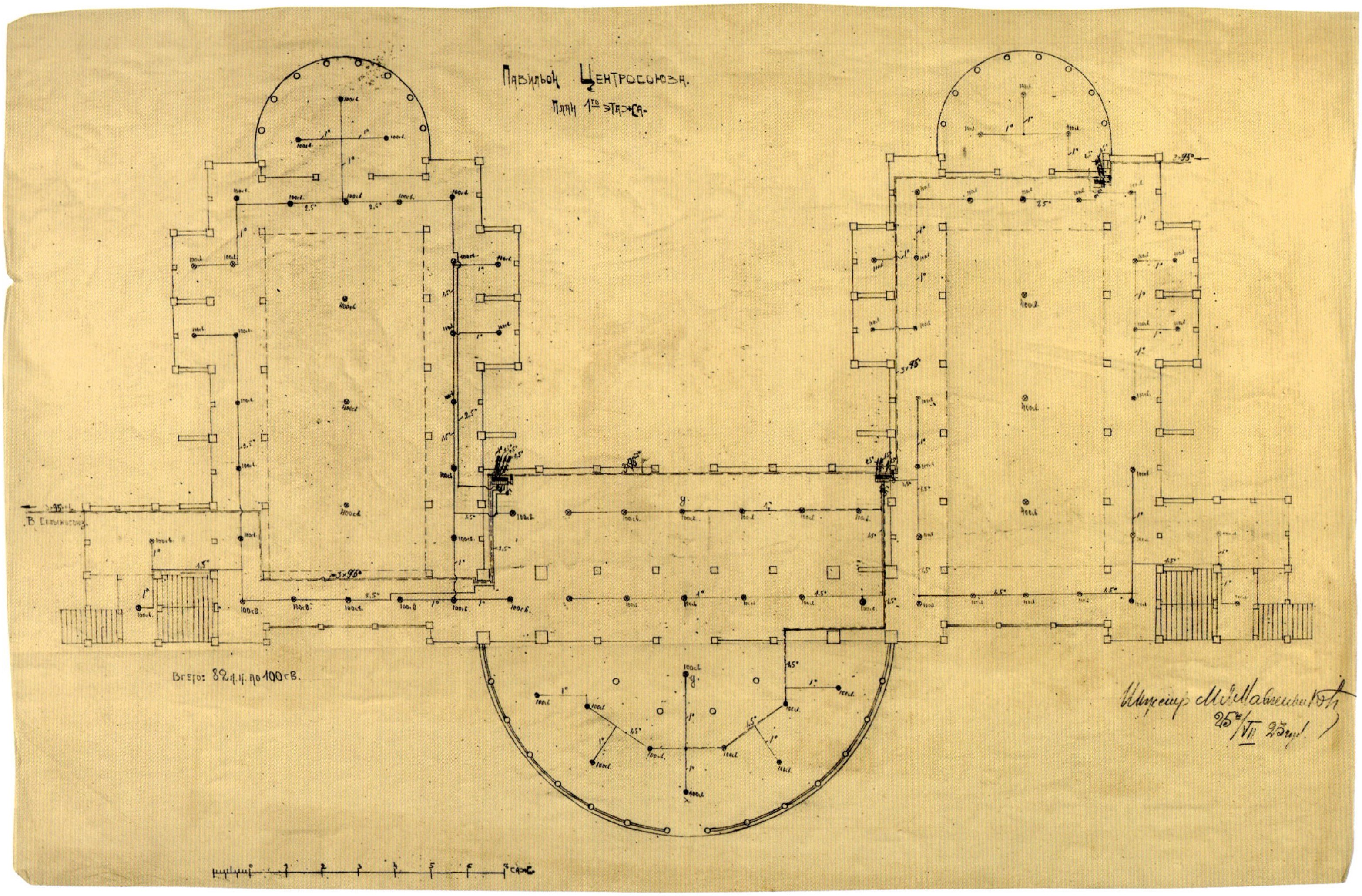
Павильон Центросоюза.
План 1го этажа.
Всего: 82 л. н. по 100 св.

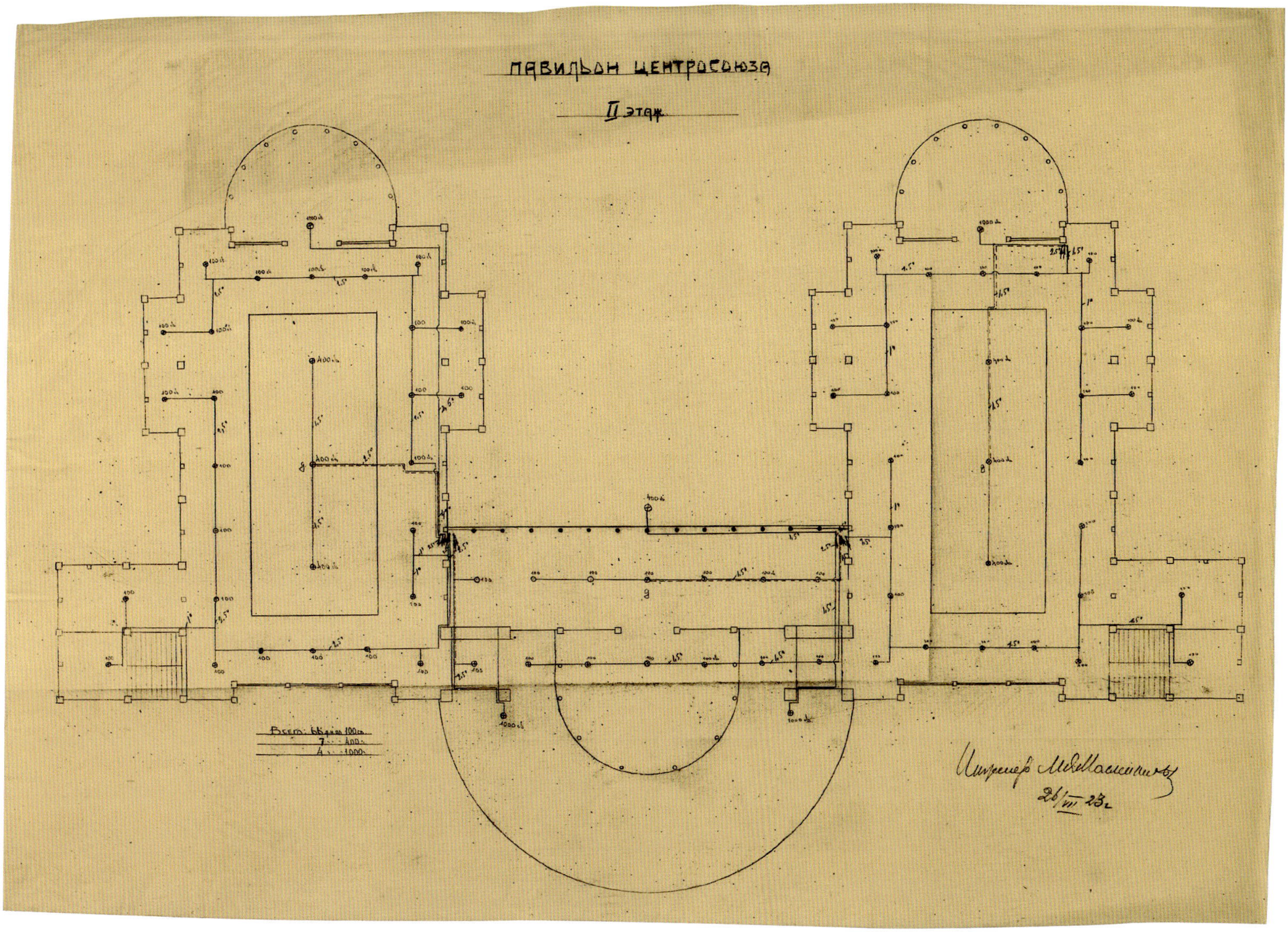

Tsentrosoyuz Pavilion
All-Russian Agricultural and Handicraft-Industrial Exhibition, Moscow (unsurviving)
1923
Engineer Maslennikov's detailed drawings

looked towards the future as a pure construction (the only real examples of decor were the two à jour stepped towers and the paintwork on the wooden panelling).

The exhibition was very colourful and diverse, with intense competition among the various architects. Alexander Grinberg designed the analogous Cooperation Pavilion, which was similarly under the authority of Tsentrosoyuz and stood to the left of Velikovsky's creation. It also had two side wings and a lowered central section with two decorative towers. Nearby was the Forest Industry Pavilion, which had four immense towers. This building likewise belonged to Tsentrosoyuz and was designed by Sergei Gruzenberg and Arkady Langman.

Against this general background, Velikovsky's pavilion looked refined and elegant. The forms of his building were sharper and more distinct, reflecting the quest for a new means of architectural expression. This was underscored by a famous photograph of the pavilion taken by Alexander Rodchenko, which was reproduced as a double-page spread in a review of the exhibition, along with the equally outstanding architecture of the Ukraine Pavilion designed by Victor Trotsenko. In both cases, the architects originally interpreted folk traditions without attempting to literally copy them.

The territory of the All-Russian Agricultural and Handicraft-Industrial Exhibition was later transformed into the Central Park of Culture and Relaxation, which was named after Maxim Gorky in 1934. In the 1930s, the former Tsentrosoyuz Pavilion was used to house the cultural centre of Gorky Park.

1 The NEP (New Economic Policy) was an attempt by the Soviet government to reintroduce elements of capitalism into the Russian economy between 1921 and 1928, following the disasters of the Civil War and the policy of War Communism. In the countryside, peasants were allowed to own land and sell produce to the state, while small businesses flourished in the towns.

Tsentrosoyuz Pavilion
All-Russian Agricultural and Handicraft-Industrial Exhibition, Moscow (unsurviving)
1923
Rear view

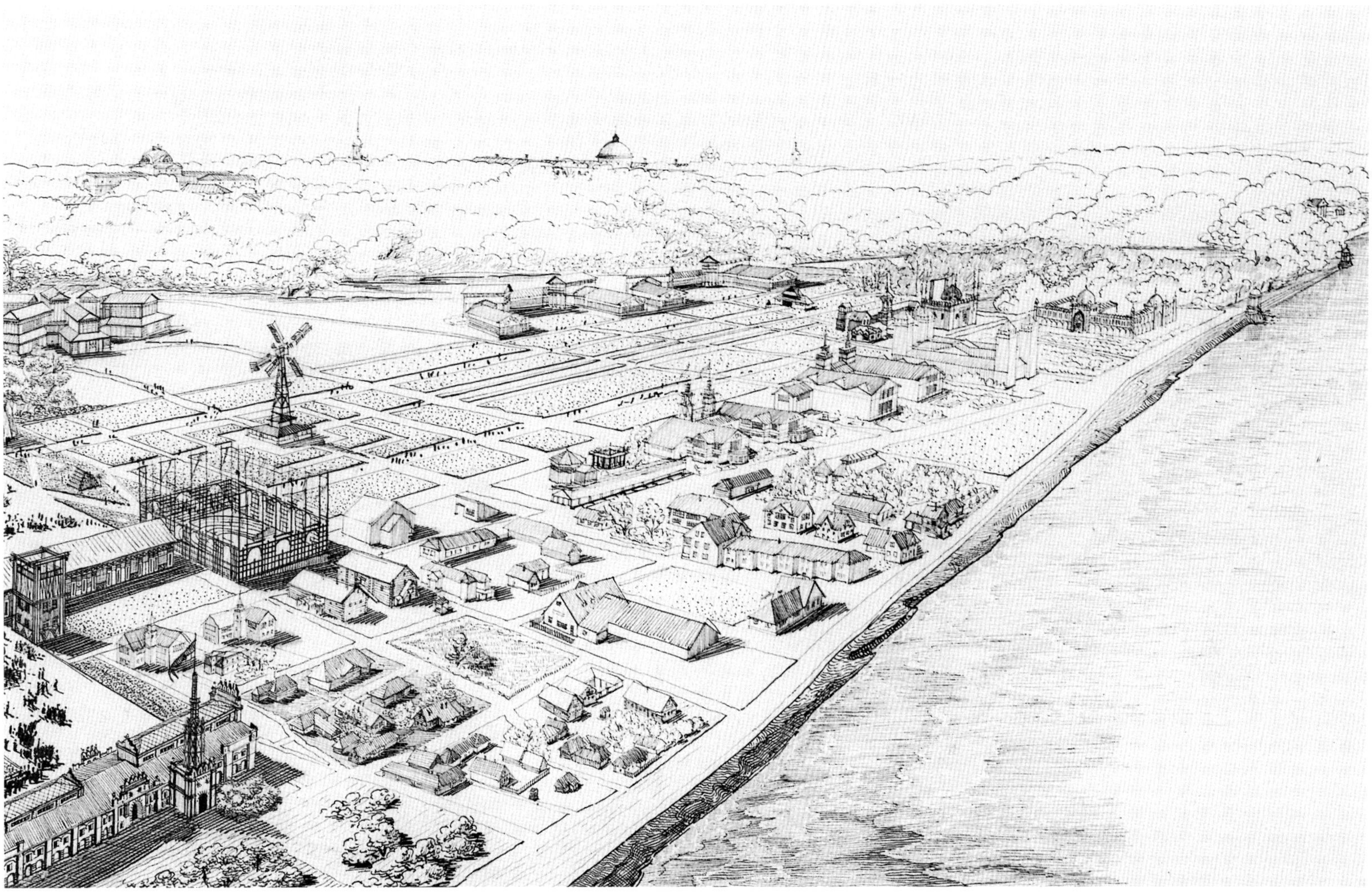

Tsentrosoyuz Pavilion
All-Russian Agricultural and Handicraft-Industrial Exhibition, Moscow (unsurviving)
1923
Bird's-eye view drawing of exhibition. Graphic reconstruction, 1950s

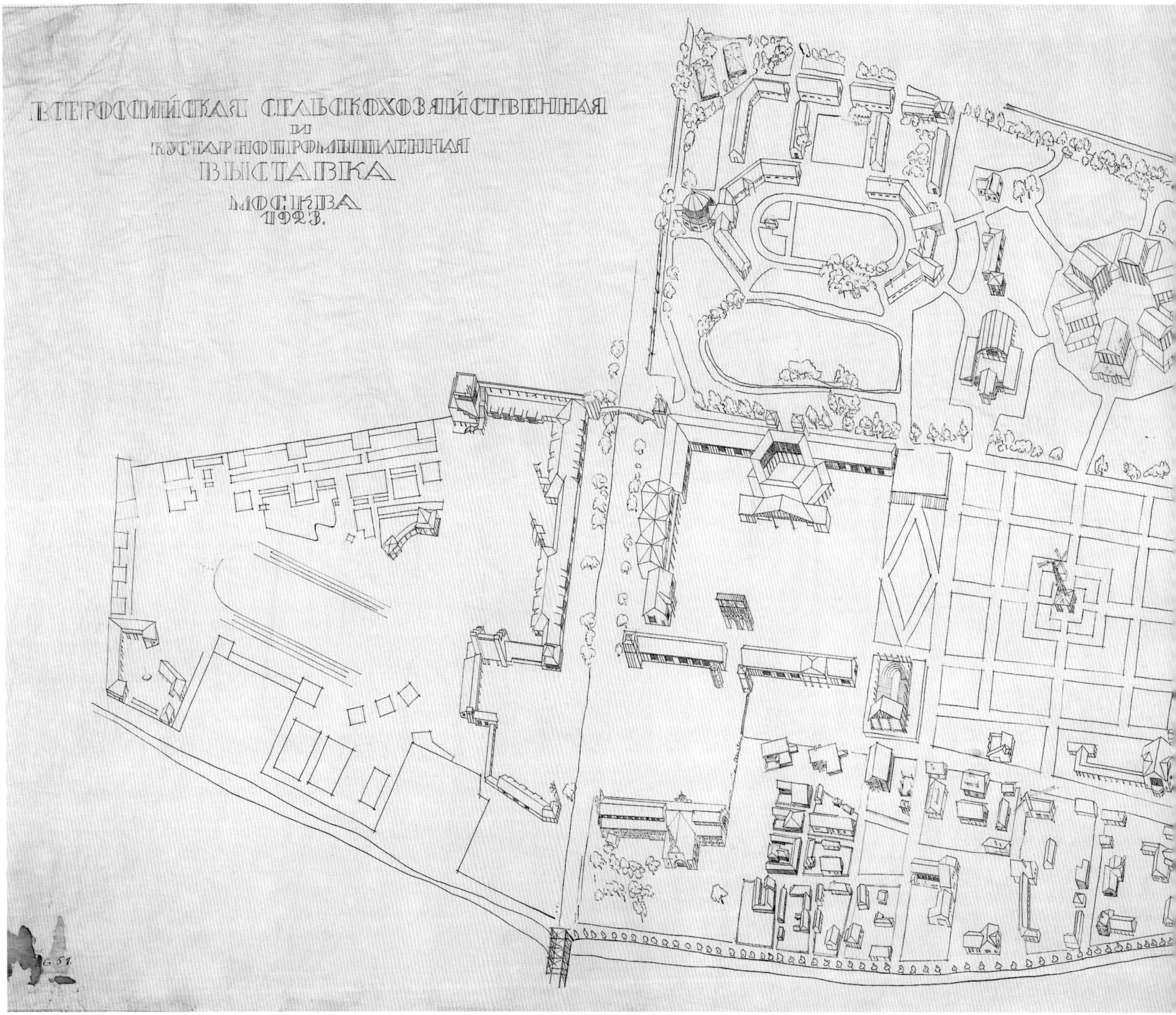

Tsentrosoyuz Pavilion
All-Russian Agricultural and Handicraft-Industrial Exhibition, Moscow (unsurviving)
1923
Exhibition plan

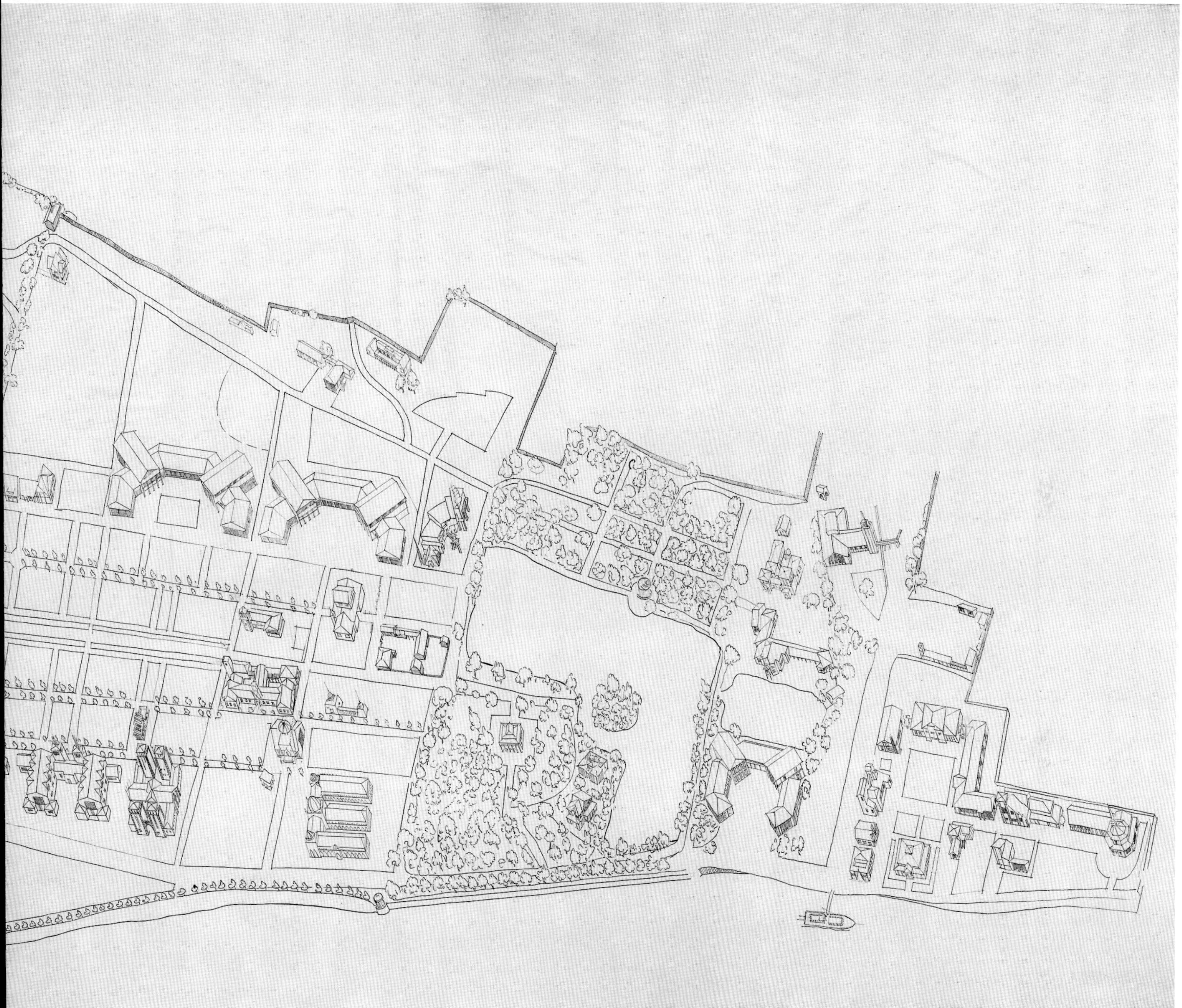

Генеральный план
поселка Дружба
северных ж.д. ст. Перловка.
Участков 265.
S
N
Экспликация.
1. Народный дом.
2, 3, 18 Администрация.
4. Дома служащих.
5. Ясли и детский дом.
6. Кооп. лавка.
7.8.9.10.11.16.20. Санит. здан.
12. Баня.
13. Прачешная.
14. Водок. башня.
15. Школа I с. т.
17. Мастерския.
19. Дом приезжих.

19

Druzhba ("Friendship") Settlement (Garden City) Near Perlovskaya station, Moscow Province 1922–1924 Architect: Boris Velikovsky

In the 1910s, several new settlements in the style of garden cities were planned to the north-east of Moscow. The most famous of them – Prozorovka and Kratovo – were designed by Vladimir Semyonov (1874–1960), who had helped to create Letchworth Garden City in England and subsequently promoted the idea in Russia. Boris Velikovsky was also a proponent of this new way of living and his Druzhba ("Friendship") settlement is now undeservedly forgotten. Both the general plan and the few surviving houses were conceived in close correspondence with what was, at that time, a very progressive idea.

At the start of 1917 a cooperative was formed with the aim of constructing the Druzhba settlement. This was even before the overthrow of the Tsarist regime in March 1917 and the Bolshevik takeover in November 1917. The post-revolutionary chaos, however, meant that the initial concept was only brought to fruition in 1924, when the settlement was presented to the public as a new model of the Soviet way of life.

The Druzhba settlement was awarded over a hundred hectares of land between the Yaroslavl Highway and the Losiny Ostrov ("Moose Forest") National Park. Velikovsky's general plan had a fan-shaped layout, which was typical of European garden cities, with small clusters consisting of eight to twelve plots of land. The triangular piece of earth in the middle was reserved for social or administrative buildings. While the latter have long been either demolished or completely rebuilt, some of the original houses in the settlement have survived. The measurements of a whole series of houses, with their gable roofs and high pediments, closely recall Velikovsky's blueprints, even though each owner has clearly adapted or altered his or her abode over the following decades.

The published projects show two types of cottage, both of them designed for two families. There were also plans to build hostels. These houses were either one-storey or two-storey

Druzhba ("Friendship") Settlement (Garden City)
Near Perlovskaya station, Moscow Province
1922–24
Druzhba settlement master plan

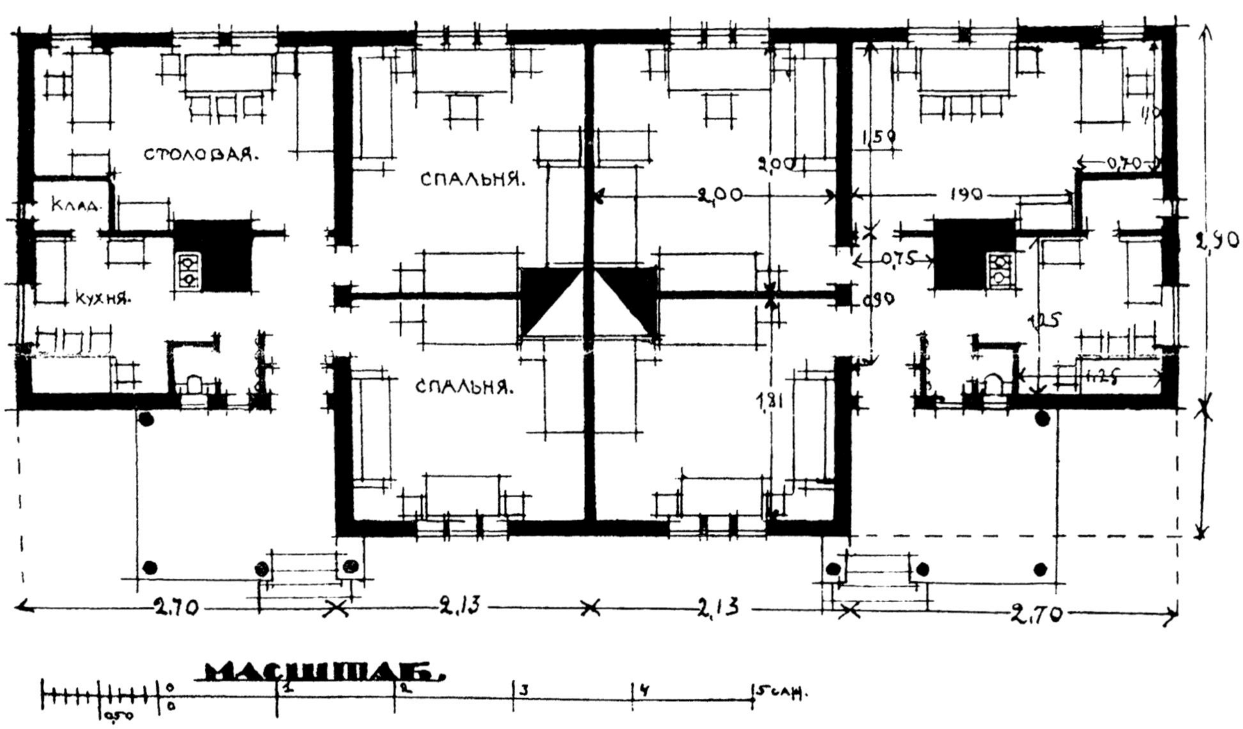

СТОЛОВАЯ.
КЛАД.
КУХНЯ.
СПАЛЬНЯ.
СПАЛЬНЯ.
2,70
2,13
2,13
2,70
2,90
МАСШТАБ.
5 САЖ.

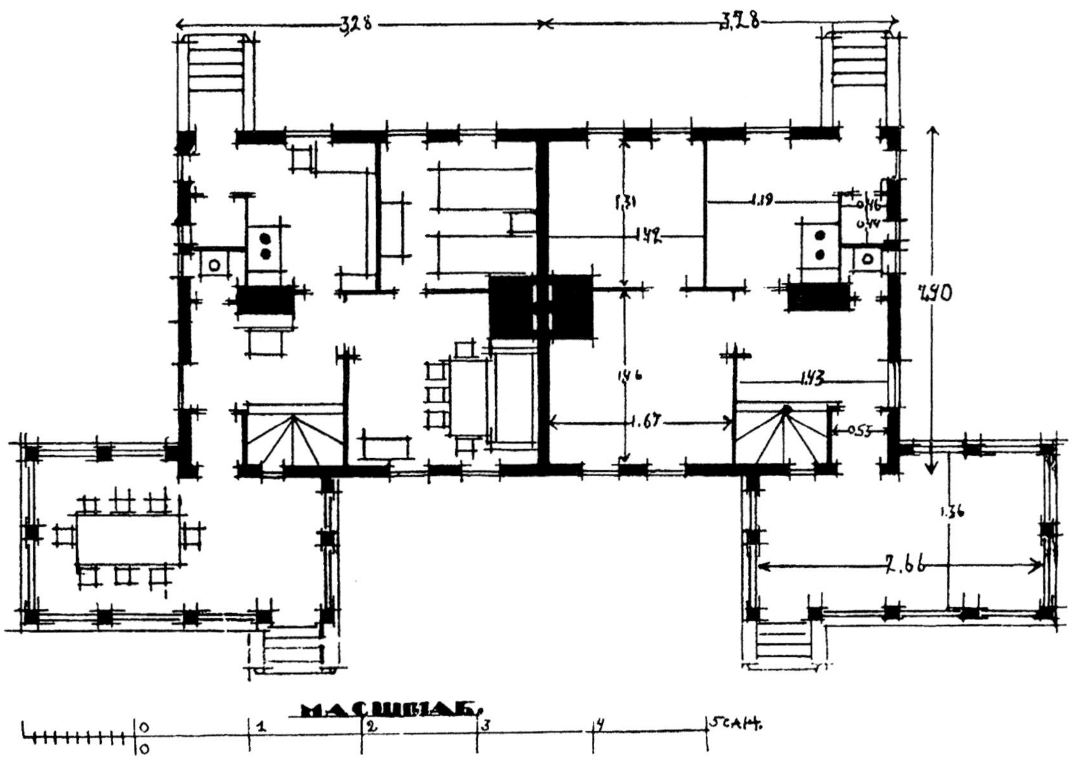

Druzhba ("Friendship") Settlement (Garden City)
Near Perlovskaya station, Moscow Province
1922–24
Cottages of varying design

wooden constructions and were very practical (both types were based on a similar principle of configuration).

The first type of house consisted of a square timber frame, covered by a gable roof, with small timber frames adjoining on two sides, also with gable roofs. Each house was split into two along the ridge of the common high roof. Stoves were placed next to the dividing wall to heat the two bedrooms in each apartment. The side timber frames were intended as kitchens with stoves in the middle and included a pantry and a dining room. The entrances to the apartments had a small indoor porch with toilet facilities nearby.

The second type of house was larger and consisted of two square timber frames (one for each family) covered by a high gable roof. This house came with an attic, which was also divided into two. The timber frames were adjoined on both sides by covered terraces.

Velikovsky's blueprints are professional masterpieces. The plans suggest that, despite the harsh winters in the countryside outside Moscow, the houses would stay snug and warm. The architect refused to become a slave to fashion, preferring to design buildings with very modest architecture and striving above all for the correct proportions. But would his ideas have withstood the pressure of the developers? This is difficult to ascertain today. The settlement has now greatly changed in appearance and has a multitude of brick houses. But there are also wooden ones with triangular pediments and large windows on the main and side facades. These particular houses recall Velikovsky's published blueprints, suggesting that more than two types of cottage were developed. It is also likely that not all the cottages corresponded to his actual designs, owing to a lack of construction materials. In addition, when new reservoirs were being created at that time, the wooden huts in flooded villages were very often dismantled and moved to the sites of new settlements – although this seems less likely in the case of the Druzhba settlement, as such reservoirs were not created to the north of Moscow until the late 1930s.

Remarkably, it was not just any old run-of-the-mill journalist, but Mikhail Bulgakov himself, before he became a famous writer, who reported on the Druzhba settlement in a newspaper. Although his article reflects the general need to condemn the situation before 1917 and to praise the social innovations after 1917, it still offers fascinating information on the pre-revolutionary concept of a garden city and its transformation after the March and November revolutions:

The idea of organising a workers' settlement outside Moscow was conceived in 1914 among a group of blue-collar and white-collar workers of three large enterprises – the Bogatyr Factory, the 1886 Power Station and the Indent Depots. The provisional government confirmed the charter of the "Friendship of 1 March 1917" settlement. Then, under Soviet power, Narkomzem[1] met the initiative group of future inhabitants halfway and, in 1918, released 102 desyatinas[2] of land in Pogonno-Losiny Ostrov, near Perlovka station. But this land was too plum a piece, and the creators of the garden city had to fight a war, first with the provincial forestry division and then with the district one. Only in late 1921 did Sovnarkom[3] supply a loan of ten billion roubles for the construction of the settlement.

The initiators of this enormous undertaking, headed by the tireless worker Sergei Shestyorkin, a former greaser at the Bogatyr Factory, then commenced the practical realisation of their cherished dream.

WHAT IS A GARDEN CITY?

Cottages in the English style will be built on 102 desyatinas of land, using the funds collected from the dues of workers wishing to settle there. Besides houses intended for families, there will also be hostels for bachelors. The settlement is intended for one and a half thousand people and will have its own power station, school, hospital and laundries. By the end of this year, the organisers plan to settle the first two hundred blue-collar and white-collar workers from Bogatyr, the power station and the depots.

ORGANISATIONAL WORK

The board has bought up the old dachas in Losiny Ostrov and is commencing their transfer to the territory of the town. Work is beginning on the uprooting of the area, and construction has started.

CELEBRATION IN PERLOVKA

The trains arriving at Perlovka station from stuffy Moscow discharge groups of guests onto the platform. Everyone walks past cottages drowning in green pines to the former dacha of Sergeyev. Its veranda is decked in green, and the sounds of music are carried far afield. Red flags flutter at the entrance.

By 3 o'clock everyone has gathered. On the terrace, which is jam-packed with the future residents of the garden city, silence falls.

Shestyorkin welcomes the arriving guests.

Comrade Divilkovsky, the deputy head of administration of Sovnarkom, takes to the floor and says: "We cannot help expressing our amazement and delight at the energy shown by the organisers of the republic's first workers' town. Despite all the difficulties of the terrible devastation through which we are living, they have managed to overcome all obstacles and realise their cherished dream – to give workers the opportunity to live not in attics and basements, where they have always suffocated, but amid greenery, wide spaces and cleanliness. Long live the energy of the proletariat! Long live Soviet power, which has allowed this wonderful idea to be accomplished!"

After Divilkovsky, other guests extend their greetings – Voznesensky, a member of the Russian Communist Party; the chairman of the district council; a representative of the Moscow Communal Services; and the representative of Tsentrosoyuz.

After each speech, the Internationale[4] blasts out.

LAYING THE FOUNDATIONS OF THE SETTLEMENT

The workers, employees and guests form rows, red posters swaying in front, and everyone proceeds to the place of the laying of the foundations, where the first foundation has already been marked out.

More speeches are made, and then comrade Divilkovsky lays the foundation of the first building in the workers' town with a metal plate carved with the following inscription: "RSFSR. 28 May 1922. Foundations laid of the Druzhba settlement – a workers' garden city. The Board."

Mikhail Bull. [pseudonym of Mikhail Bulgakov]

Rabochyi ("Worker") newspaper, 30 May 1922

1 Narkomzem (*Narodnyi komissariat zemledeliya*, or People's Commissariat of Agriculture) was the government ministry responsible for planning and managing the agricultural industry in the RSFSR from 1917 and the USSR from 1929 to 1946.

2 The desyatina was a land measurement used in pre-revolutionary Russia and equivalent to 2,400 square sazhens or 2.702 acres. An area of land measuring 102 desyatinas would be approximately 276 acres.

3 Sovnarkom (*Sovet narodnykh komissarov*, or Council of People's Commissars) was the name for the governing cabinet of ministers of first the RSFSR from 1917 and then the USSR from 1923. The institution existed until 1946, when it was replaced by the Council of Ministers.

4 Poem originally written by French revolutionary Eugène Pottier after the defeat of the Paris Commune in 1871 and set to music by Pierre De Geyter in 1888. Besides being claimed by various socialist and other left-wing groups, the Internationale was the Soviet national anthem from 1918 to 1944.

20

Gostorg Building
47 Myasnitskaya Street, Moscow
1927
Architects: Boris Velikovsky and Vyacheslav Vladimirov with contributions from Mikhail Barsch, Georgy Wegmann, Maria Gaken and Arkady Langman

The project of the Gostorg building was developed in 1925, when the new style of Constructivism was just beginning to emerge. In 1924, Moisei Ginzburg published a book entitled Style and Epoch, which used the term "Constructivism" to describe architecture that regarded the construction itself as an artistic phenomenon.

Rather symbolically, the seven-storey administrative headquarters of this all-powerful Soviet organisation recalled a machine. The building was conceived with a fourteen-storey tower placed right in the middle. Such completely symmetric designs were rarely applied in Constructivist projects, which preferred to position towers at the corners of buildings, increasing the dynamic perception of all the forms. The rational composition of the Gostorg building was intended to conjure up associations with a mechanism working like clockwork. In this particular design, Velikovsky betrays his successful previous experience of work in the Neoclassical Revival style, which favoured symmetric plans, facades and architectural details.

The construction has a regular trapezoid form, slightly narrowing at the back. The recessed section of the main facade, where the main entrance from Myasnitskaya Street is located, is flanked by two protruding avant-corps with bay windows. On either side of the vestibule are entranceways, through which cars could enter the narrow courtyards.

The external asceticism of the building continued in the interiors, which were divided not by massive walls but by the measured columns of the

Gostorg Building
47 Myasnitskaya Street, Moscow
1927
Left wing detail, 2016

frame of the construction. Almost all the facades are completely glazed and show the frame. Interestingly, the spacing of the ceilings and the heights of the windows have been lowered on the upper floors. This is because the demonstration areas were at the bottom and the offices were at the top.

Velikovsky noted that seventy per cent of the total area of the building was covered by glass and that the interiors could have been designed with less light. Complete glazing was fashionable at that time but led to increased expenditure on heating in the cold Russian winters and to the overheating of the premises in summer. The architect originally wanted to make the construction even more transparent, employing a metallic frame, but he was forced to use the more practical and less expensive reinforced concrete.

Gostorg was the state export-import office of Soviet Russia and was subordinated to the People's Commissariat of Foreign Trade. Gostorg was responsible for exporting traditional Russian products (furs, flax, hemp, wheat and fish) and using the proceeds to buy machines, tools and other technical equipment. In the early 1920s, Gostorg was spread out over almost thirty buildings in Kitai-Gorod, inevitably leading to calls for the construction of a single headquarters, where all its numerous offices, departments and branches might be concentrated.

The new Gostorg building on Myasnitskaya Street was as revolutionary on the inside as it was on the outside. Instead of the usual checkpoint with a security guard at the entrance, the employees recorded their own times of arrival and departure using a special clock with numbers around the dial. Each employee moved the lever to his or her personal number and pressed a button, and the clock automatically marked the time on a piece of paper.

The ground floor contained a vestibule, offices and demonstration halls, occupying two

Gostorg Building
47 Myasnitskaya Street, Moscow
1927
Perspective view of preliminary design

thousand square metres. The vestibule had an enormous wardrobe capable of serving several thousand people. The basement also acted as an exhibition room, where visitors could see examples of the technical equipment purchased by Gostorg – and admire another technical innovation, a hoist capable of lifting and lowering loads weighing up to ten tons.

The first floor housed the accounts department and the operations room of the financial department. For the first time in the Soviet Union, a new document management system was brought into operation here. Rather than writing in thick ledgers, the employees entered debit and credit information on special pieces of cardboard with the help of perforations, using a digital cipher. The punched cards were then processed by the Power accounting machine, which drew up the final balance sheet.

The rooms from the second floor upwards were used for offices, while the top floor contained a canteen, kitchen, sports hall, library and an assembly room with capacity for a thousand people. The kitchen was equipped with such modern gadgets as mechanical bread slicers, meat cutters and dishwashers and was capable of serving up to five thousand people a day.

The flat roof was employed as a terrace and an exercise area in good weather. Downstairs, an orange sign the size of the whole vestibule wall read: “Everyone to morning exercises! Every day – on the roof of the building! A special instructor has been invited.” The various floors were connected by staircases and four paternoster elevators.

Gostorg Building
47 Myasnitskaya Street, Moscow
1927
Perspective view of approved design

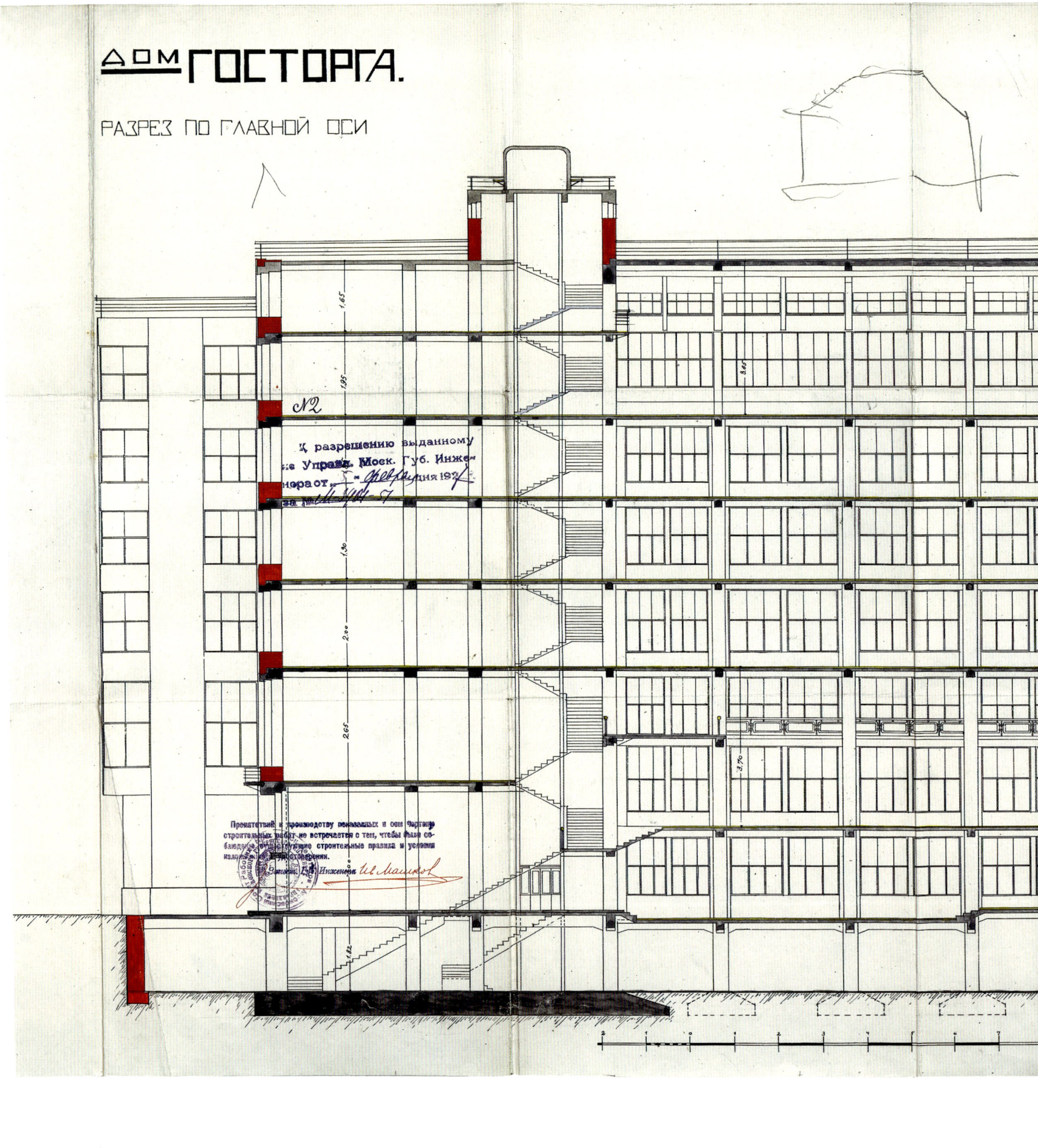
ДОМ ГОСТОРГА.
РАЗРЕЗ ПО ГЛАВНОЙ ОСИ
№2
К разрешению выданному
Управл. Моск. Губ. Инже-
нера от
дня 192
строительных работ не встречается с тем, чтобы были со-
строительные правила и условия
Инженера

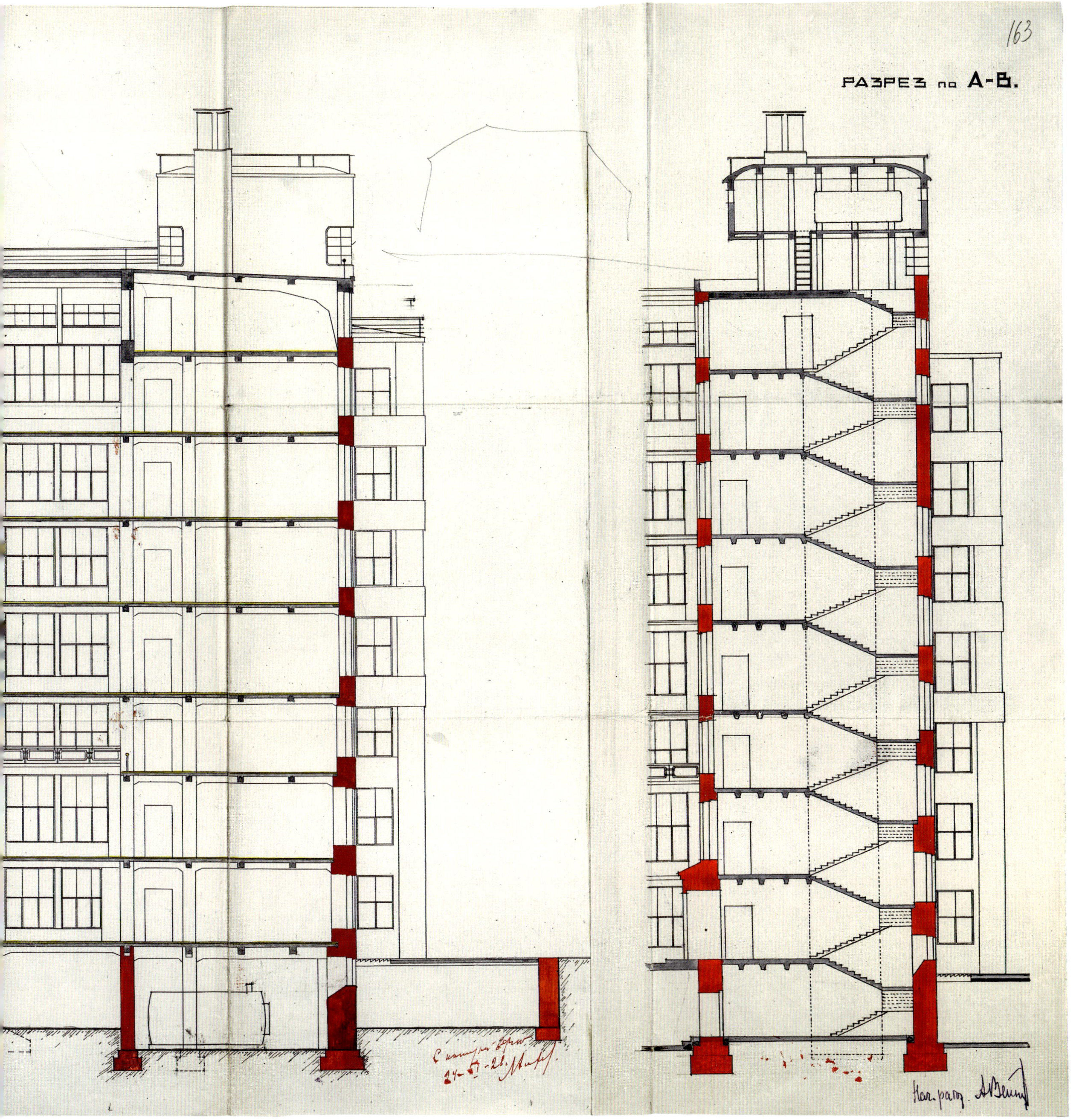

Gostorg Building
47 Myasnitskaya Street, Moscow
1927
Stairwell and longitudinal sections

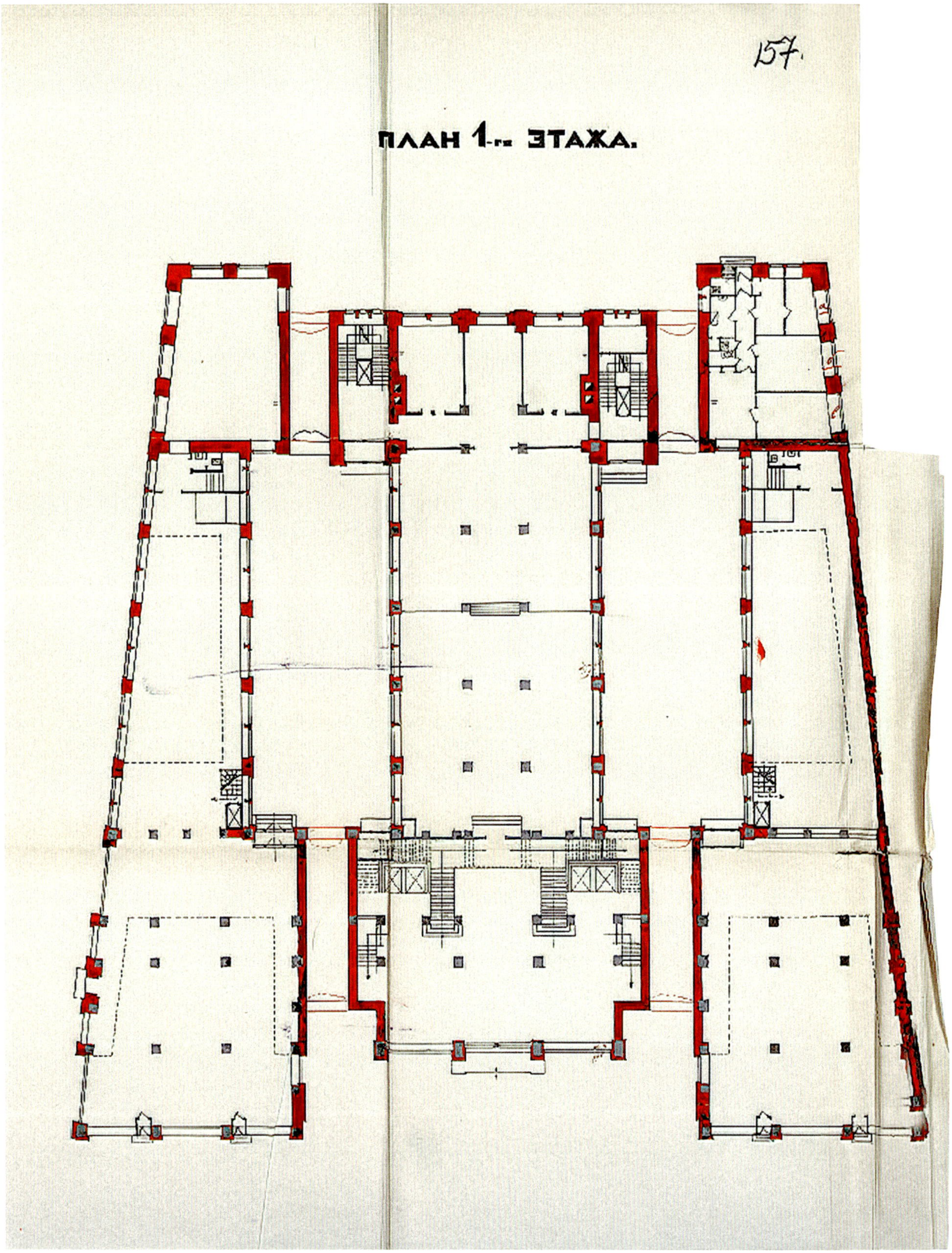

Gostorg Building
47 Myasnitskaya Street, Moscow
1927
Floor plans

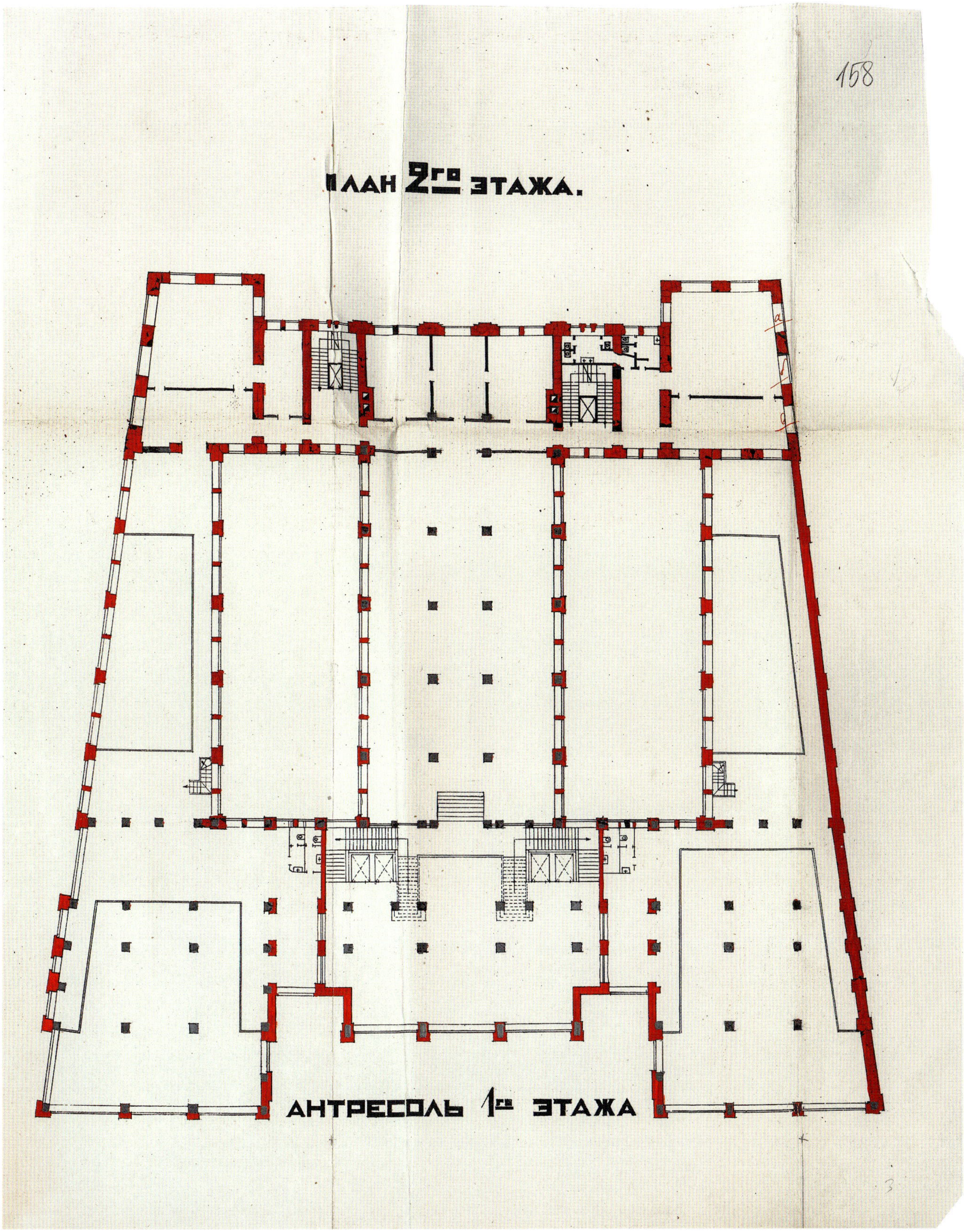
158
ПЛАН 2го ЭТАЖА.
АНТРЕСОЛЬ 1го ЭТАЖА

ХРОНИКА СТРОИТЕЛЬСТВА 1925–6–7

ДОМ ГОСТОРГА

GOSSTORG-GEBAUDE IN MOSKAU ERBAUT VON ARCHITEKT B. M. WELIKOWSKY

На фоне начинающего широко развиваться жилищного и промышленного строительства, строительство административных и общественных зданий занимает пока еще довольно скромное место.

Последнее обстоятельство объясняется не отсутствием нужды в подобного рода зданиях, а лишь недостатком средств.

Среди административно-промышленных зданий наиболее острая нужда ощущается в строительстве зданий типа конторских зданий — Bürohaus, приспособленных к новейшим потребностям советского хозяйства. Отчасти в связи с перенесением административных и торгово-промышленных центров, а отчасти в виду возникновения новых организаций типа трестов, синдикатов и т. д. наличность помещений для указанной цели оказывается далеко не отвечающей потребности, как в отношении размера, так и в смысле ее целесообразного использования.

По необходимости под многие административные помещения занята и жилая площадь.

Такое положение вещей ухудшает и жилищную ситуацию и неудовлетворительно разрешает и вопрос конторского помещения.

В особенности эти обстоятельства имеют место в Москве, Харькове и в других новых центрах. Правда, Москва и раньше служила торгово-промышленным центром, но совершенно другого типа — типа торгово-складочной торговли.

В Китай-городе, где располагались главным образом торгово-промышленные помещения, последние строились по принципу вертикальных ячеек, так называемых амбаров, причем внизу устраивались магазины, в верхних этажах—склады, а на самом верху — конторы. Многие здания были построены таким образом, что первые два этажа занимались под конторы, верхние же под жилье. Лишь в самые последние годы были оборудованы здания новейшего образца, как Деловой Двор, дом, занятый ЦК ВКП, Наркомземом, Наркомздравом и т. п.

Назначение всех этих домов было промежуточным между конторой и складом.

Народившиеся сейчас большие наркоматы, учреждения трестов, синдикатов, кооперативных центров и проч. вынуждены были расселиться в этих готовых домах и помещениях, далеко не отвечающих задачам нового потребления.

Благодаря такому несоответствию и получились чрезвычайно большие неувязки как в смысле нерационального использования, так и в отношении санитарных условий.

Очень многим крупным учреждениям пришлось дробиться на ряд мелких контор, так как подобрать одно удовлетворяющее их потребности помещение в несколько десятков тысяч метров было невозможно.

Такое существование учреждения обусловливало излишние затраты на эксплоатацию и вызывало ряд неудобств в смысле сношений.

Таково было положение и одного большого учреждения в Республике — Госторга — в 1925 г.

Громадный аппарат его в несколько тысяч человек, состоящий из Центрального Управления и 12 контор, вынужден был расселиться в 12 помещениях, причем две из этих контор, за отсутствием помещений в Москве, переехали в Ленинград.

Значительная часть помещений, занятых под эти конторы, чисто жилищного характера, и не приходится доказывать, насколько нерационально было использование подобных помещений и насколько затруднительна была в них жизнь самого учреждения. Кроме того, оплата всех помещений обходилась Госторгу чрезвычайно дорого и выразилась в солидной сумме — около 1/2 миллиона рублей в год.

Вышеуказанные условия заставили Правление Госторга принять меры к сосредоточиванию всех своих контор в одном месте, построить такой дом, который отвечал бы запросам, предъявляемым новыми потребностями.

В этих целях летом 1925 г. Госторг решил приступить к постройке своего дома.

В выборе участка Госторг остановился на улице 1-го мая (Мясницкой), как на главной артерии нашей технической промышленности, с одной стороны, а с другой, как на улице, соединяющей центр города со всеми внутренними вокзалами.

Против участка расположена небольшая площадь, образующаяся скрещиванием улицы 1-го Мая, Мясницкого проезда и Козловского переулка.

Это обстоятельство было учтено при составлении проекта дома на предмет увеличения высоты в средней части здания, так как она не будет затемнять прилегающие дома.

Занятый под здание участок имеет около 48000 $м^2$.

В целях увеличения площади впереди дома и образования

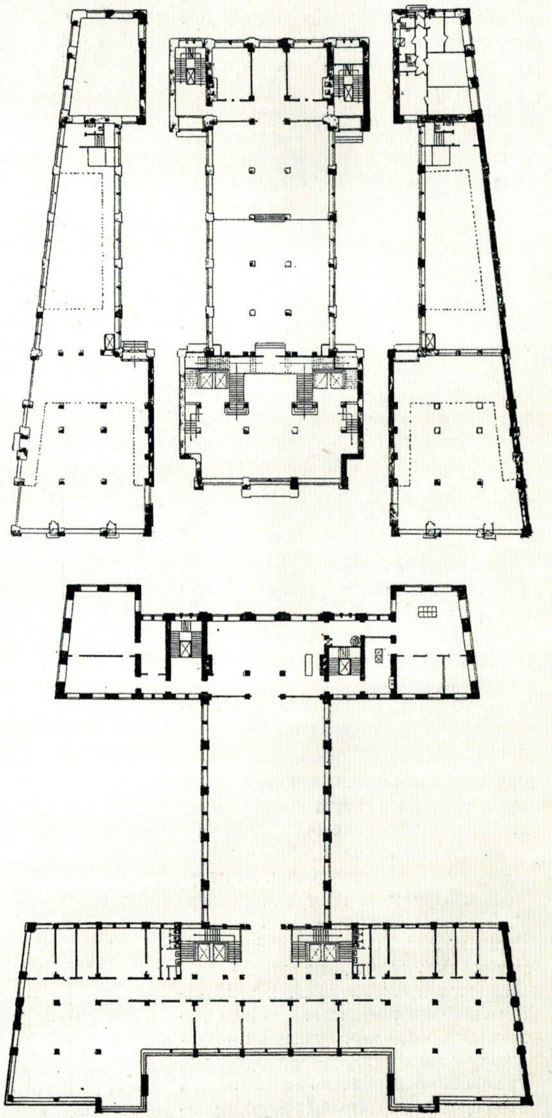

28

Gostorg Building
47 Myasnitskaya Street, Moscow
1927
Stroitelstvo Moskvy (Construction of Moscow) magazine article and photographs, 1927

ШОКОЛАД
МОНПАНСЬЕ
КАРАМЕЛЬ

Gostorg Building
47 Myasnitskaya Street, Moscow
1927
Courtyard view by Boris Ignatovich, late 1920s

Gostorg Building
47 Myasnitskaya Street, Moscow
1927
Main entrance view by Boris Ignatovich, late 1920s

Gostorg Building
47 Myasnitskaya Street, Moscow
1927
Photographs from various magazines and postcards of the 1920s

Gostorg Building
47 Myasnitskaya Street, Moscow
1927
Interior photo of "SA"
(Sovremennaya Arkhitektura)
magazine, 1927

Gostorg Building
47 Myasnitskaya Street, Moscow
1927
Stairway detail

Gostorg Building
47 Myasnitskaya Street, Moscow
1927
Interior photo of "SA" (Sovremennaya Arkhitektura) magazine, 1927

Gostorg Building
47 Myasnitskaya Street, Moscow
1927
Interior photo of "SA" (Sovremennaya Arkhitektura) magazine, 1927

173 Gostorg Building

47
МЯСНИЦКАЯ
Листья

МИСАТО
MISATO
МИСАТО
MISATO
МИСАТО

Gostorg Building
47 Myasnitskaya Street, Moscow
1927
pp. 174–175. Main facade, 2012
pp. 176–177. Left wing courtyard, 2016
pp. 178–179. Left wing rear view, 2016

Gostorg Building
47 Myasnitskaya Street, Moscow
1927
Left wing detail, 2016

Gostorg Building
47 Myasnitskaya Street, Moscow
1927
Roof terrace entrance, 2015

МАЛАЯ БРОННАЯ

21

Muniets Residential House
11–13 Malaya Bronnaya Street, Moscow
1928–1930
Architect: Boris Velikovsky

This five-storey construction was designed for members of the Muniets house-building association, a cooperative of employees of MUNI.[1] The house is a typical example of the residential constructions built for the workers of large bureaucratic organisations in the Soviet Union. All of them were, as a rule, located in the centre of Moscow.

The general plan of the plot of land shows that not only does the gable end of the new building adhere to the frontage line of Malaya Bronnaya Street, but the house also continues the flow of pedestrians along Bolshaya Bronnaya Street towards Spiridonovka Street. In this way, the natural movement of passers-by is logically controlled within the surrounding buildings.

The house consists of four sections. Each section contains one two-room apartment and one three-room apartment. Their spatial arrangement does not follow the standardised "Mossovet sections" that lay at the heart of many mass-housing constructions at that time.

The gable-end apartments differed from the other flats inside the house. They had basements for a boiler room, a laundry, a drying room and an assembly hall for meetings of the cooperative. By including public areas in the house, the architect was taking into account the movement towards greater communal living in the late 1920s.

The extremely modest facades are typical of this period. They are not plastered and they lack decor. The only sculptural and expressive notes are the slightly protruding avant-corps with three windows, which extend approximately by the equivalent of the thickness of the wall. This architectural device was intended to draw attention to the middle part

Muniets Residential House
11–13 Malaya Bronnaya Street, Moscow
1928–1930
View from the north, 2016

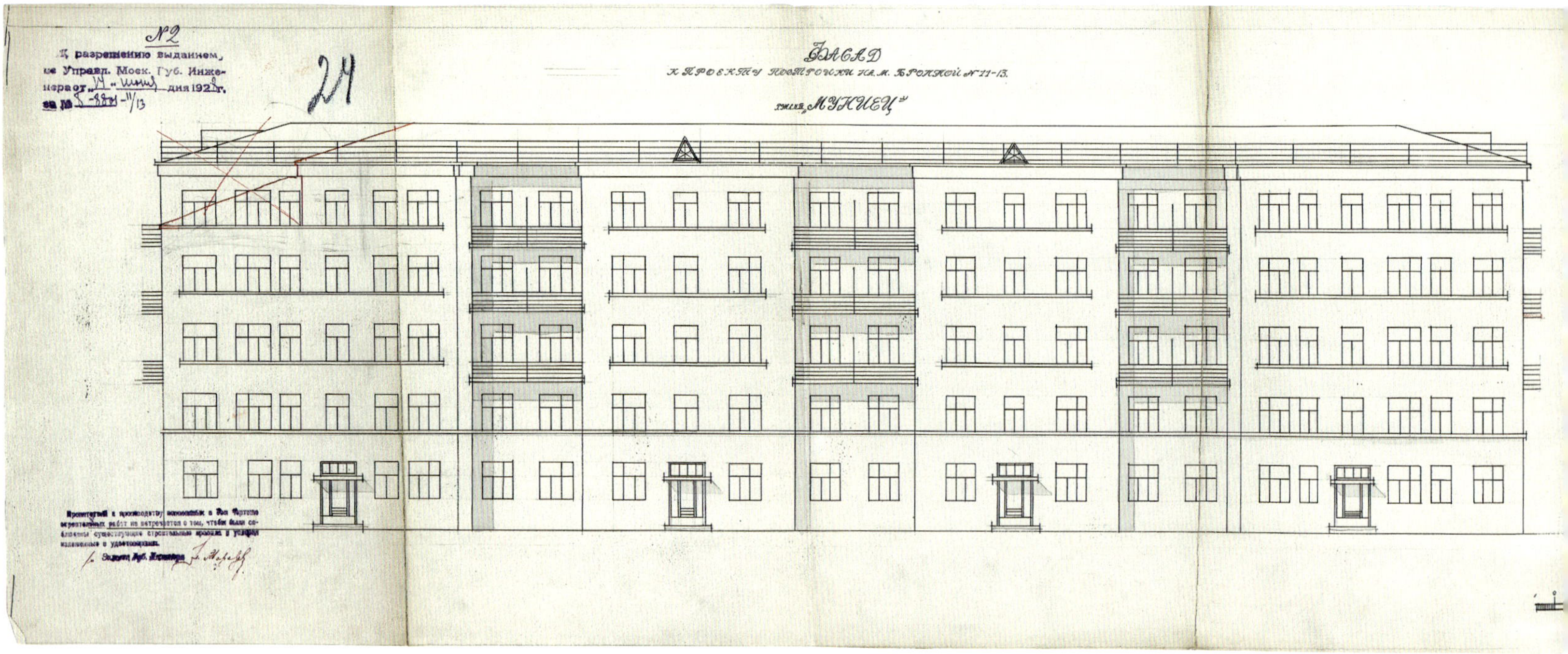
№2
Фасад
к проекту постройки на М. Бронной № 11-13.
24

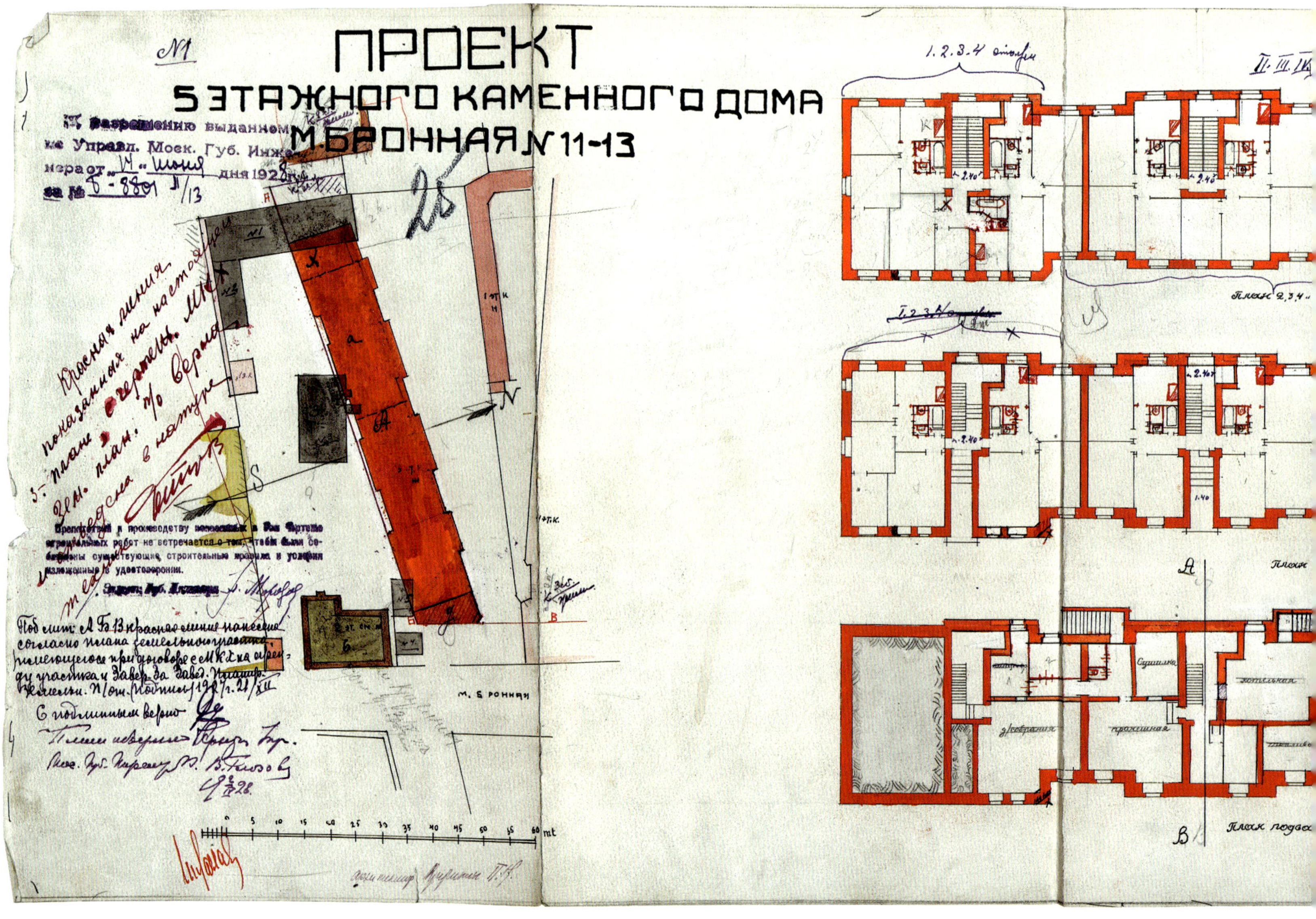
№1
ПРОЕКТ
5 ЭТАЖНОГО КАМЕННОГО ДОМА
М. БРОННАЯ № 11-13
25
М. БРОННАЯ

of each section. There are also balconies set in niches between the protuberances. All of these elements create a play of light and shade on the main facade.

The layout of the stairwells envisaged entrances on both sides of the house. This allowed lifts to be added from the northern (courtyard) side in the 1960s.

1 MUNI (*Moskovskoe upravlenie nedvizhimym imuschestvom*, or Moscow Directorate of Immovable Property) was the real-estate department of Moscow City Council. The department existed from 1922 to 1929 and was headed by Nikolai Philippovich Popov (Sibiryak).

Muniets Residential House
11–13 Malaya Bronnaya Street, Moscow
1928–1930
Drawings of site plan, floor plans and facades.

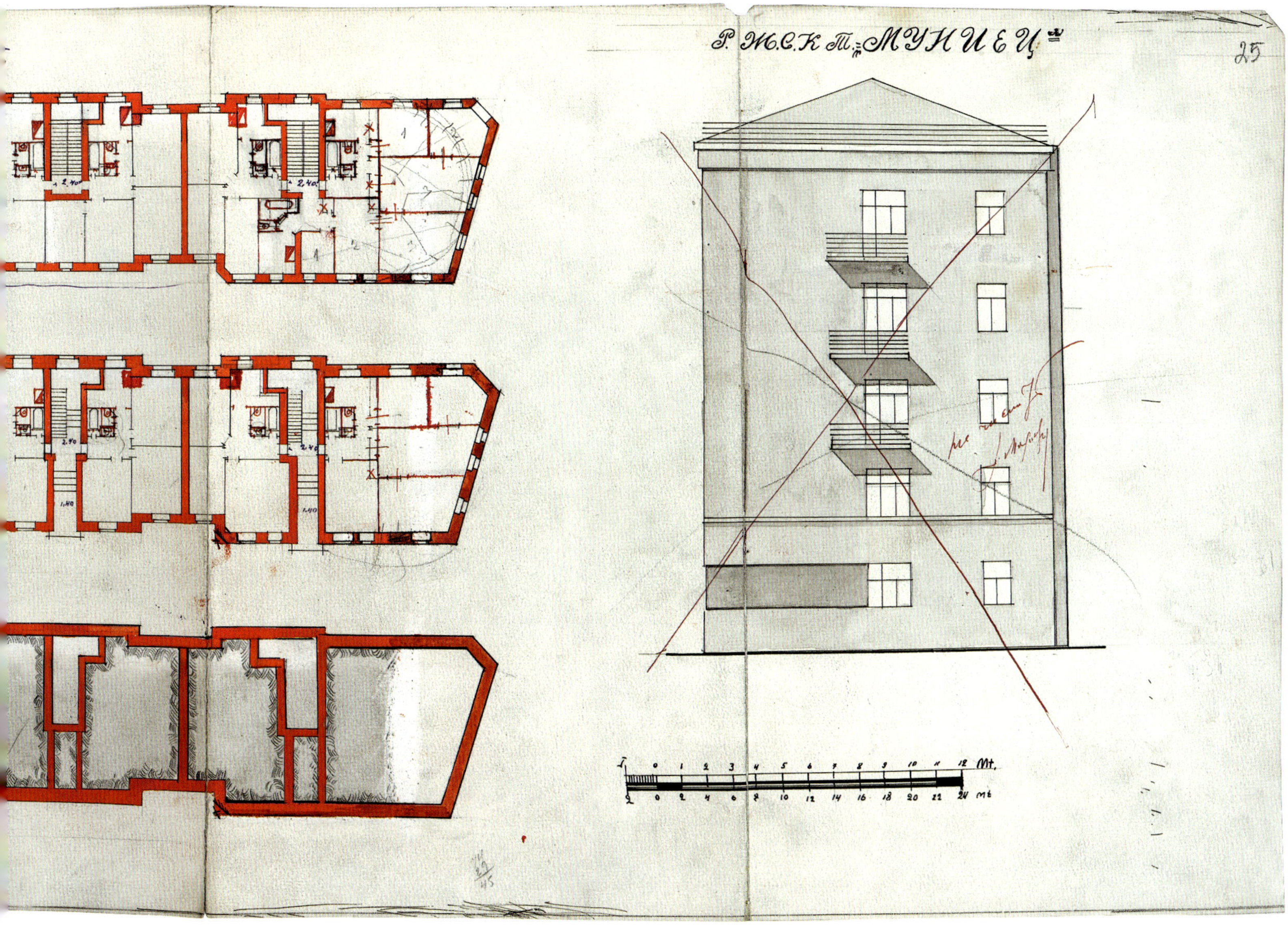

22

Lnotorg Worker Residential House 36 Malaya Bronnaya Street, Moscow 1925–1926 (extended upwards in 1932) Architects: Boris Velikovsky and Ivan Mashkov

This cooperative residential house was designed for employees of Lnotorg[1] *and originally had a different number of floors – four on the side of the street and five on the courtyard side. The large avant-corps extends into the courtyard, while its two other wings go out onto the street. This particular composition ensured excellent insolation.*

Velikovsky masterly configured two sections with different layouts. The two-apartment section with the arched entranceway on the ground floor is placed along the street. The second section contained three apartments. The plan of the building demonstrates the whimsical combination of the rooms and corridors in the different apartments. The house contained five four-room flats, seven two-room apartments and thirteen three-room flats. All the apartments had cross ventilation, while the largest (the four-room flats) faced three sides.

All the apartments in the Lnotorg House were originally equipped with fitted cupboards and had convenient kitchens and toilets, as well as exits onto private balconies. There was also a long common balcony, which ran along the third floor, in the left-hand section of the main facade. This added a sense of dynamism to the overall architectural composition.

Velikovsky's creative approach was based on his vast experience of designing pre-revolutionary tenements. *Stroitel'stvo Moskvy* (1927, No. 2) published a special article on the building, including fascinating data on the cubic measurements of the premises and the cost of construction. The author of the article especially praised the inner layout and the fittings in all the different apartments.

1 Lnotorg (Flax Trading Agency) was responsible for the purchase and sale of flax and hemp in Soviet Russia in the 1920s.

Lnotorg Worker Residential House
36 Malaya Bronnaya Street, Moscow
1925–1926 (extended upwards in 1932)
View from the south, 2016

*Lnotorg Worker Residential House
36 Malaya Bronnaya Street,
Moscow
1925–1926 (extended upwards
in 1932)*
Main facade detail, 2016

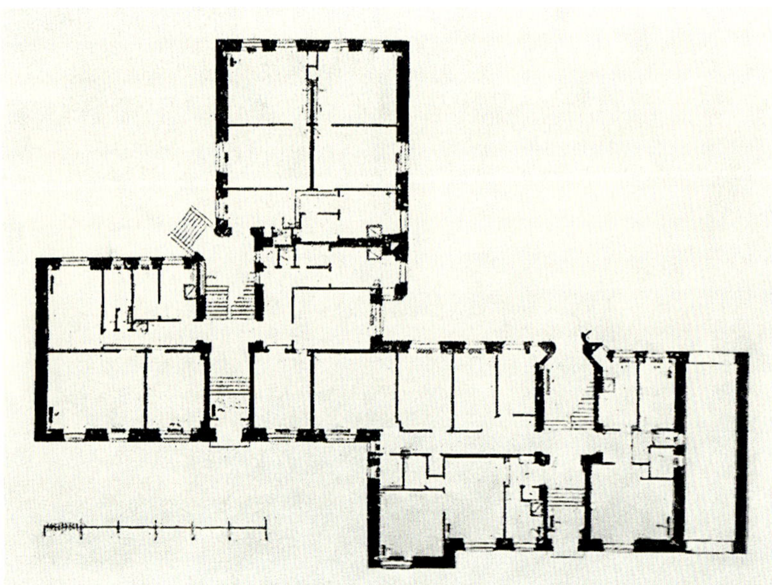

*Lnotorg Worker Residential House
36 Malaya Bronnaya Street,
Moscow
1925–1926 (extended upwards
in 1932)*
Floor plan

*Lnotorg Worker Residential House
36 Malaya Bronnaya Street,
Moscow
1925–1926 (extended upwards
in 1932)*
View from the east, 2016

23
Koopstroi Residential House
21 Sadovaya-Kudrinskaya Street, Moscow
1927–1928 (extended upwards in the late 1940s)
Architect: Boris Velikovsky

This multi-sectional residential house was designed for the construction cooperative of the Supreme Soviet of the National Economy and differs from many other mass-housing developments of that time. The architecture is a curious mixture of the refined layouts of pre-revolutionary tenements and the Soviet aspiration towards a standardised design of apartments. The simplistic decor on the facades recalls the Suprematist (non-objective) paintings of the 1910s and 1920s.

The project was submitted for approval in January 1927. Velikovsky followed the pragmatic approach towards house design in that period and kept architectural expression to a bare minimum. Later – possibly after discussions with the clients – he decided to embellish the facades with balconies and rectangular bay windows. In the final version of the project, they lend a sense of vitality to the architecture of the house, which now had a dynamic layout. The plan had a broken form and surrounded the courtyard from the north-west. The sections adjoin one another with a slight shift, which is underscored by the bay windows (their asymmetric positioning and simplified, smooth forms are particularly interesting).

The balconies were originally protected by slender railings. This imparted a sense of elegance to the brutal architectural forms, although these railings have since been replaced.

The house has four sections. Each section has either two, three or four apartments, and each flat has either two, three or four rooms. All the apartments have cross ventilation.

This elegant four-storey building was extended upwards in the late 1940s, when the country was experiencing a post-war housing crisis. Unfortunately, the two new floors with high mansard roofs and pointless small-scale details have distorted the masterful proportions of Velikovsky's original design.

Koopstroi Residential House
21 Sadovaya-Kudrinskaya Street, Moscow
1927–1928 (extended upwards in the late 1940s)
Corner detail, 2015

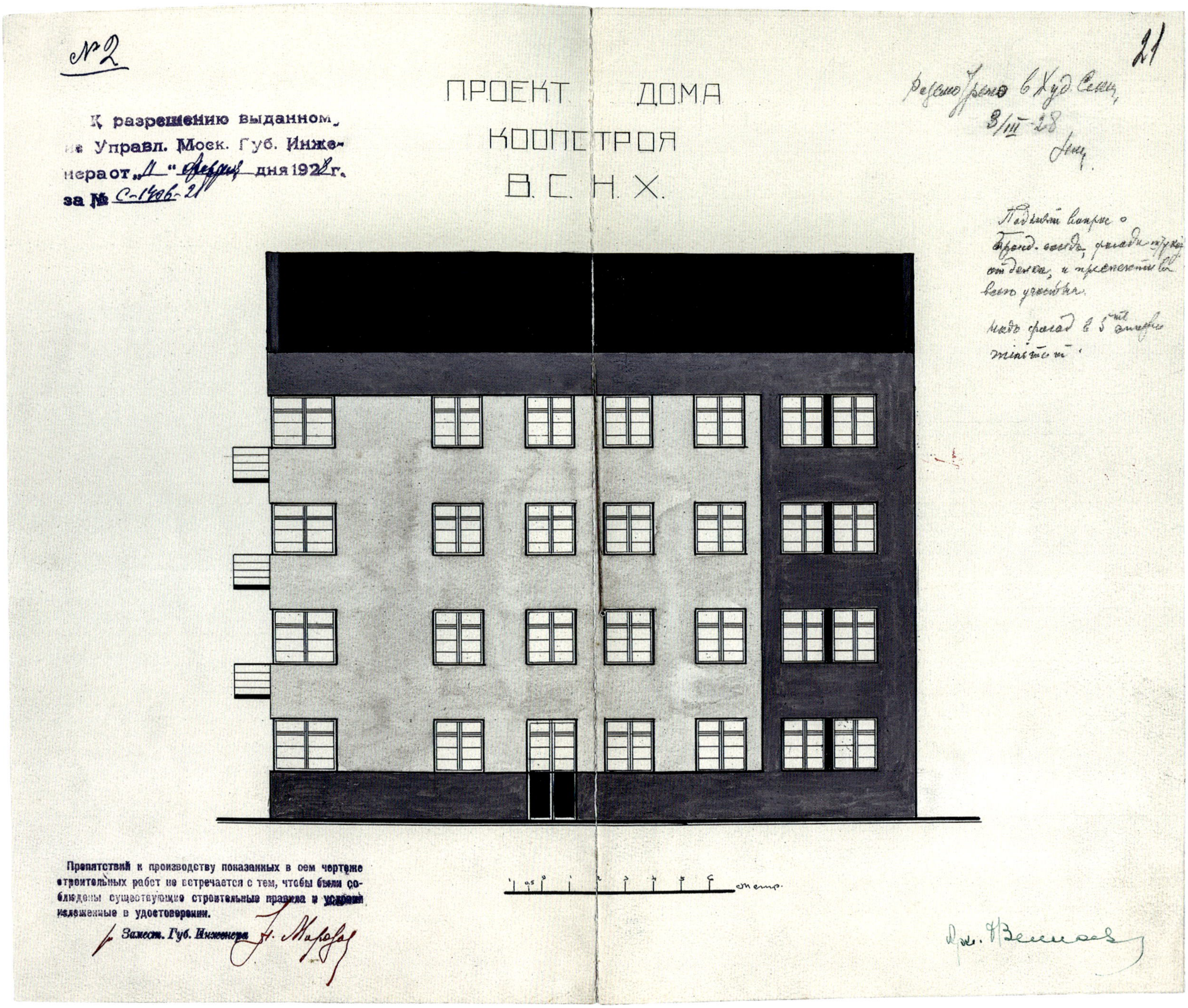
№2
21
ПРОЕКТ ДОМА
КООПСТРОЯ
В. С. Н. Х.
К разрешению выданному Управл. Моск. Губ. Инженера от „11“ дня 1928 г.
за № С-1406-21
Препятствий к производству показанных в сем чертеже строительных работ не встречается с тем, чтобы были соблюдены существующие строительные правила и условия изложенные в удостоверении.
Замест. Губ. Инженера
метр.

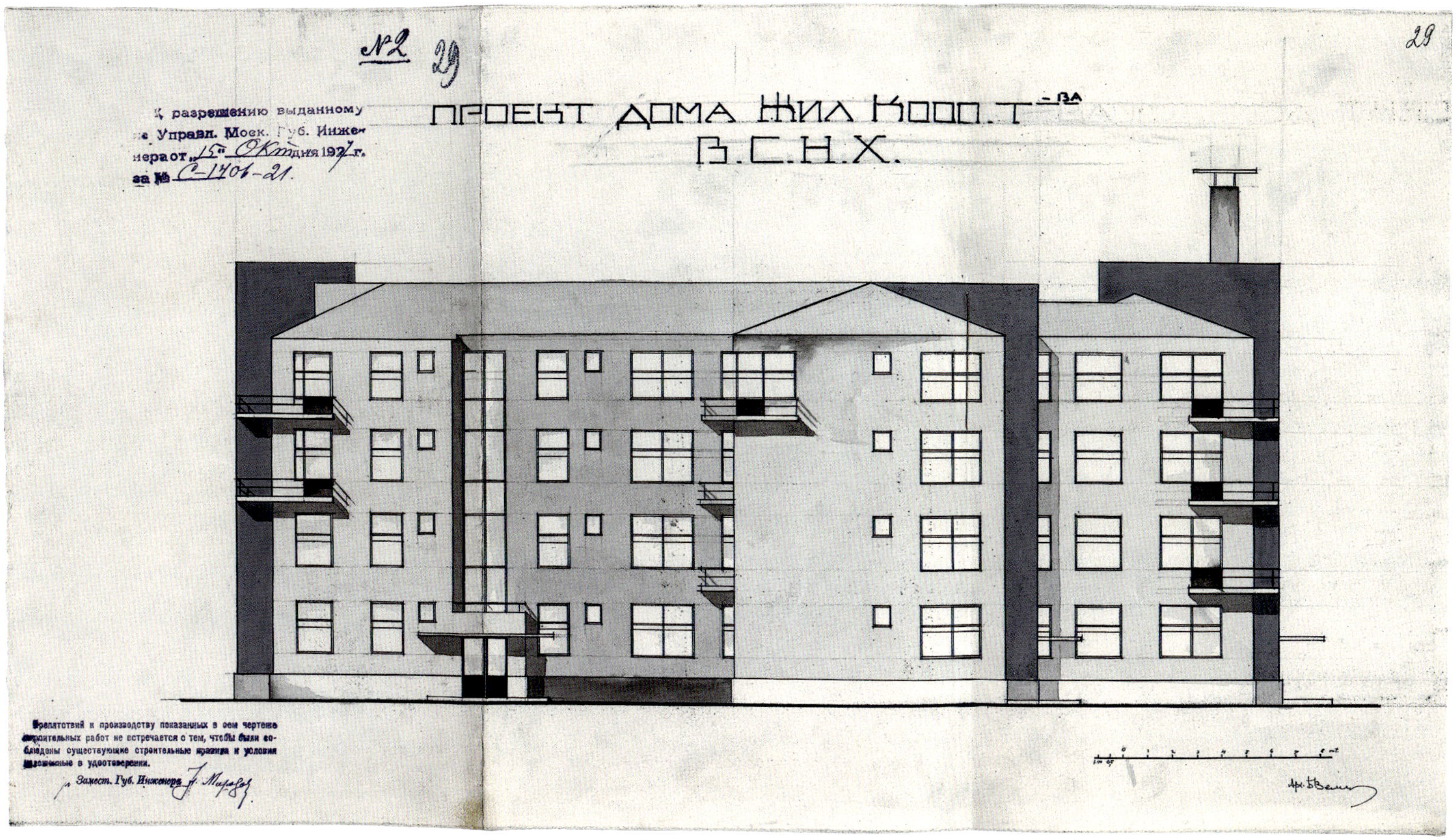

Koopstroi Residential House
21 Sadovaya-Kudrinskaya Street, Moscow
1927–1928 (extended upwards in the late 1940s)
Drawings of facades

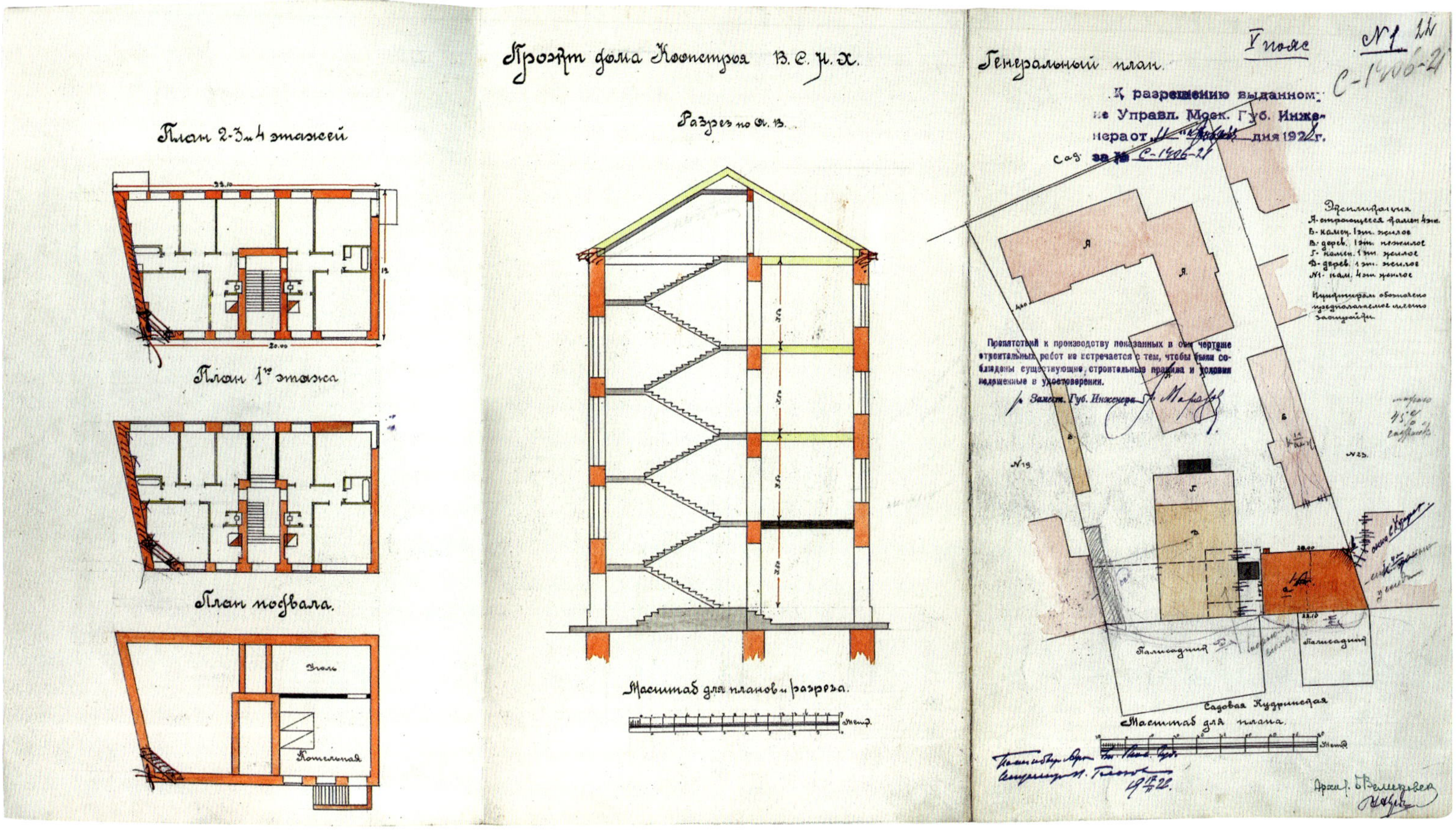
Проэкт дома Коопстроя В.С.Н.Х.
План 2-3 и 4 этажей
План 1го этажа
План подвала
Котельная
Разрез по А.В.
Масштаб для планов и разреза.
Генеральный план.
V пояс
№1
С-1406-21
К разрешению выданному
Управл. Моск. Губ. Инженера от дня 1927 г.
за № С-1406-21
Препятствий к производству показанных в сем чертеже строительных работ не встречается с тем, чтобы были соблюдены существующие строительные правила и условия изложенные в удостоверении.
Замест. Губ. Инженера
Палисадник
Садовая Кудринская
Масштаб для плана.

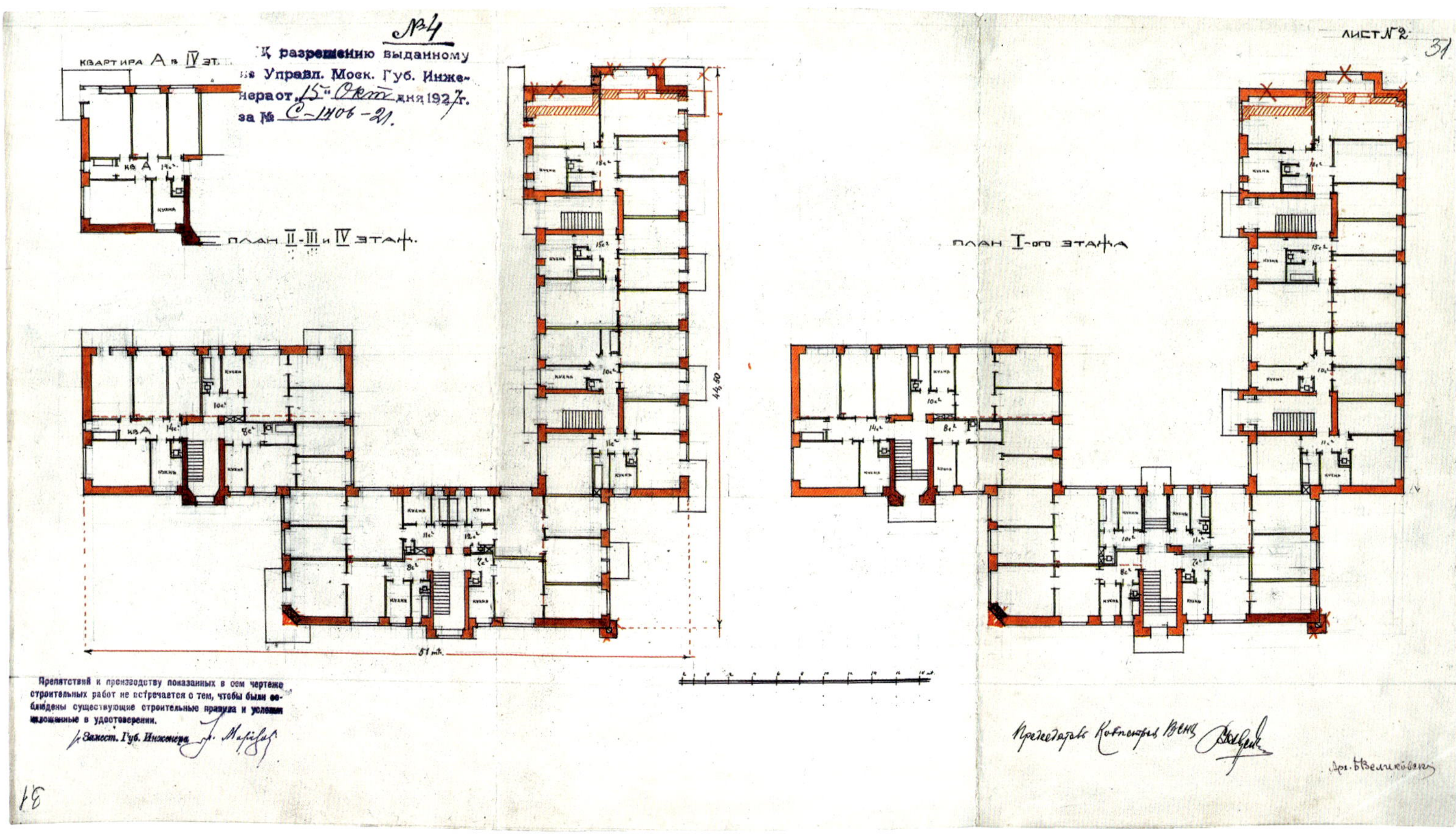
№4
Квартира А в IV эт.
К разрешению выданному
Управл. Моск. Губ. Инженера от 15 Окт дня 1927 г.
за № С-1406-21.
План II-III и IV этаж.
План I-го этажа
Лист №2
Препятствий к производству показанных в сем чертеже строительных работ не встречается с тем, чтобы были соблюдены существующие строительные правила и условия изложенные в удостоверении.
Замест. Губ. Инженера

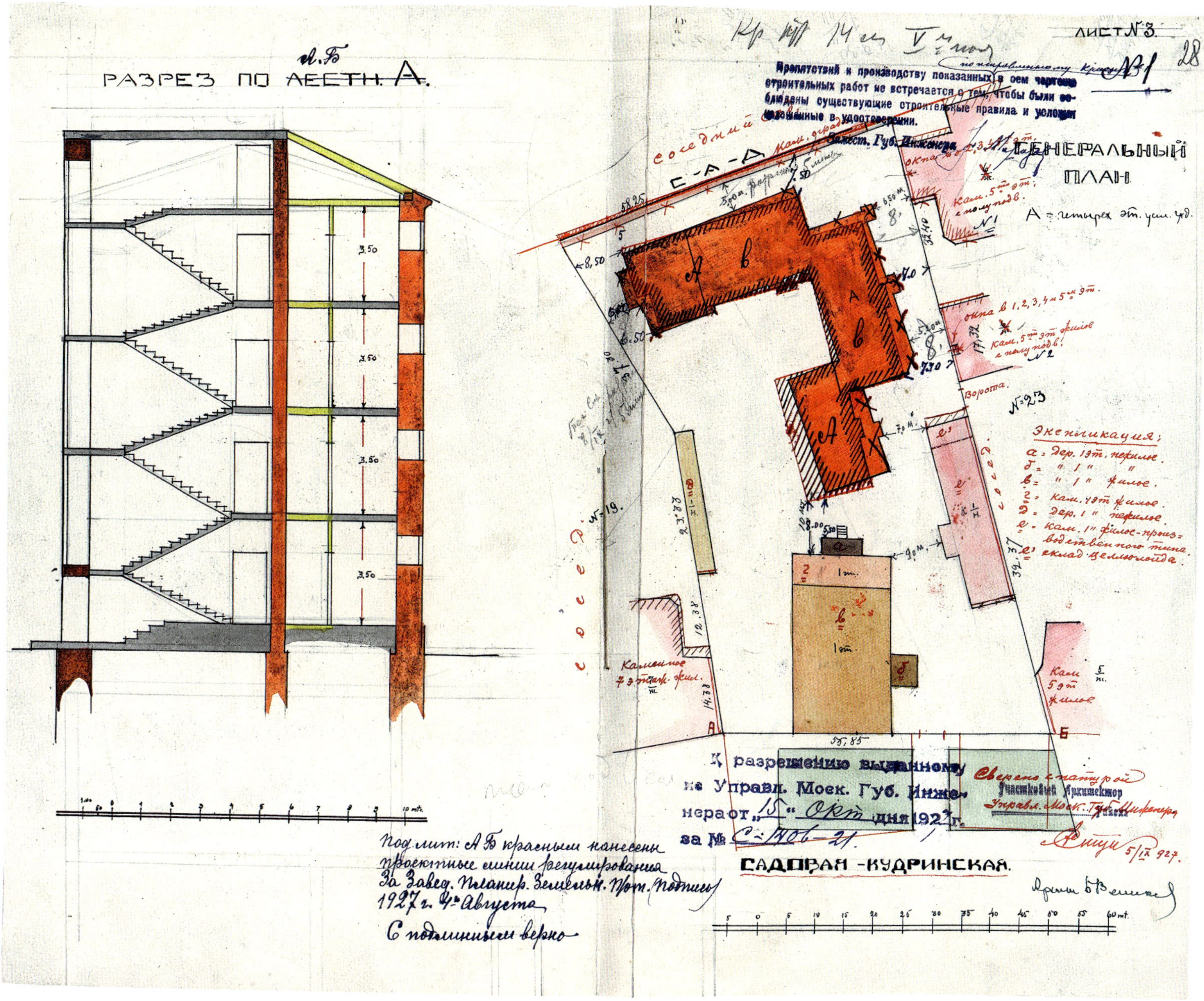

Koopstroi Residential House
21 Sadovaya-Kudrinskaya Street, Moscow
1927–1928 (extended upwards in the late 1940s)
Drawings of site plan, floor plans and stairwell sections

24
Gosstrakh Residential House
Durnovsky Lane, Moscow (unsurviving)
1926–1927
Architect: Boris Velikovsky

In the mid-1920s, Gosstrakh commissioned the construction of two experimental residential houses, which were both very typical for that time. In the course of their design and construction, this led to inevitable comparisons between the two different approaches of the two different architects – Moisei Ginzburg (one of the leaders of the Constructivists) and Boris Velikovsky (his friend). Ginzburg built a surviving apartment block on Malaya Bronnaya Street (with contributions from Vyacheslav Vladimirov), while Velikovsky built an unsurviving house on Durnovsky Lane (renamed Composers' Street in 1952).

Selim Khan-Magomedov[1] wrote: "The house designed by Moisei Ginzburg was constructed on Gosstrakh's own resources, while the other was built using deductions paid into the fund for improving the way of life of blue-collar and white-collar workers. These two houses became landmark events in the development of housing. Firstly, they were the first residential constructions in which the new stylistic movement was clearly expressed. Such formal devices of avant-garde architecture as flat roofs and corner glazing were employed (principally in the house designed by Moisei Ginzburg). Secondly, they were the first residential houses in which modern fittings were used."

In both cases, the architects were obliged to accommodate a broad range of residential units, ranging from five-room apartments to a corridored hostel. In the two lower floors of his house, Velikovsky designed two three-apartment sections, which were not standard types or like the widely applied "Mossovet sections". Although the twelve apartments on these two floors were initially created as three-room flats, the plans of the house demonstrate the possibility of their transformation into larger or smaller housing units, depending on the number of proposed inhabitants in each apartment. A similar possibility of turning large flats into smaller apartments (and vice versa) was employed around

Gosstrakh Residential House
Durnovsky Lane, Moscow
(unsurviving)
1926–1927
Photograph of the construction process

the same time by Alexei Schusyev when designing a residential house for the actors of the Moscow Art Theatre.

Velikovsky created a spacious hostel of fifty-one rooms on the three upper floors (with seventeen rooms on each floor). The doors of each room opened onto a common corridor, which provided access to the washing and toilet facilities. The corridor had a complex form and was well lit by three windows.

The general contour of Velikovsky's building was zigzag-shaped (two staircases were placed in the resulting inner corners). As was typical of the mid-1920s, the facades of the house were left virtually bare. The only elements of decoration were the balconies, which differed in length and in their location on each facade. Velikovsky employed a similar device in the Koopstroi house, which he designed around the same time.

The two residential houses built for Gosstrakh enjoyed two very different fates. While Ginzburg's apartment block was constantly published at the various stages of design and construction and has survived to this day, only one short piece was written about Velikovsky's house, which was later pulled down. So the only known details about the interior decor and fittings relate to Ginzburg's house. However, all the evidence suggests that the house on Durnovsky Lane was no worse than the block on Malaya Bronnaya Street, which was described in the same article by Selim Khan-Magomedov: "The top floor of the house has been turned into a hostel of twelve rooms with a large common kitchen, two bathrooms and two toilets. The other floors contain two-, three- and four-room apartments. The ground floor has been partially occupied by a shop. The house is equipped with waste-disposal units, while all the apartments have balconies and bay windows. The kitchens have wide, fitted wall cupboards: the upper sections are occupied by closed and open shelves, while the middle sections contain a disappearing bed (for the housemaid). The structure of the building also includes several elements of communal living. The flat roof, which is intended for relaxation (rain water is removed by the internal gutters), has flowerbeds in reinforced-concrete boxes, reinforced-concrete benches and a rain canopy. The attic contains a clothes dryer, while the basement has a laundry and storage rooms for each apartment."

Although Velikovsky's inclined attic roof was not innovative, it would pass the test of time today, whereas Ginzburg's flat roof did not catch on and was later reconstructed. Velikovsky immediately rejected this device, despite it being very fashionable in the 1920s. The evidence suggests that his approach to other matters concerning the fixtures and fittings inside his house was equally circumspect, and probably more realistic, reflecting his greater experience as a pre-revolutionary architect.

1 Selim Omarovich Khan-Magomedov (1928–2011) was a Soviet historian who specialised in the architecture of the Russian avant-garde and the indigenous nations of Dagestan. He published books on many Soviet modernist architects, including Konstantin Melnikov, Alexander Vesnin, Ilya Golosov and Moisei Ginzburg.

Gosstrakh Residential House
Durnovsky Lane, Moscow
(unsurviving)
1926–1927
Stroitelstvo Moskvy (Construction of Moscow) magazine article, 1927

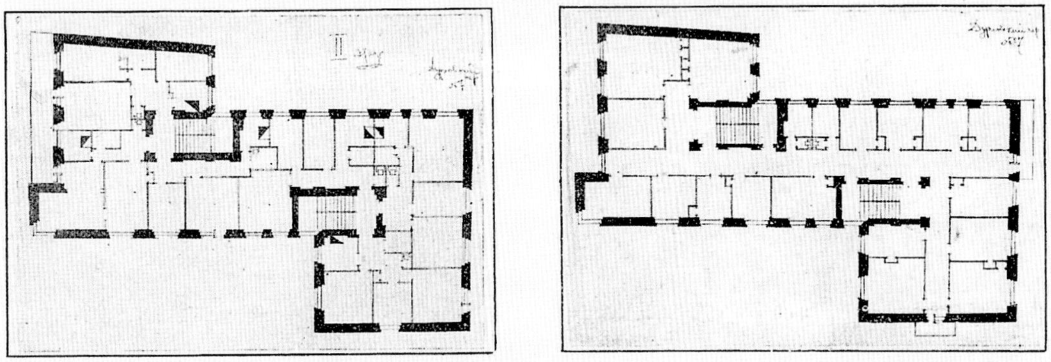

Арх. Б. М. Великовский. План 2-го этажа (слева) и 3, 4 и 5-го этажей (справа) дома Госстраха в Дурновском пер.

Арх. Б. М. Великовский. Дом Госстраха в Дурновском пер.

Постройка дома началась в июле 1926 г. В настоящее время здание уже закончено и заселено. Стоимость всех строительных работ выразилась в сумме около 270.000 рублей. Кубическая сажень обошлась, следовательно, в 325 р.

Здание по Дурновскому пер. несколько больше по размерам. Оно пятиэтажное, об'емом в 10.300 куб. м. Нижние два этажа заняты 12 трехкомнатными квартирами, в верхних же трех этажах устроено общежитие из 51 комнаты. Полезной площади в нем 402 кв. саж., жилой—266 кв. саж.

Затраты на сооружение дома исчислены в сумме около 300.000 р. Стоимость куб. сажени постройки — 290 руб., — несколько ниже, чем на Мал. Бронной. Об'ясняется это, главным образом, отсутствием здесь таких исключительных удобств, какие предоставляются жильцам того дома. Начато здание сооружением в сентябре прошлого года. Закончено должно быть к концу августа текущего года.

Снаружи оба дома частью оштукатурены, частью облицованы особой смесью, отделанной под гранит.

Все строительные работы, в том числе и специальные, велись хозяйственным способом.

С. П.

РСПЕКТИВА ЛАБОРАТОРИИ
ГАЛЕН МОСКВА
ГАЛЕН

25

Galen Cooperative Building
Vysheslavtsev Lane, Moscow (unsurviving)
1927–1928
Architect: Boris Velikovsky

The Galen cooperative was a chemical-pharmaceutical enterprise, and the design of its unsurviving building on Vysheslavtsev Lane in northern Moscow was a complicated process. Boris Velikovsky was asked to come up with conveniently interconnected premises over a compact three-storey building. The interiors all had very different functions and included a laboratory, industrial workshops, soap-making works, a packaging department, a kitchen, a canteen and offices.

Velikovsky created a striking composition which looked particularly stunning when viewed from the corner. The most noteworthy features were the protruding avant-corps of the staircase with two vertical windows and the large round window above the corner balcony. The avant-corps rose above the partially flat roof. The architect successfully placed the pool with the liquid chemicals (raw materials) at the top of the avant-corps. In doing so, he was not just paying tribute to a form which was fashionable at that time; he had previously employed a similar approach when designing factories in the pre-revolutionary period. Back then, he had created water towers in the form of an avant-corps, attached to the factory workshop and designed in the style of a medieval turret or bell tower.

The inner layout of the Galen cooperative building is extremely laconic. The chain of production is organised so that the initial processing of the raw materials occurs at the top, while the filling and packaging takes place at the bottom. A similar principle for the organisation of production along vertical, rather than horizontal, lines was proposed by Konstantin Melnikov in his famous Makhorka Pavilion for the tobacco industry at the All-Russian Agricultural and Handicraft-Industrial Exhibition in Moscow in 1923. In both cases, these were carefully planned and deliberate actions, incorporating the latest principles for the organisation of production in a confined space. The upward growth of construction in Moscow, the increased size of enterprises and the relocation of industry outside the city influenced the subsequent fates of such small buildings, explaining why this particular example, which was very typical of the 1920s, has sadly not survived.

Galen Cooperative Building
Vysheslavtsev Lane, Moscow
(unsurviving)
1927–1928
Perspective view (from Stroitelstvo Moskvy (Construction of Moscow) magazine article, 1928

Galen Cooperative Building
Vysheslavtsev Lane, Moscow
(unsurviving)
1927–1928
Floor plan (from Stroitelstvo Moskvy (Construction of Moscow) magazine article, 1928

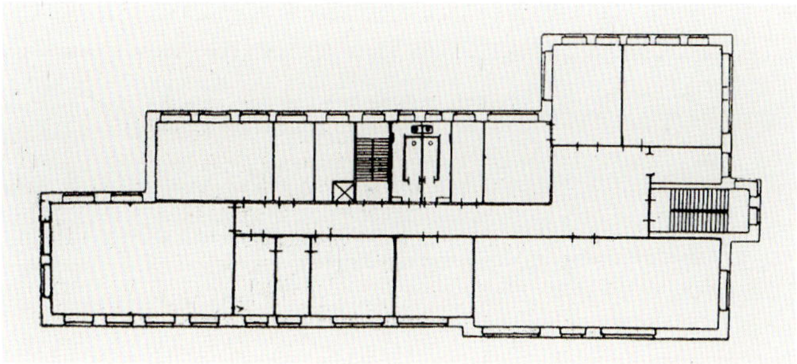

XII СЕЗД
ЦЕНТР

26

Competition to Design the Tsentrosoyuz Building 39 Myasnitskaya Street, Moscow 1928

Tsentrosoyuz (Central Union of Consumer Societies) was founded in 1896. After the revolution, in1918, all consumer cooperative unions were amalgamated with Tsentrosoyuz. The following year, Tsentrosoyuz became a government organisation, controlling the production, trade and acquisition from the population of agricultural products. In the NEP period, a large percentage of Soviet consumer goods was produced by cooperative artels, whose activities were also overseen by Tsentrosoyuz.

The competition held in 1928 to design a new building for Tsentrosoyuz developed into one of the most important in the architectural life of the Soviet Union. It was organised by the Society of Civil Engineers, one of the country's oldest professional organisations. The results of the first round were announced on 19 June 1928. The main task was to design a monumental facade on Myasnitskaya Street, bearing in mind the important role of this thoroughfare, where the headquarters of many important trade and industrial organisations were located.

In 1926, Tsentrosoyuz was awarded a large plot of land on Myasnitskaya Street, between numbers 35 and 43, running far back from the road. The imposing facades of the enormous new building were expected to dominate the proposed routes of two new thoroughfares. These two new streets were developed by engineer Sergei Shestakov[1] in his "Greater Moscow" plan (1921–25) and had already been approved by the planning department of Moscow City Council. In reality, however, only one of the streets was ever laid out – Novo-Myasnitskaya Street, which ran parallel to the old Myasnitskaya Street. The planned boulevard uniting both these streets remained on paper. Incidentally, Boris Velikovsky was also assigned to the redevelopment of this part of Moscow[2] and was shortly afterwards commissioned to design the House of the Book at the end of the new street (1930–34).

The competition stipulated that the ground floor of the Tsentrosoyuz building was to be raised above the earth and that the bearing constructions were to be made of reinforced concrete. The decoration of the facades was left to the discretion of the competing architects.[3] The entrants were also asked to divide the

Competition to design the Tsentrosoyuz building
39 Myasnitskaya Street, Moscow
1928
1st prize competiton design
by B. Velikovsky with
contributions from V. Voinov

щают интересную перспективу со стороны бульвара».

4-я премия присуждена: а) девизу «*F*», автор—гр. инж. Б. М. Великовский, б) девизу «Зеленый треугольник», автор—арх. С. Е. Чернышев, в) девизу «Арктика», авторы—арх. Н. А. Троцкий, С. И. Казан (Ленинград).

5-я премия присуждена: а) девизу: «Нем», авторы—арх. В. Р. Цабель, В. М. Кусаков, б) девизу: «Зиф», авторы—студ. МВТУ—Ф. Я. Бялостоцкая и З. М. Розенфельд, в) девизу «Копеечная марка», авторы—гр. инж. А. В. Розенберг и М. И. Бабицкий, г) девизу «Красный круг», автор—арх. М. Г. Рубинштейн, д) девизу «Е. Р.», автор—гр. инж. А. Д. Крячков и е) девизу «Голубая черта», автор—гр. инж. Б. В. Ефимович.

Приобретены проекты: 1) арх. Л. М. Яругского, 2) арх. Я. И. Райх, Б. И. Вендерова, 3) С. П. Иванова и Г. С. Райц.

Заключение по проектам, представленным на второй, закрытый конкурс дала комиссия, приглашенная Центросоюзом. Комиссия о проекте **английских** архитекторов Бернет и Тейт говорит: «По композиции—примитивен, интереса не представляет и не отвечает современным архитектурным требованиям. К разработке не может быть принят».

Проект архит. М. Таут (Берлин). «В проекте привлекательна ясность схемы плана с одним двором, но вследствие: 1) неудовлетворительного разрешения главного входа с Мясницкой в одном углу плана деловой части и недостаточной разработанности входа с Ново-Мясницкого просп.; 2) неудачного решения клуба, недопустимого размещения квартир и отсутствия входа с Бульварного проезда,—проект в основу для окончательной разработки принять нельзя».

Проект архит. Ле-Корбюзье и Жаннере (Париж). «Четкость плана в размещении административных, оперативных и общественных частей Центросоюза, хорошо запроектированные входы и вестибюли, наличие значительного отступа от Мясницкой ул., удачное решение раздевален и стоянки автомо-

Проект группы архитекторов Центросоюза

Модель здания

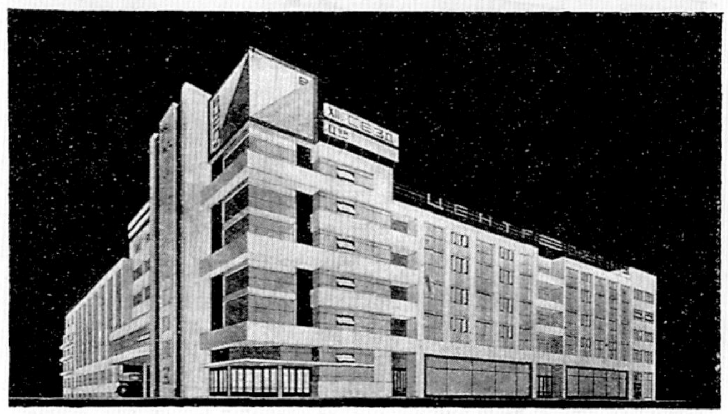

1-я премия
Перспективный вид

2-я премия
Перспективный вид

5

Competition to design the Tsentrosoyuz building
39 Myasnitskaya Street, Moscow
1928
Article on competion from "SA" (Sovremennaya Arkhitektura magazine), 1928. Velikovsky's entry in centre

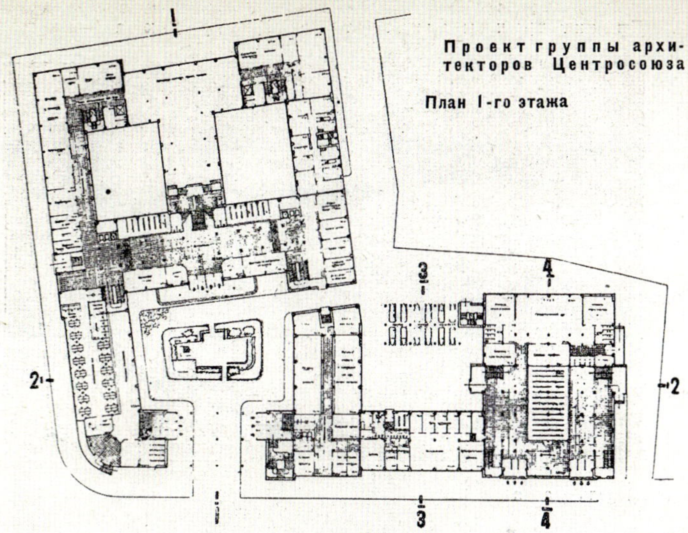

Проект группы архитекторов Центросоюза

План I-го этажа

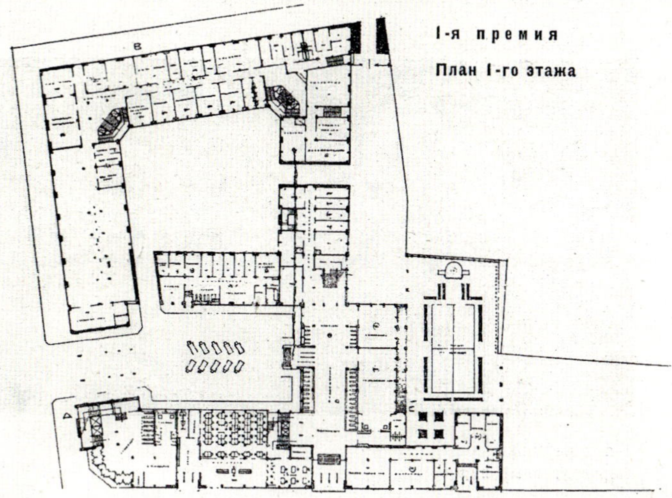

I-я премия

План I-го этажа

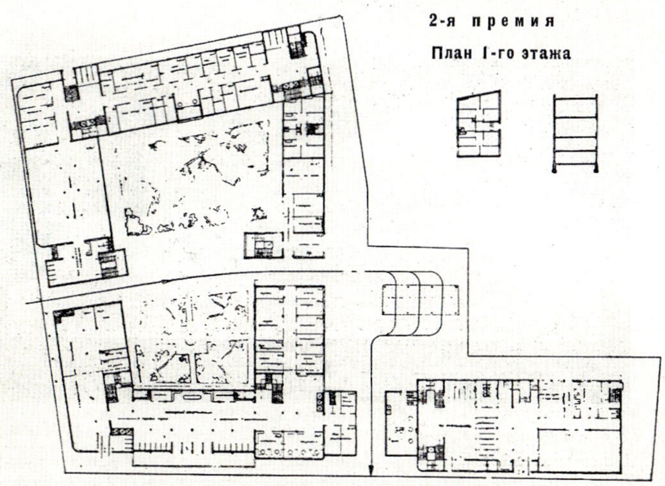

2-я премия

План I-го этажа

6

билей, своеобразное разрешение клуба и общая насыщенность проекта новыми решениями, переходящими в изобретательность, дают все основания *для рекомендации проекта Корбюзье к дальнейшей разработке.*

К недостаткам проекта следует отнести застройку вплотную к границам соседнего владения, сложную конструкцию перекрытия над залом собраний, недостаточную освещенность раздевальни, недостаточное обособление помещений клуба от остальных помещений Центросоюза.

Проект управления по постройке складов Центросоюза. «Наиболее продуманный и разработанный проект. План здания задуман хорошо, размещение и взаимная связь частей Центросоюза, входы и раздевальные разрешены хорошо. К недостаткам проекта Комиссия относит интенсивную застройку участка, недостаточную использованность фронта Мясницкой ул. под деловую часть здания, где расположен клуб, и недостаточно выразительный в'езд на парадный двор. *Проект следует признать вполне пригодным к дальнейшей разработке* с устранением замеченных недостатков.

Комиссия считает необходимым разработку окончательного проекта силами русских зодчих с учетом всех замечаний Комиссии и положительных сторон выделенных проектов».

Результат приведенных двух конкурсов дает вполне отчетливую картину наиболее правильных решений проектировки будущего дома Центросоюза и поэтому Правление Центросоюза организовало третий, закрытый конкурс, заказав проекты: 1) арх. Оль, 2) гр. инж. Никольскому (Ленинград), 3) акад. Жолтовскому, 4) арх. бр. Весниным, 5) гр. инж. Самойлову и Нахману, 6) О-ву Соврем. Архитекторов (ОСА) (Москва) и 7) проф. П. Беренс (Берлин) к сроку 20 октября с. г.

Результаты этого интереснейшего третьего конкурса мы осветим в одном из ближайших №№ «Строительства Москвы».

Гр. инж. Е. ТАТАРИНОВ.

Competition to design the Tsentrosoyuz building
39 Myasnitskaya Street, Moscow
1928
Article on competion from "SA" (Sovremennaya Arkhitektura magazine), 1928. Velikovsky's entry of the ground-floor in centre

building into separate zones (blocks) for a total of two thousand employees. Zone A was for the managerial staff and would include the accounts office and the various forecasting, planning and administrative departments. Zone B would contain the commercial departments, while Zone C would have a club, a canteen, a library and a first-aid room. Zone D was for the auxiliary premises, garage, workshops and service apartments.

Velikovsky had already worked for Tsentrosoyuz in the early 1920s and entered two designs in the first (open) round of the competition. He was awarded first prize for his joint project (designed in collaboration with Vasily Voinov) and third prize for his personal project.

Twenty-three teams of architects submitted projects during the first stage. The first prize was awarded to the project of Boris Velikovsky and Vasily Voinov, while the second prize went to Anna Kapustina and Leonid Saveliev. The third prize went to the project of Ivan Zvezdin and Ivan Zaporozhets, while the fourth prize was awarded to Noi Trotsky, S. N. Kazak and Theresa Zelikman.

Velikovsky's experience of designing the Gostorg building undoubtedly played a role in his victory. Gostorg was the country's first truly modern office block and had even impressed Le Corbusier. The architecture of the Gostorg building had also influenced Nikolai Popov (Sibiryak), the head of MUNI (Moscow Directorate of Immovable Property), who now associated the future of Myasnitskaya Street with buildings made of glass and concrete. Popov had sharply criticised the "New Moscow" general plan, developed under the leadership of Alexei Schusyev (1918–23), which had aimed to preserve the historical buildings on Myasnitskaya Street. Incidentally, Popov had also been Velikovsky's client in the project to design the residential house for MUNI employees.

In this way, Velikovsky played a major role in forming the tastes of those responsible for commissioning large administrative buildings. Back in 1925–26, when the Gostorg headquarters were being built, he had already shown in practice how the Moscow of the future might look. And this meant architecture on a truly European level. So it is perhaps unsurprising that preference was given to him in the first round – and then, ultimately, to the great European architect Le Corbusier.

Jean-Louis Cohen, a leading expert on Le Corbusier, quotes the explicit desires of the customer, contained in the letter of invitation sent to the Swiss-French architect: "The architecture should be in the distinctly expressed style of an official administrative building; close attention should be paid to the external surfaces and the silhouette; wherever possible, the beauty and grandeur of the building should proceed from the simplicity of the forms; the use of decorative details should be avoided. As it will be encircled on three sides by major thoroughfares, the Tsentrosoyuz building should have a single image."

Not only historical houses were demolished on the piece of land assigned for construction; one of the oldest churches in Moscow – St Nicholas in Myasniki (sixteenth–eighteenth century) – was also pulled down. Tsentrosoyuz assigned half a million roubles to construct new apartments for those who lost their homes, although it is not known exactly how this sum was spent.

A review of the competition projects was published in the Construction of Moscow *magazine (1928, No. 1): "Commencing construction of*

Competition to design the Tsentrosoyuz building
39 Myasnitskaya Street, Moscow
1928
1st prize competiton design of the floor plan by B. Velikovsky with contributions from of V. Voinov

a grandiose office building for its own needs, the board of Tsentrosoyuz approached the question of the design of the building in an extremely serious manner. In accordance with the scrupulously developed programme, they held a total of three competitions to compile the project. The first, which was an open competition, was organised by the Society of Civil Engineers."

The project most unlike all the others turned out to be, as expected, the version offered by Ivan Leonidov: "The idea of locating all the business premises in one multistorey block running along the boulevard should, as a result of the close communication links and the most convenient use of the space, be regarded as very successful. Thanks to the high density of construction, the designer has managed to avoid enclosed courtyards and to ensure good lighting of the premises located inside the block." Leonidov, however, either ignored or completely reinterpreted

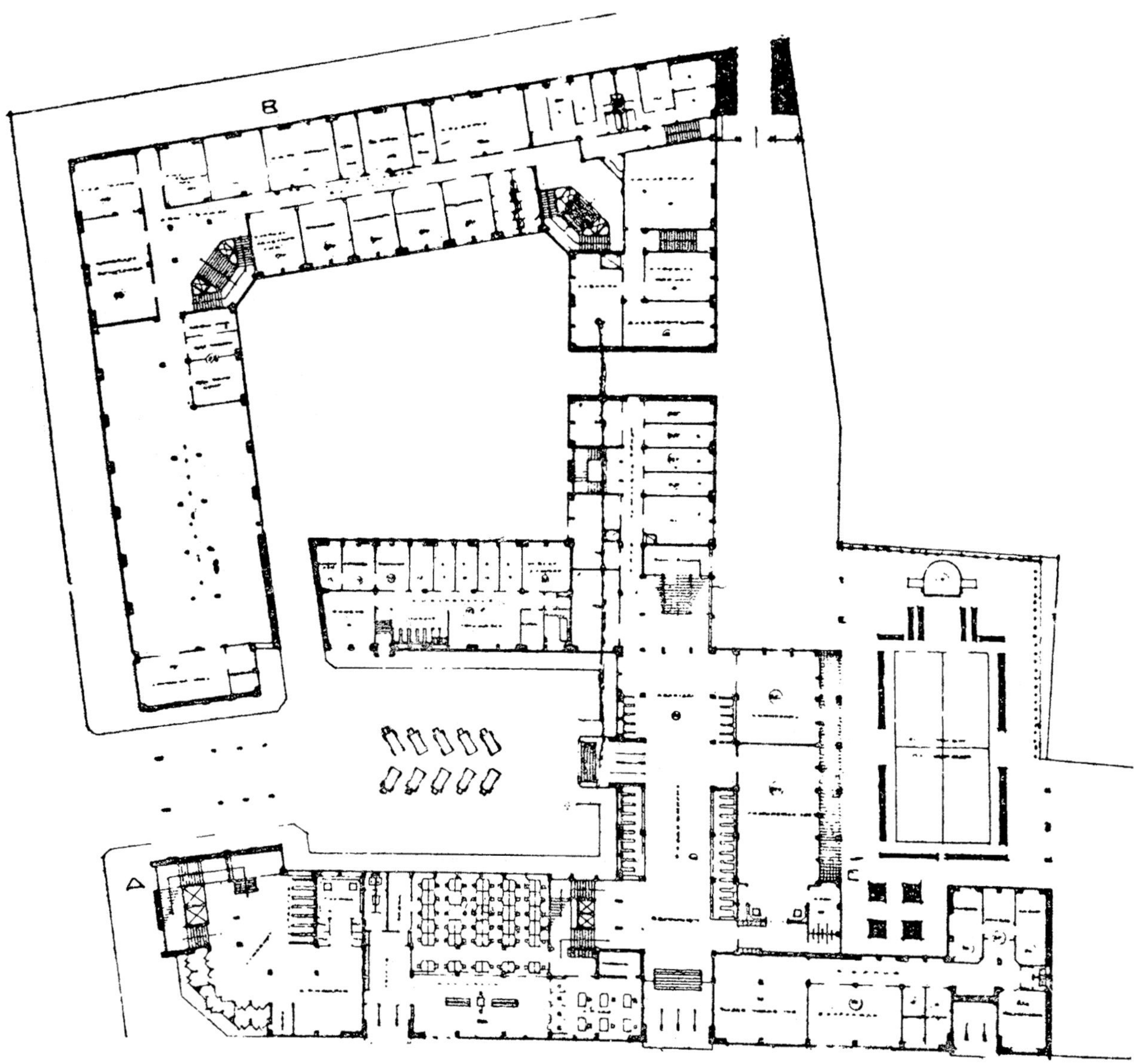

the customer's recommendations: "Besides the box-like building, he brought to the forefront on Myasnitskaya Street a museum, which was included in the project programme in the form of a two-storey block with an open colonnade; this was acknowledged to be 'unwarranted', while his design of the facades was 'monotonous'. Alexander Nikolsky followed the same approach as Leonidov, rejecting courtyards in favour of a single large block. His proposed universal and multifunctional spaces evoked doubt, as did the facades, which were regarded as 'not representing any interest'."

The second (closed) round was held among leading foreign architects who had received special invitations – Le Corbusier (Paris), Max Taut (Berlin), Peter Behrens (Berlin), Burnet and Tait (London) – and the Tsentrosoyuz team of architects.

The Construction of Moscow *magazine continued: "After a painstaking examination and study of all the designs from the first two competitions, a third and final competition was held, taking into account all the submitted materials. The following architects took part: the Vesnin brothers, Pavel Nakhman and Anatoly Samoilov, Andrei Ol, the OSA Group (Alexander Pasternak, Vyacheslav Vladimirov, Lyubov Slavina and Nina Vorotyntseva), Ivan Leonidov, Alexander Nikolsky, Ivan Zholtovsky, Le Corbusier and Professor Behrens (Berlin). At the start of November, a commission of representatives from Tsentrosoyuz, Mossovet, Mosstroi and other organisations examined all the commissioned projects, collected all the opinions and came to a decision about the compilation of the final project."*

The project of Velikovsky and Voinov, which was awarded first prize in the first round, differed greatly from the Gostorg building. Judging by the published plan of the ground floor, the two architects proposed an asymmetric composition (although again with two courtyards). Despite Velikovsky's own involvement in the development of Novo-Myasnitskaya Street, the main accent was placed on the corner of old Myasnitskaya and the new boulevard (which was never actually built), where a large glazed vestibule was planned. To the left of this vestibule would be an entranceway into the first courtyard, which would contain another vestibule for those employees arriving by car. There were two other entrances from Myasnitskaya Street. A large cloakroom was located where the main flows of people intersected. The planned building was completely closed off on Novo-Myasnitskaya Street, although one could enter the block running along this thoroughfare via other vestibules located in the corners of the second inner courtyard.

The distinct division of the socle floor into different zones for different purposes was appreciated by the jury. This device ensured that the flow of employees would not mix with the streams of outside visitors. However, while the jury considered the project to be realistic and heedful of many vital factors, it also noted several digressions from the competition programme.

Velikovsky and Voinov's project looks like the image of an existing building, or even the reconstruction of a previously existing building. The architectural plasticity corresponds closely to the pragmatic "functionialist" approach of the late 1920s. Their main competitors, however, offered larger and more monumental forms, and this gave them the edge in the final round of the competition. Velikovsky and Voinov's main rivals were clearly the Vesnin brothers, who won all the significant architectural contests of that time. The only person whom the three brothers could never hope to outperform was such an authoritative European master as Le Corbusier. All innovative

Russian architects were greatly inspired by both his designs and his fiery articles in *L'Esprit nouveau*, and he naturally came up with the most original project for the Tsentrosoyuz building.

L'Esprit nouveau published some of the responses of the commission members to the designs submitted in the third round. There is no mention of Velikovsky, who was not invited to enter a project at this final stage. The revue noted that the project of the Vesnin brothers "should be ranked among the best from the point of view of the composition of the plan. Two blocks parallel to the boulevard, with a central master link, provide a simple and clear way to conveniently locate all the administrative premises of Tsentrosoyuz within the bounds of each block and, forming two open courtyards, take into account the varying significance of Staro-Myasnitskaya Street and Novo-Myasnitsky Prospekt."

This approach was, in many ways, similar to the first project of Velikovsky and Voinov, which greatly influenced the final stage of the competition. The design submitted by the Vesnin brothers in the third round was more monumental than most. In this sense, it was comparable to the project of Le Corbusier, whose composition also rejected sculptural details and subdivisions in favour of large, smooth surfaces and rounded volumes.

Le Corbusier's interpretation of the Tsentrosoyuz building also far from completely corresponded to the set task. However, it did correspond to the requirement for a separation into functions of different character. At the same time, everything about his composition looks integrated. The building faces both streets with striking, yet dissimilar facades. Unlike his competitors, Le Corbusier applied parabolic elements in the plan – an auditorium and ramps. This imparted a memorable image to his creation. The ramps were subjected to criticism, but the master insisted on their implementation in combination with paternoster elevators. The facades in his version, it should be confessed, look monumental – as was required.

The projects of Max Taut and Peter Behrens also represented compositions of numerous blocks with simple forms. Behrens paid more attention than Le Corbusier to the facades. He clearly reflected the decorative tendencies in the architecture of his time, as was noted by the jury. Taut, on the contrary, acted very pragmatically, masterly configuring the individual blocks. Each element of his edifice was shown more distinctly on the dummy model, down to the individual blocks with columns of mesh of different density. The other projects were much more stereotypical (for example, that of Nakhman and Samoilov).

Whatever the outcome of the competition, Velikovsky could clearly compete on an equal footing with the leading stars of modern architecture, even when orientated on extremely widespread professional devices (devices which he himself had helped to make so widespread). The architect relied above all on the practical experience he had accumulated over the past two decades, and the exterior forms of his Gostorg building acted as the prototype for virtually all the Russian entrants in the competition.

1 Sergei Sergeyevich Shestakov (1862–1929) was a Russian engineer who graduated from the Imperial Technical College in Moscow in 1886. He designed the Fraternal Cemetery in the village of Vsekhsvyatskoe to the north-west of Moscow (1914–15) and worked on the "Greater Moscow" plan for the redevelopment of the city (1921–25). He was arrested and died in prison in 1929.

2 See B. M. Velikovsky, "Novaya Myasnitskaya ulitsa", *Arkhitektura SSSR*, No. 1/11, 1933, p. 57.

3 See E. Tatarinov, "Dom Tsentrosoyuza v Moskve", *Stroitel'naya promyshlennost'*, No. 6/9, September 1928; "Dva konkursa na dom Tsentrosoyuza", *Stroitel'stvo Moskvy*, No. 5/11, November 1928.

КИНОПЛОВ
КИНОПЛОВ

27

House of the Book
3 Orlikov Lane, Moscow
1930–1934
Architect: Boris Velikovsky with contributions from Pavel Antonov, Klimovich, Yuly Savitsky, Vladimir Vereschagin and Alexei Volkhonsky

Boris Velikovsky's work for Gosizdat[1] was possibly the most important in his creative biography. The success of his magnum opus of the 1920s – the Gostorg building – helped the architect to secure this particular commission.
The project to build the House of the Book was conceived as part of the general drive to develop the capital's new administrative and business centre, which was already springing up around the intersection of the Sadovaya ("Garden") Ring and Novo-Myasnitskaya Street (renamed Novokirovsky Prospekt in 1985 and Academician Sakharov Prospekt in 1990). Velikovsky played a vital role in assimilating this district, which he envisaged as a new urban axis stretching from the Kremlin through the central squares around Kitai-Gorod to Kalanchyovskaya (Komsomolskaya) Square.

The building of the House of the Book was intended to usher in a new stage in the architectural development of this part of Moscow. This move began with the construction of the Gostorg building on Myasnitskaya Street (designed by Boris Velikovsky and Vyacheslav Vladimirov, 1927) and the Orgametall[2] building on Kalanchyovskaya Street (designed by Oswald Schneidratus, D. I. Fränkel and B. A. Gaidu, 1927–28). Other prominent buildings were placed nearby, including Narkomput[3] (designed by Ivan Fomin, 1927–32), Narkomzem (designed by Alexei Schusyev with contributions from Alexander Grinberg, Dmitry Bulgakov, Isidor Frantsuz and Georgy Yakovlev, 1928–33) and Tsentrosoyuz (designed by Le Corbusier, Pierre Jeanneret and Nikolai Colley, 1930–36). Velikovsky had further contributed to the

House of the Book
3 Orlikov Lane, Moscow
1930–1934
View from south-east, 2016

development of this district when he won first prize in the first round of the competition to design the Tsentrosoyuz building in 1928.

Conceptually, the House of the Book was expected to be similar to the *Izvestiya* and *Pravda* newspaper complexes. The planned building was to combine both administrative premises (the numerous editorial offices of all the publishing houses) and printing rooms.

The chosen plot of land ruled out any horizontally extended designs, obliging the architect to come up with a vertical composition. In 1930, two competitions had already been held but had not provided any acceptable solutions – except that all the entrants had understood the need for a complex form of skyscraper. A total of thirty-five projects were submitted to the first competition, while the second contest attracted five projects.

The architect Ivan Lamtsov wrote a critical article on the project, entitled "An Unsuccessful Competition". At the end of his piece, he noted, "Even whilst developing the control project and holding the competition, the necessity of expanding the programme had already become obvious. What the competitions have given us, therefore, no longer corresponds to the increased demands of GIZ."

The project was finally commissioned from Boris Velikovsky as an experienced architect capable of overcoming difficult functional problems. In 1931, construction work began on the basis of his design, despite a public scandal, which was covered in the press.

Following the work specially held to test the sub-foundation area, the go-ahead has been given for a skyscraper design. For the first time, the principle of Le Corbusier has been employed – placing the building on pilotis, which will allow the lower premises to be used as a car park.

All the main prerequisites of the project, such as the surface area and so forth, were agreed by GIZ with the municipal organisations (Sokolniki district). For the first time, a dual competition was held (for both the idea and the project development), but this did not provide any satisfactory results. As a consequence, in May of this year, GIZ was obliged to commence the project development using administrative methods, relying on the young architects of its own construction department (comrades Volkhonsky, Vereschagin, Klimovich and others). The architect Velikovsky, who had sufficiently proved himself with the construction of Gostorg and other buildings, was invited to join the staff of the construction department as a consultant.

By 15 June of this year, the project of the House of the Book had been basically developed and passed at all levels. At this point, the regional department of the Union of Constructors suddenly announced that work on the design of the House of the Book was being conducted in a "non-transparent" fashion, in the form of a "private commission". In connection with this announcement, the regional department of the Union of Constructors asked MOVANO (Moscow Regional Department of the All-Union Architectural-Scientific Society) to organise a public review and revision of the project.

MOVANO is a young professional organisation which brings together all the trends in Soviet scientific and architectural thought. However, the commission selected by the board of MOVANO regarding the House of the Book has proven to be of little authority and extremely tendentious. Instead of an objective appraisal of the project at the public examination of 15 August of this year, the MOVANO commission, in the form of its chairman, comrade Friedman, opposed the project of the House of the Book

House of the Book
3 Orlikov Lane, Moscow
1930–1934
1930s photograph showing part of House the Book (right), Gostorg (left) and Alexei Schusev Narkomzem (centre) as well as a section of the cooperative building of 1927 (far left)

(worked out by a collective method) with [...] the one-man project of comrade Friedman.

As has been established from the archive materials of the construction department of GIZ, comrade Friedman contacted GIZ last year with the proposal to commission the design for the House of the Book from a group of urbanist architects. However, GIZ learnt that the suggested "group" at that moment consisted of only two members, headed by the maestro Friedman, and, naturally, did not consider it possible to establish what would virtually be a one-man commission.

At the present moment, all the preparatory work on the territory earmarked for the House of the Book (the corner of Orlikov Lane and Novo-Myasnitskaya Street) is coming to an end. The sub-foundation area has already been tested and the foundation pit has been dug. On 17 August, in view of its lack of authority, the MOVANO commission was formally dissolved. However, the formation of a new authoritative commission has been swept under the rug. And the MOVANO commission continues to terrorise the construction department of GIZ, threatening to prohibit building work.

At the request of GIZ, a special government commission is being created. It faces the task of unravelling the tangle of contradictory announcements surrounding the project of the House of the Book and dispelling the atmosphere thickening around it.[4]

In the project documents, submitted for approval on 28 May 1930, Boris Velikovsky is listed as the main architect (and not a consultant), while the well-known engineer Arthur Loleit is named as the constructor. The House of the Book was intended to be a high-rise building with as many as twenty floors. The planned building would

House of the Book
3 Orlikov Lane, Moscow
1930–1934
Preliminary design side view

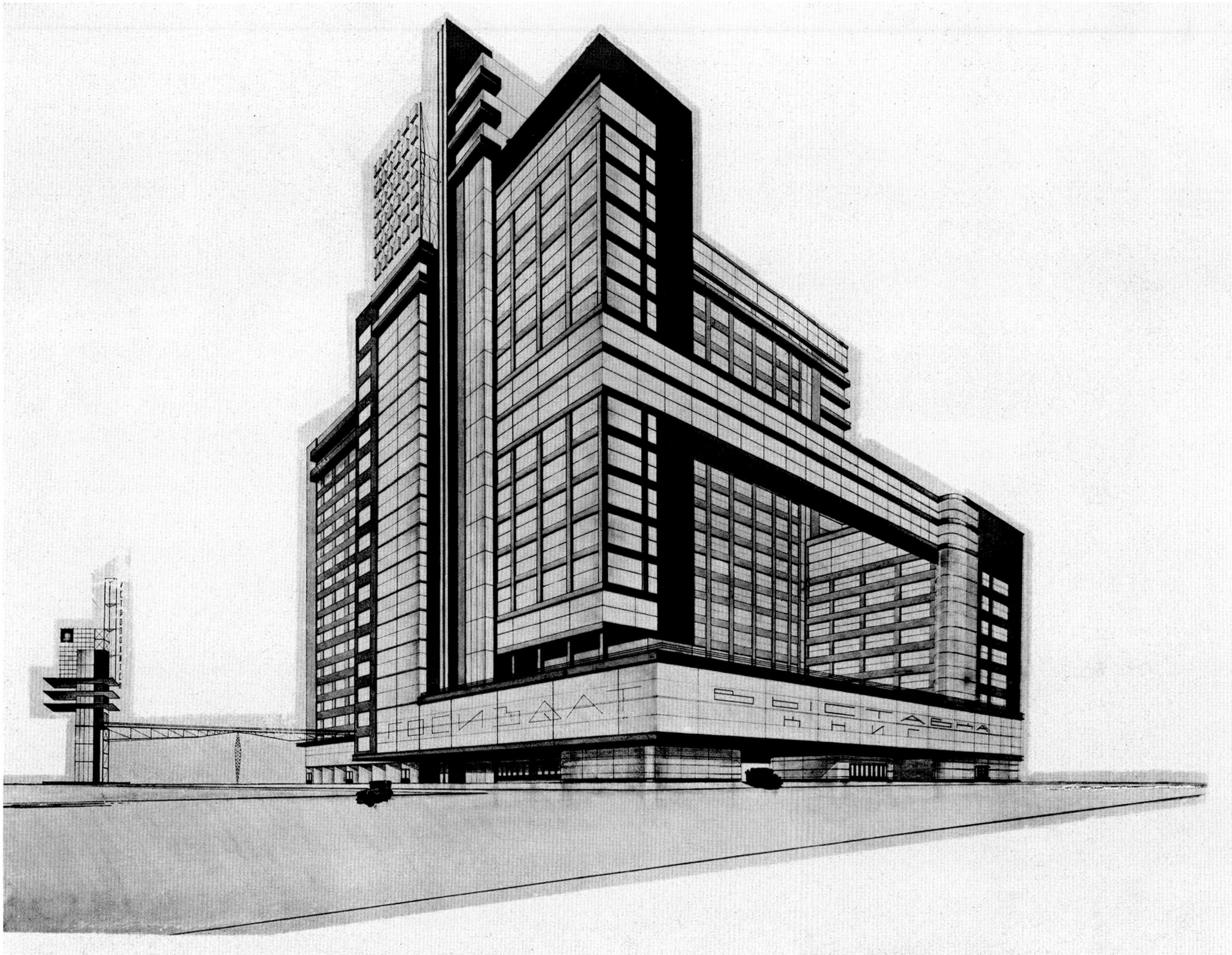

House of the Book
3 Orlikov Lane, Moscow
1930–1934
Perspective drawing of preliminary design from the north-west

consist of several blocks, girdled by a common glazed stylobate two floors in height. Spaces were left at the bottom for entranceways into the inner courtyard – two on Novo-Myasnitskaya Street and one on Orlikov Lane. The building was conceived with an enormous amount of glazing. The highest part would be set far back from the street. The courtyard in front of it would be enclosed by the stylobate and flanked on two sides by rectangular blocks, which would be joined together by a hanging gallery sixty metres in length. Viewed from the north-east, from Kalanchyovskaya (Komsomolskaya) Square, the building would have a striking, asymmetric, tower-like silhouette.

The implementation of Velikovsky's plan was halted at the stage of the construction of the frame of the socle floor. The next known project for the House of the Book was developed in 1934 at the Mossovet No. 4 architectural design bureau, under the leadership of Ilya Golosov (the younger brother of Panteleimon Golosov, designer of the *Pravda* newspaper complex). He successfully resolved the new tasks he was given, although he was better known as an avant-garde master of the 1920s.

Ilya Golosov was asked to utilise the already constructed parts of the House of the Book – the foundations and the socle floor. The new programme envisaged the same premises as before – printing rooms, storerooms, a library, a central bookshop, designers' studios, sound-recording studios, a canteen for 750 visitors and office space for 5,500 workers (increased from 4,000 in Velikovsky's plan).

The new project was designed in an Art Deco style typical of its time. The building was still based on Velikovsky's volumetric plan, however, although it now had a symmetric axial composition. The tower was increased by four floors, while the side wings were lowered. But construction never commenced, and a central building for all the Soviet publishing houses never actually appeared.

Unfortunately, Velikovsky's published project of 1930 does not offer any insight into the planned inner layout. Neither is it clear why his project was never implemented. This could have been a consequence of the MOVANO scandal, or perhaps an episode similar to the story of the redesign of the Hotel Moskva occurred. Construction of the Hotel Moskva initially began on the basis of the Constructivist project of Leonid Saveliev and Oswald Stapran. But the changing tastes of the Party leaders meant that academician Alexei Schusyev was then brought in to add Neoclassical decor – when the Constructivist frame had already been built. This evoked the indignation of the original designers, leading to a public scandal and the myth that the asymmetric facade was caused by Stalin's direct interference in the design process. A similar incident occurred over the *Pravda* newspaper complex, which was first built in a stark Constructivist style and then given decorative interiors. As a result, the architect (Panteleimon Golosov) refused to continue work on the project.

Whatever the case, Velikovsky dates his work on the House of the Book to the years 1930–34 in his autobiography. At the present moment, the southern and eastern facades of the building still survive (along Orlikov Lane). They have features similar to his project of 1930, although there are also noticeable differences.

On the 1930 blueprint of the facade, the block running along the frontage line of Orlikov Lane has six floors, increasing to ten floors above

House of the Book
3 Orlikov Lane, Moscow
1930–1934
Eastern facade detail, 2016

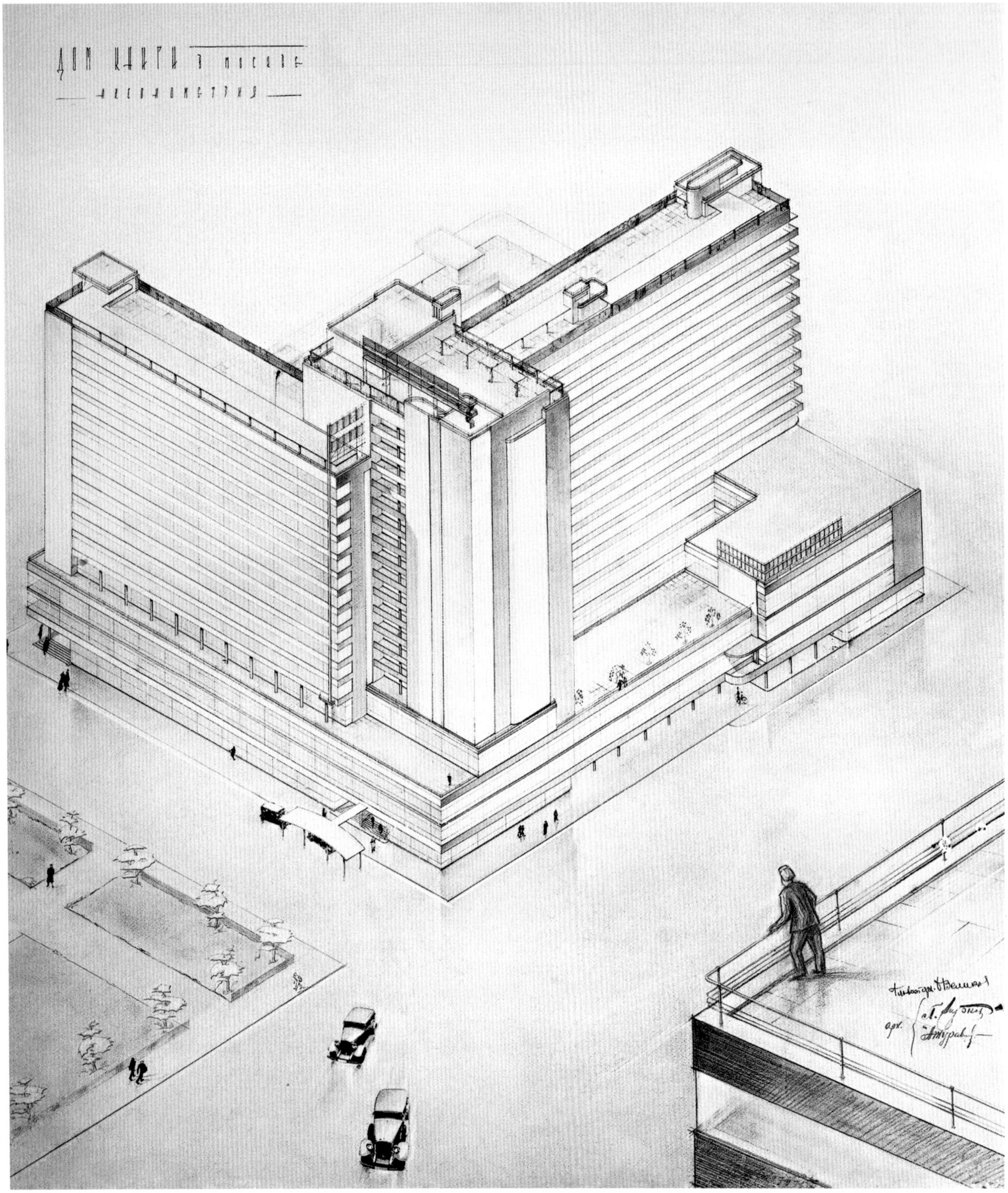

House of the Book
3 Orlikov Lane, Moscow
1930–1934
Perspective view of preliminary design

the arched entranceway. In reality, however, the building is six-storeys along the entire length of the lane. The section looking out onto Academician Sakharov Prospekt was built in the 1970s (when that avenue was finally completed and the pre-revolutionary constructions on the former Domnikovka Street were demolished).

The slightly asymmetric configuration of the blocks with the corner entranceway is visible from Orlikov Lane. The protruding avant-corps of the staircase with vertical glazing at the right-hand corner can also be seen. The round windows of the corner vestibule on the ground floor have been filled in. The loggia above the vestibule has been paned with glass, and the upward extending ribbon glazing has lost its original casing.

Velikovsky repeated the same approach in the House of the Book as in the Gostorg building. The heights of the floors are not identical and they decrease at the top. From the ground to the second floors the height is much greater. The heights of the windows also alternate from high to low. The windows of the first and second floors have the greatest heights, while those of the ground, third and fifth floors have reduced heights. An open gallery with cylindrical pillars was built on the last (sixth) floor, an architectural device still in fashion at that time.

The lower floors were designed to be occupied by areas open to the public, with a bookshop, a canteen, halls, a cloakroom, staircases and lifts. Like Le Corbusier's Tsentrosoyuz building, the facades were lined with Armenian tufa. In 1934, the Central Scientific Agricultural Library of the Vladimir Lenin All-Union Academy of Agricultural Sciences moved into the partially completed construction (the institution was controlled by Narkomzem, whose own headquarters stood next door, at 1 Orlikov Lane).

On 30 July 1930, the Central Committee of the All-Union Communist Party (Bolsheviks) published a resolution "On the work of Gosizdat of the RSFSR and on the Unification of Publishing." The text noted that the development of this industry had fallen behind the demands of the age of Socialist reconstruction and that the task of its structural reorganisation had been established, based on the proposed standardisation of all publishing houses. On 8 August 1930, Sovnarkom of the RSFSR passed a resolution, according to which, instead of a multitude of independent publishing houses, the country would have one single and virtually monopolistic organisation – the Unification of State Book and Magazine Publishers (OGIZ) under the auspices of Narkompros[5] of the RSFSR. The functions of OGIZ were exhaustive: its tasks included the planning, management and technical oversight of all printing, publishing and book-retail enterprises; deliveries, finances and the extension of credit; construction and infrastructure; and the training and allocation of employees.

Twenty-seven large and small publishing houses, with all their subordinated enterprises, were integrated into the composition of OGIZ. This included Gosizdat, which became the nucleus of the new organisation (its head, Artashes Khalatov, was appointed the chairman of the board and director of OGIZ), Land and Factory, Moscow Worker, Young Guard, Soviet Encyclopaedia, Education Worker, Gostekhizdat, Gosmedizdat, Gosyurizdat, Gosselkhozizdat, Goskhimizdat, Atheist, Physical Culture and Tourism *and the publishing houses of the Communist Academy, Sverdlov University, Osoaviakhim and the NKVD.*

Originally, there were thirteen publishing houses in the composition of OGIZ, which released books on specific subjects or for certain groups of readers. These were UchpedGIZ (educational), SotsekGIZ (social-economic), MasspartGIZ (mass political), Gostekhizdat (technical), SelkolkhozGIZ (agricultural), Medizdat (medical), GIKhL (fiction), Yundetizdat (young children), VoenGIZ (military), MuzGIZ (music), Yurizdat (law), IzOGIZ (art) and the Dictionary-Encyclopaedic Publishing House. At the start of 1931, three more publishing houses were added to OGIZ – Gostransizdat, SnabkoonGIZ and the recreated Physical Culture and Tourism. Besides these, OGIZ included nineteen regional publishing houses.

Academia, Federation, Tsentroizdat, the publishing house of the Academy of Sciences of the USSR and several others remained outside the OGIZ system but under its common leadership and control.

Departmental scientific-research institutions and educational establishments were also transferred to the OGIZ system.

Besides publishing houses, such trusts as Poligrafkniga and Poligraf were also under the jurisdiction of OGIZ.[6]

1 Gosizdat (also known as GIZ) was the State Publishing House, founded in Moscow in 1919 to publish political literature and oversee the book trade in Soviet Russia. In 1930, it was expanded to include almost all other state publishing houses in the Soviet Union and renamed OGIZ (Ob'edinennoe gosudarstvennoe izdatel'stvo, Unification of State Book and Magazine Publishers).

2 Orgametall was created in 1924 as a subdivision of the People's Commissariat of Machine Building. The aim of the organisation was to introduce technological advances in the spheres of metalworking, tools and machinery in order to raise productivity and the quality of industrial output in the Soviet Union.

3 Narkomput (*Narodnyi komissariat putei soobscheniya*, or People's Commissariat of Transportation) was the government ministry responsible for overseeing the railways and other forms of transport in the RSFSR from 1917 and the USSR from 1923 to 1946.

4 M. Melenevskaya, "Okolo kazyonnogo piroga. Delo o proyekte 'Doma knigi' i 'del'tsy' iz MOVANO", *Vechernyaya Moskva*, September 1930.

5 Narkompros (*Narodnyi komissariat prosvescheniya*, or People's Commissariat of Education) was the government ministry responsible for all cultural, artistic and educational matters in the RSFSR from 1917 and the USSR from 1923 to 1946.

6 From the book *Istoriya knigi*, ed. Alexander Govorov and Tatyana Kupriyanova, Moscow, 1998.

House of the Book
3 Orlikov Lane, Moscow
1930–1934
Perspective view of approved design from the north-west

ДОМ КНИГИ
ВЫСТАВКА

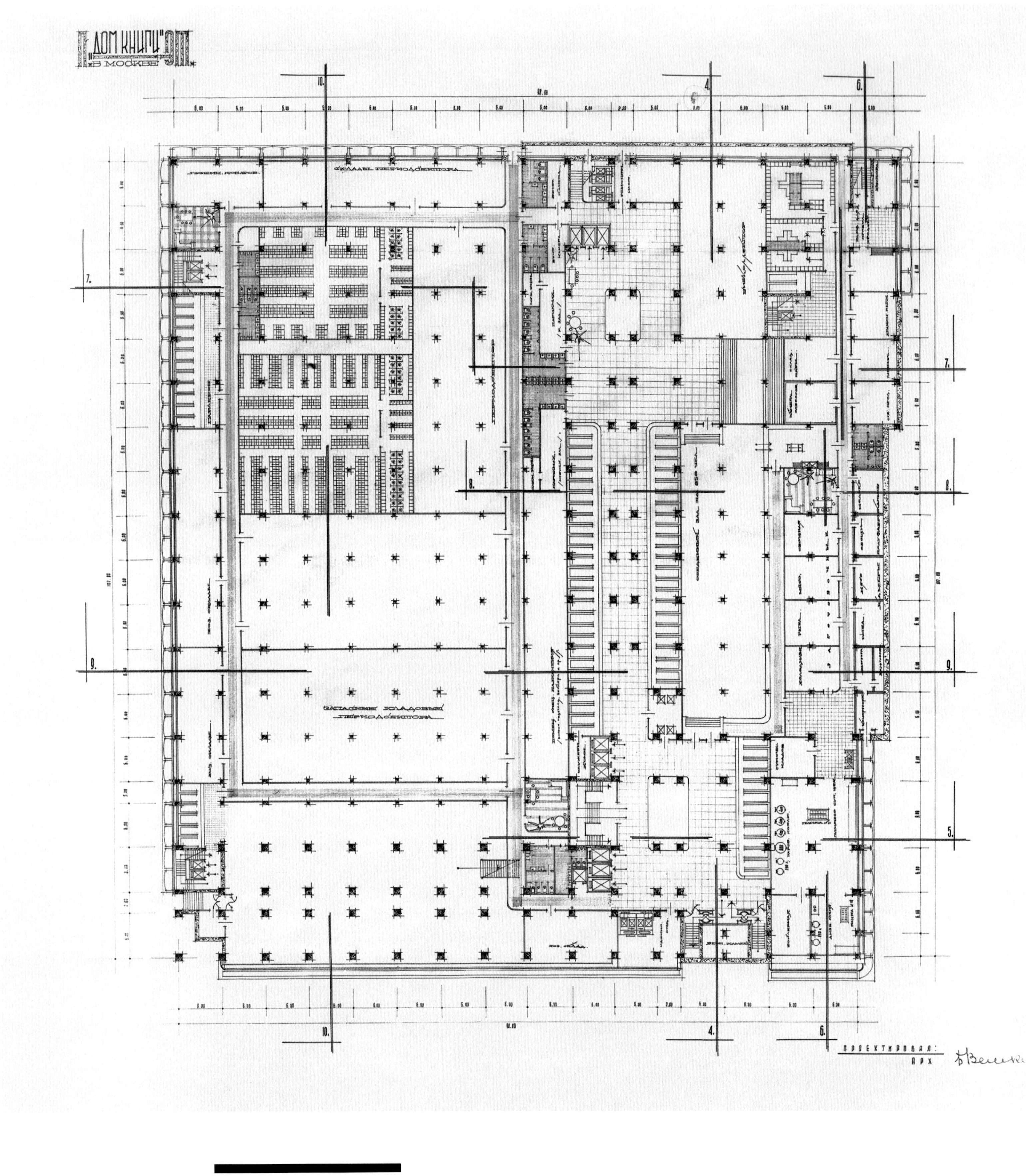

House of the Book
3 Orlikov Lane, Moscow
1930–1934
Ground-floor plan

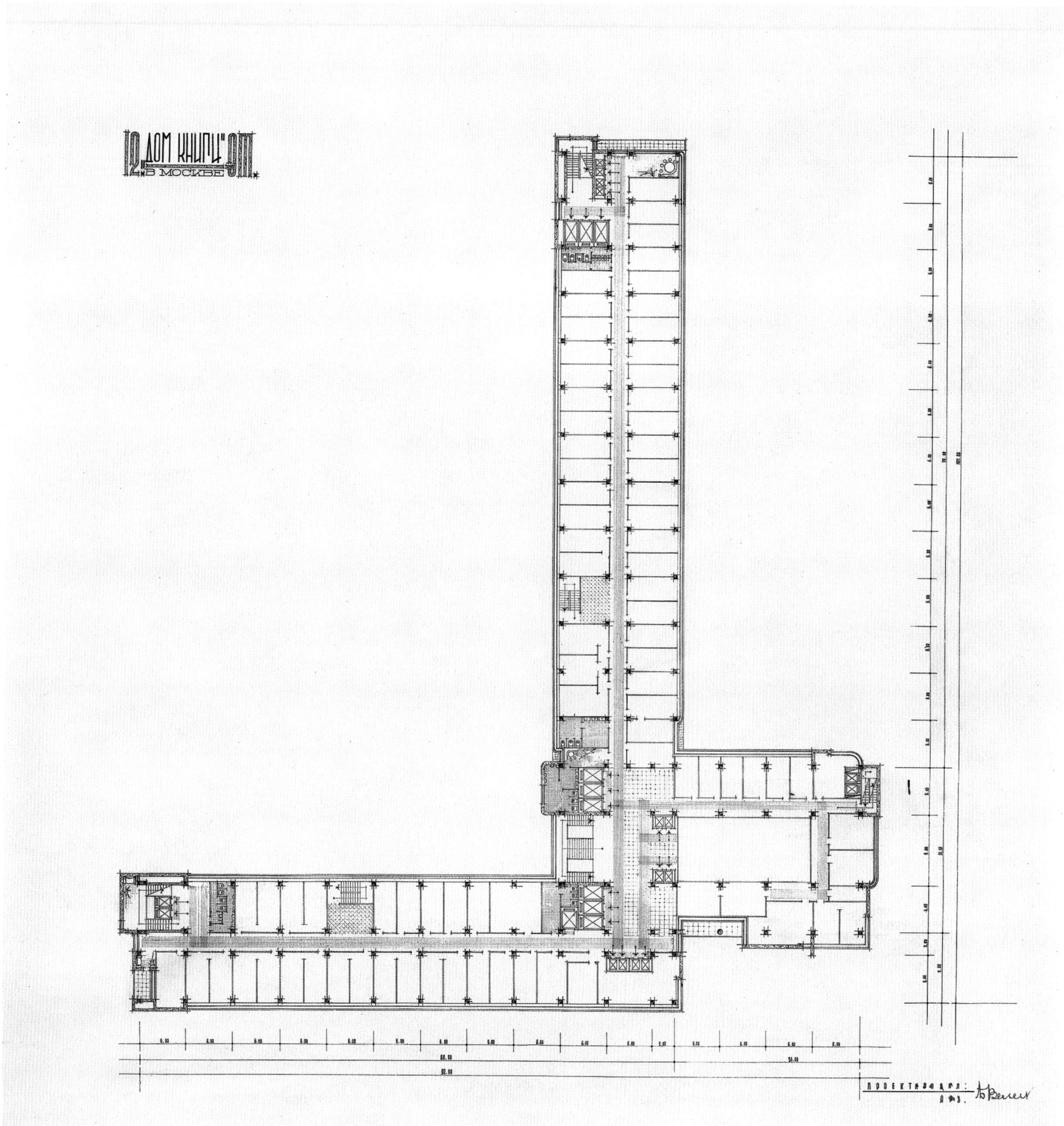

House of the Book
3 Orlikov Lane, Moscow
1930–1934
Typical floor plan of the topmost section

House of the Book
3 Orlikov Lane, Moscow
1930–1934
View from the north-west (showing a section completed in 1970s), 2016

House of the Book
3 Orlikov Lane, Moscow
1930–1934
View from the north-east, 2015

28

OGIZ Book Depot
15A Chkalov Prospekt, Leningrad
1930–1936
Architect: Boris Velikovsky with contributions from Yakov Tartakovsky, Tamara Kvin-Pivovarskaya and others

While heading the architectural studio of OGIZ (Unification of State Book and Magazine Publishers) as part of the project to build the House of the Book in Moscow, Velikovsky also designed the new blocks of a large printing complex on the Petrograd Side in Leningrad (St Petersburg), an area of the city which was home to both fashionable tenements and many factories. This particular complex was based on a printing house constructed by academician Leonty Benois (with contributions from Ludwig Schröter) between 1907 and 1910.

The original composition represented a square (*carré*) of three large buildings. Velikovsky supplemented this with a new block, thereby enclosing the existing courtyard. He then placed a second block parallel to the first one, running along the street. In this way, Velikovsky not only completely preserved Benois's creation but also added the "finishing touch" to his original concept. Externally, however, the new blocks radically differed from the previous ones, despite the identical heights of the floors.

A smaller two-storey auxiliary block was placed between the two new buildings. This third block was designed in a more classical style, with a symmetric facade divided by four pilaster strips with small capitals of a simplified order system. The slightly inclined roof was concealed beneath a stepped attic.

Velikovsky's first (production) block was a four-storey building, which towered above the old three-storey constructions. His second block, where the book warehouse and shop were located, had five floors yet was the same height as

OGIZ Book Depot
15A Chkalov Prospekt, Leningrad
1930–1936
Printing plant stairwell, 2015

OGIZ Book Depot
15A Chkalov Prospekt, Leningrad
1930–1936
pp. 228–229. Bridge over coutyard between storage and printing facilities, 2016

OGIZ Book Depot
15A Chkalov Prospekt, Leningrad
1930–1936
Courtyard view, 2016

OGIZ Book Depot
15A Chkalov Prospekt, Leningrad
1930–1936
Storage facility side view, 2016

OGIZ Book Depot
15A Chkalov Prospekt, Leningrad
1930–1936
Street and courtyard views of storage facility, 2015

the first block. The facades of both buildings were designed in a deliberately laconic style. They had ribbon windows, while the interfenestration was painted to create the effect of a continuous band. Both blocks were united by a covered bridge-passageway at the height of the first floor.

Small attics were created above the staircases at both ends of the first (production) block, giving the building a more striking silhouette. The first block is topped with a cylindrical vault, while the second has a slightly inclined gable roof. This design was more practical than the flat roofs which were fashionable at that time. Both buildings were constructed using monolithic reinforced-concrete frames. As a result, they have a free layout inside and can be regarded as an excellent example of the assimilation of new building technologies. The original terrazzo floors and metal bannisters have survived on the staircase landings. Unfortunately, most of the workshops have now been partitioned off by the tenants into smaller, individual premises. Nevertheless, the struts and beams of the reinforced-concrete frame can still be seen to this day inside the building. They lend a special expressiveness to these industrial premises, just like the red brickwork of the pre-revolutionary blocks.

OGIZ Book Depot
15A Chkalov Prospekt, Leningrad
1930–1936
View from the south, 2015

29

First Exemplary Printing House 71/5 Pyatnitskaya Street, Moscow First half of the 1930s Architect: Boris Velikovsky

This complex developed the famous pre-revolutionary printing house of Ivan Sytin on Pyatnitskaya Street in the centre of Moscow. Two new sections were constructed on the side of the territory – a long building extending along the side lane, followed by an adjoining three-storey block.

Although the facades had very few decorative details, individual elements – the profiles of the cornices and the rods of the window frames – reflected the desire to add something else, visible close-up, to the very basic Constructivist design, which was intended to contrast the original block in the Art Nouveau style. The two new sections were constructed using a reinforced-concrete frame. The larger block had a record area of glazing – at least for that time in a building in the historical centre of Moscow (until Le Corbusier's Tsentrosoyuz was completed in 1937).

As was typical of industrial architecture, the main facade of the large block was occupied by three ribbon windows, each covering the height of the entire storey. The glazing on the ground floor is interrupted by imposts – elements of the frame which continue inside the surfaces of the walls above. The top floor is interspersed with rectangular vertical windows, creating the impression of a bulky mass soaring above the lane.

The second building is designed in a slightly more decorative manner. The first two floors are interspersed with square windows and partitioned with simplified pendant pilasters in the spirit of Ivan Fomin's "proletarian classicism". The attic above the cornice has vertical windows with more extended proportions. Unlike the larger building, this block has a gable roof, which the silhouette of the symmetric facade does not conceal.

First Exemplary Printing House
71/5 Pyatnitskaya Street, Moscow
First half of the 1930s
View from the north-east, 2002

First Exemplary Printing House
71/5 Pyatnitskaya Street, Moscow
First half of the 1930s
2002

30

Smolensk Hotel
11/30 Glinka Street, Smolensk
1935–1939
Architects: Boris Velikovsky and Ilya Golosov

Boris Velikovsky's final major project was an hotel in the centre of Smolensk. This building project coincided with a difficult time for architects, following the multi-stage competition to design the Palace of the Soviets, when each successive round had seen the government officials and public figures on the jury increasingly favour pompous and symmetric compositions. The Hotel Moskva was being built at the same time right outside the Moscow Kremlin and became the prototype for Velikovsky's hotel, which was also located near the Kremlin in Smolensk.

Soviet architects of the 1930s were expected to design classically inspired buildings, reflecting the new image of the USSR as a superpower. The government wanted something strict, severe and imposing, in the spirit of the communiqués read out over the radio in a steely voice by the state announcer Yury Levitan. As a result of these changes in the stylistic guidelines, the project of the Hotel Moskva had to be reworked after its construction had already begun, inspiring a popular legend that the asymmetric facade was caused by Stalin's direct interference in the design process. Whatever the truth, the architects of the Hotel Moskva (Leonid Saveliev and Oswald Stapran) were obliged to make their original design more "decorative". The hotel was then completed in the required spirit under the guidance of Alexei Schusyev.

A similar incident occurred with the Vysevolod Meyerhold Theatre. A competition to redesign the facades was held in 1934. But when the chosen design was virtually completed in 1938, new orders suddenly descended from above and the Constructivist theatre found itself transformed into the Peter Tchaikovsky Concert Hall with a retrospective decor. The creators of the project (Mikhail Barkhin and Sergei Vakhtangov) were forced to reject their original designs and their project was reworked by Dmitry Chechulin (the chief architect of Moscow).

Velikovsky, as always, brilliantly handled both a tricky situation and the set task. When

Smolensk Hotel
11/30 Glinka Street, Smolensk
1935–1939
Left wing facade detail, 2016

designing the Smolensk Hotel, he managed to strike a compromise between what appeared to be mutually exclusive architectural devices. On the one hand, he configured the building in a dynamic and asymmetric manner, in the spirit of Constructivism. On the other, he successfully employed Neoclassical decorative elements.

Velikovsky joined two blocks at a right angle, leaving a small public space in front of the main entrance and creating a courtyard inside the territory. The complicated form of the building was a direct result of the unfortunate shape of the acute-angled plot of land at the corner of 11 Glinka Street and 30 Bolshaya Sovetskaya Street. Although unable to fully utilise as much territory as he desired, the architect managed to overcome the problem in an unconventional manner.

The hotel is composed of several blocks of different heights, reflecting the various functions of each separate part – the imposing vestibule, the standard rooms, the deluxe rooms, the restaurant and other services. The highest part of the hotel has seven floors and is located close to the corner of the building. To this day, it is still one of the highest structures in the city centre. The section on the very corner, however, has only six floors. The five-storey block on Glinka Street looks onto the new town centre, while the four-storey wing faces the historical part on Bolshaya Sovetskaya Street, which was previously known as Blagoveschenskaya ("Annunciation") Street.

In the 1930s, Neoclassical architecture was popular all across Europe, within the general bounds of the Art Deco movement. In the Soviet Union, this tendency was reflected in the Palladianism of Ivan Zholtovsky[1] and even more complicated versions of the style, which Velikovsky also addressed. In this particular case, he masterly combines an asymmetric composition with symmetric exterior decor. The main entrance has a portico and a loggia above the protruding vestibule. The portico extends over three floors and adds a sense of pageantry to the bare main facade with its rhythmically arranged square windows. A similar effect is created by the statues placed in the corners above the cornice of the portico and in the two arched niches at the bottom. A second stylised portico acts as the entrance to the restaurant (two thick pylons support the extended balcony on top). There is also a balustrade with decorative vases running along the terrace above the vestibule.

Velikovsky created a much simplified order system for the decor of the hotel. The different scales and the different levels of detailing reflected the varying importance of each individual part of the entire composition. This approach softens the overall impression of the hotel as a monolithic cliff and helps to explain why the building found its way into so many films and photographs of the 1930s to 1950s. Velikovsky's creation evokes comparisons with the works of such leading Leningrad architects as Yevgeny Levinson, Noi Trotsky and Ivan Fomin, although a better comparison would be with the oeuvre of Lazar Khidekel. In the 1920s, Khidekel had been a student of Kazimir Malevich and he later constructed real buildings inspired by Malevich's "architectonas".[2] Working in the 1930s, Khidekel also combined the brutal forms of the avant-garde period with elements of a classical order in such works as the Moskva Cinema at 6 Old Peterhof Prospekt in Leningrad (1939).

In the mid-1930s, imposing architectural ensembles appeared in many Soviet towns, including Smolensk, where the local branch

Smolensk Hotel
11/30 Glinka Street, Smolensk
1935–1939
1950s

of Gosbank was clearly influenced by the new side-wings designed by Ivan Zholtovsky for the Gosbank headquarters in Moscow. Other local examples included the October Cinema and the District House of Officers. But only Velikovsky was capable of bringing the genuine scale of the capital to Smolensk, without resorting to directly copying any building in Moscow. The secret was his ability to interpret the classics while rejecting professional dogmas. For example, he even included classical features – such as a generally symmetric (albeit brutal) composition – in the "Constructivism" of his famous Gostorg building.

Boris Velikovsky died of heart problems at his home in Moscow in 1937. The Smolensk Hotel was completed after his death by another famous Russian architect – Ilya Golosov.

1 Ivan Vladislavovich Zholtovsky (1867–1959) was a Russian architect born into a Catholic family in the town of Pinsk in modern-day Belarus. He graduated from the Imperial Academy of Arts in St Petersburg in 1898 and closely studied Palladian architecture in Italy in the 1910s and 1920s. Zholtovsky worked in a Neo-Renaissance style before the 1917 revolution and in a Stalinist Neoclassical style in the 1930s and 1940s. He even lived to design the first Soviet pre-fab housing under Khrushchev in the 1950s.

2 Architectonas were architectural models of the future developed in the early 1920s by avant-garde artist Kazimir Malevich (1878–1935). They took the form of geometric sculptures, representing a free combination of squares, crosses and rectangles – a spatial form of Suprematism. The artist's term for these models dates from 1925 and was originally *architectona*, although the correct spelling in Russian is now *architecton*.

Smolensk Hotel
11/30 Glinka Street, Smolensk
1935–1939
Entrance of left wing with restaurant, 2016

Smolensk Hotel
11/30 Glinka Street, Smolensk
1935–1939
Main entrance facade view, 2016

Smolensk Hotel
11/30 Glinka Street, Smolensk
1935–1939
pp. 244–245. View from city wall
pp. 246–247. Attic sculpture view, 2016

Smolensk Hotel
11/30 Glinka Street, Smolensk
1935–1939
Main entrance terrace view, 2016

Smolensk Hotel
11/30 Glinka Street, Smolensk
1935–1939
View from the east, detail, 2016

Smolensk Hotel
11/30 Glinka Street, Smolensk
1935–1939
Main attic sculpture and portico details, 2016

Smolensk Hotel
11/30 Glinka Street, Smolensk
1935–1939
Column details, 2016

List of Buildings in Russian

01. Church of St George
Церковь Св. Георгия
1907–1912
Novo-Kharitonovo, Gzhel District, Moscow Province
Ново-Харитоново, близ Гжели, Московская область

02. Gryaznov Textile Mill
Текстильная фабрика Грязнова
1906–1908
Ivanovo-Voznesensk (now Ivanovo)
Иваново-Вознесенск (сейчас Иваново)

03. Ivan Kuznetsov Porcelain and Faience Factory Complex
Фаянсовая фабрика
1911–1912
Gruzino, Chudovo District, Novgorod Province
Грузино. Чудовский район. Новгородская область

04. Gribov Mansion
Особняк Грибова
1909–1911
15 Khlebny Lane, Moscow
Хлебный переулок, 15, Москва

05. Ivan Kuznetsov Tenement
Доходный дом Ивана Кузнецова
1909–1912
15 Myasnitskaya Street, Moscow
Мясницкая, 15, Москва

06. Lunts Tenement
Доходный дом Михаила Лунца
1910–1911
9 Krivokolenny Lane, Moscow
Кривоколенный переулок, 9, Москва
Архитекторы: Борис Великовский, Алексей Милюков, при участии Виктора Веснина

07. Serafima Davydova (Spiridonova) Tenement
Доходный дом Серафимы Давыдовой (Спиридоновой)
1898 and 1913 (extended upwards in 1934)
13 Myasnitskaya Street, Moscow
Мясницкая, 13, Москва

08. Merkel Tenement
Доходный дом Аркадия Меркеля
1911–1914
7 Arkhangelsky Lane, Moscow
Архангельский переулок, 7, Москва

09. Prowe Tenement
Доходный дом Прове
1912–13, late 1920s (attached block)
16 Novaya Basmannaya Street, Moscow
Новая Басманная, 16, Москва

10. Myasnitskaya Housing Association Tenement
Доходный дом Мясницкого товарищества
1913–1914
12 First Basmanny Lane, Moscow
1-й Басманный переулок, 12, Москва

11. Doctor Eberlin House
Доходный дом-клиника доктора Эберлина
1912–1913
9/1 Klimentovsky Lane, Moscow
Климентовский переулок, 9/1, Москва

12. Mikhail Alexeyev Tenement
Доходный дом Михаила Алексеева
1912–1913
42/2 Bolshaya Polyanka Street, Moscow
Большая Полянка, 42/2, Москва
Борис Великовский, Алексей Милюков, Вячеслав Корчагин

13. Ivan Kuznetsov Tenement
Доходный дом Ивана Кузнецова
1915–1916
27/21 Zagorodny Prospekt, St Petersburg
Загородный проспект, 27/21, Санкт-Петербург
Борис Великовский, Александр Розенберг и Давид Бурышкин

14. Alexander Herzenberg Tenements
Доходный дом Александра Герценберга
1912–1914
Structures 4 and 5, 22 Tsvetnoy boulevard, Moscow
Цветной бульвар, 22, Москва

15. Felicia Mansbach German Gymnasium
Немецкая гимназия Фелиции Мансбах
1913–1914
10 First Basmanny Lane, Moscow
1-й Басманный переулок, 10, Москва

16. Polyakov Mansion
Особняк Полякова
1911–1916
10 Bolshaya Bronnaya Street, Moscow
Большая Бронная, 10, Москва

17. Kovrov Armaments Factory (Block A, Block B, boiler house)
Оружейный завод
1916–1921
Kovrov, Vladimir Province
Ковров, Владимирская область

18. Tsentrosoyuz Pavilion All-Russian Agricultural and Handicraft-Industrial Exhibition, Moscow (unsurviving)
Павильон Центросоюза (не сохранился). Всероссийская сельскохозяйственная и кустарно-промышленная выставка
1923
Борис Великовский. Инженер
Михаил Масленников

19. Druzhba ("Friendship") Settlement (Garden City)
Поселок "Дружба"
1922–1924
Near Perlovskaya station, Moscow Province
Станция "Перловская", Московская область
Московская область

20. Gostorg Building
Госторг. Административное здание
1927
47 Myasnitskaya Street, Moscow
Мясницкая, 47, Москва
Борис Великовский, при участии Михаила Барща, Вячеслава Владимирова, Георгия Вегмана, Марии Гакен, Аркадия Лангмана

21. Muniets Residential House
Жилой дом кооператива "Муниец"
1928–1930
11–13 Malaya Bronnaya Street, Moscow
Малая Бронная, 11-13, Москва

22. Lnotorg Worker Residential House
Жилой дом РЖСКТ "Льноторг"
1925–1926 (extended upwards in 1932)
36 Malaya Bronnaya Street, Moscow
Малая Бронная, 36, Москва
Борис Великовский, Иван Машков

23. Koopstroi Residential House
Жилой дом кооператива "ВСНХ"
1927–1928 (extended upwards in the late 1940s)
21 Sadovaya-Kudrinskaya Street, Moscow
Садовая-Кудринская, 21, Москва

24. Gosstrakh Residential House (unsurviving)
Жилой дом Госстраха (не сохранился)
1926–1927
Durnovsky Lane, Moscow
Дурновский переулок (Композиторская улица), Москва

25. Galen Cooperative Building (unsurviving)
Производственно-административное здание кооператива "Гален". Проект. Перспектива (не сохранился)
1927–1928
Vysheslavtsev Lane, Moscow
Вышеславцев переулок, Москва

26. Competition to Design the Tsentrosoyuz Building
Конкурсный проект здания Центросоюза. 1-й тур
1928
39 Myasnitskaya Street, Moscow
Мясницкая, 39, Москва

27. House of the Book
"Дом книги"
1930–1934
3 Orlikov Lane, Moscow
Орликов переулок, 3, Москва
Борис Великовский, при участии Павла Антонова

28. OGIZ Book Depot
Книжная база ОГИЗ
1930–1936
15A Chkalov Prospekt, Leningrad
Чкаловский проспект, 15А, Ленинград
Борис Великовский, при участии Якова Тартаковского, Тамары Квин-Пиворварской и др.

29. First Exemplary Printing House
1-я Образцовая типография
First half of the 1930s
71/5 Pyatnitskaya Street, Moscow
Пятницкая, 71/5, Москва

30. Smolensk Hotel
Гостиница "Смоленск"
1935–1939
11/30 Glinka Street, Smolensk
Улица Глинки, 11/30, Смоленск
Борис Великовский, Илья Голосов

Conclusion

Judging by the long list of his works, Boris Velikovsky willingly accepted any commission. The architect's creations are incredibly diverse in both the scale and purpose of each building. For example, he constructed a series of canteens in industrial towns outside Gorky (Nizhny Novgorod), including Dzerzhinsk (Rastyapino) and Bogorodsk. He also designed unsurviving settlements for the Railway Transport Scientific Research Institute in the towns of Mytischi and Scherbinka near Moscow. Velikovsky worked on the project of the Agricultural Institute in Smolensk, where he built a hotel in the 1930s (his final creation). In the last decade of his life, the House of the Book in Moscow occupied a special place in his oeuvre. Although the architect's project was not fully implemented, his acknowledged authority led to consultations on the development of similar buildings in other cities.

The architecture of Soviet government buildings inevitably reflected the policies being conceived and implemented inside these same buildings. This meant that, in the early 1930s, architects were forced to abandon their former avant-garde philosophies. A totalitarian style began to rapidly take over Soviet architecture. All sorts of previously diverse and innovative masters, such as Ivan Leonidov, Ilya Golosov and Alexander Vlasov, were obliged to revisit the historical heritage. In Velikovsky's oeuvre, this movement is reflected in his project of the Smolensk Hotel in the second half of the 1930s. This monumental building fits perfectly into the required image of a Soviet city centre, even if the master was unable to fully apply all his skills, talents and experience in this period.

Summary in German

Boris Mikhailovich Velikovsky (1878–1937) wurde in dem kleinen Städtchen Propoisk in der Provinz Mogilyov im ehemaligen Russischen Reich in eine jüdische Familie hineingeboren. Der Ort Propoisk wurde 1945 in Slavgorod umbenannt und ist mittlerweile Teil des heutigen Weißrusslands. Velikovsky erhielt als Junge ausgezeichneten Hausunterricht und wurde 1898 am Institut für Bauingenieurwesen der Polytechnischen Universität St. Petersburg zugelassen.

Während seiner Studienzeit am Institut trat er der revolutionären Bewegung bei und wurde für ein Jahr suspendiert. Ihm war es allerdings gestattet, seine Ausbildung in dieser Zeit fortzuführen und er schloss sein Studium 1904 ab. Im direkten Anschluss an sein Studium erhielt er eine Anstellung im Designstudio von Sergei Solovyov, einem der maßgeblichsten Architekten Moskaus seinerzeit.

Velikovsky trat dem Architekturbüro von Sergei Solovyov in einer Zeit bei, in der dieses an der Entstehung verschiedener bedeutender Gebäude in Moskau arbeitete. Zum Designteam gehörten der junge Architekt Ilya Golosov (ein späterer Vertreter der avantgardistischen Bewegung der russischen Architektur) sowie der bekannte Ingenieur Vladimir Shukhov (Erfinder des thermischen Crackverfahrens und der erste Ingenieur weltweit, der Gitterschalen aus Stahl zum Bau von Gebäuden und Türmen einsetzte).

Ab 1906 begann Velikovsky als Partner von Alexei Milyukov, einem erfahrenen Architekten, private Aufträge anzunehmen. Neben der eigenständigen Gestaltung einer Textilmühle in der Stadt Ivanovo-Voznesensk (1906–08) arbeitete Velikovsky zusammen mit Milyukov an einem privaten Herrensitz (1909–11) und einer Reihe von Wohnhäusern in Moskau (1909–13). Er erbaute auch ein Wohnhaus für Ivan Kuznetsov in St. Petersburg, dem viele Fabriken in Russland gehörten. Kuznetsov wurde zu seinem wichtigsten und prestigeträchtigsten Kunden. Für ihn entwarf Velikovsky zwischen 1907 und 1912 eine Arbeitersiedlung, eine Kirche und ein Pflegeheim in dem kleinen Dorf Novo-Kharitonovo außerhalb von Moskau, wo die bekannten Gzhel-Keramiken hergestellt wurden.

Die frühen 1910er Jahre gehörten zu den erfolgreichsten in der Karriere Velikovskys. Zu dieser Zeit entwickelte er sich zu einem bedeutenden Vertreter des neoklassizistischen Revivals im Bereich der Architektur, einer Variante des Art Nouveau, die sich maßgeblich des klassizistischen Erbes bediente. Dank ihrer gut durchdachten Entwürfe für den Innenbereich, der gelungenen Raumaufteilung und der hochwertigen Bauausführung waren Velikovskys vorrevolutionäre Bauten hoch angesehen.

Zwar ist Velikovsky heute vor allem für seine Wohngebäude bekannt; jedoch hat er vor der Revolution ebenfalls eine Reihe von Industriebauten entworfen. Dabei handelte es sich um Bauwerke für einige der wichtigsten Unternehmen des Landes. Velikovsky entwickelte seine eigene Variante des Backsteinbaus und schuf ein gleichermaßen auffälliges wie zweckmäßiges Fabrikdesign.

Ein großer Erfahrungsschatz sorgte dafür, dass sich das Talent des Architekten auch nach der Revolution ungebrochen großer Nachfrage erfreute. 1918 wurde der Sitz der Regierung nach Moskau verlegt; die Stadt musste eilig wiederaufgebaut werden, um die neuen Organe der Planwirtschaft beherbergen zu können und dem Status Moskaus als Hauptstadt des ersten kommunistischen Staates der Welt gerecht zu werden. Velikovsky gewann mehrere bedeutende Ausschreibungen und aus einem seiner Projekte aus den 1920er Jahren, dem Entwurf für das neue Gostorg-Verwaltungsgebäude in der Myasnitskaya-Straße 47, entstand der erste innovative Bürokomplex Moskaus.

Velikovsky arbeitete auch für den Zentrosojus, den Zentralverband der Konsumgenossenschaften der Sowjetunion. Im Jahr 1923 entwarf er anlässlich der „Landwirtschafts- und Gewerbeausstellung der Unionsrepubliken" einen der beiden Pavillons für den Zentrosojus auf dem Gelände des heutigen Gorki-Parks. Darüber hinaus nahm er 1928 am Wettbewerb um die

Ausschreibung für die Planung des neuen Hauptgebäudes des Zentrosojus teil, bei dem er in der ersten Runde sowohl den ersten als auch den dritten Preis gewann (den Wettbewerb entschied schließlich der berühmte schweizerisch-französische Architekt Le Corbusier für sich).

Obgleich er hauptsächlich in Moskau arbeitete, war Velikovsky vom neuen städtebaulichen Konzept der Gartenstadt fasziniert, das er für die perfekte Lösung der Probleme der urbanen Zersiedelung und der Verschmutzung in den Städten der Sowjetunion hielt. Eines dieser Projekte war die Siedlung Sokol im Nordosten von Moskau. Velikovsky entwarf die erste Version des Generalplans für Sokol zusammen mit dem Ingenieur Pavel Nakhman. Ihr Entwurf wurde jedoch später überarbeitet und weiterentwickelt, so dass heute übersehen wird, dass der ursprüngliche Entwurf für dieses revolutionäre Projekt von Velikovsky stammte.

Besser bekannt ist er für seine maßgebliche Beteiligung am Entwurf für die Siedlung Druzhba ("Freundschaft") im Nordosten Moskaus. Während der Entwurf dieser klassizistischen, in Fächerform angelegten Gartenstadt Parallelen zu den entsprechenden europäischen Gegenstücken aufweist, waren die Häuser selbst ganz eindeutig an die lokalen Gegebenheiten angepasst. Velikovsky entwarf zweckmäßige Doppelhäuser für jeweils zwei Familien – Holzhütten mit Eckveranden und einem gemeinsamen Dachboden. Velikovsky versuchte darüber hinaus auch, Lösungen für die akute Wohnraumknappheit in Moskau in den 1920er Jahren zu finden. Bei seinen Entwürfen für neue Wohnblöcke, die von den Wohnbaugenossenschaften gebaut wurden, griff er auf seine umfangreichen Erfahrungen der Planung vorrevolutionärer Wohnhäuser zurück. Derartige Gebäude wurden für gewöhnlich anhand von Standardentwürfen errichtet; dieses Vorgehen lehnte Velikovsky jedoch ab. Er fertigte für jeden Block einen individuellen Entwurf an, wodurch interessantere und komfortablere Innenräume entstanden und mehr Wohneinheiten geschaffen wurden.

Es gelang ihm dabei immer, die richtige Balance zwischen moderner Baukunst und traditioneller Architektur zu finden, indem er neue Stile auf seine ganz eigene unvergleichliche Weise interpretierte. Erstaunlicherweise lehnte er Elemente des Neoklassizismus, der Stilepoche, deren maßgeblicher Vertreter er vor der Revolution gewesen war, nun ab.

Andere frühere Meister des russischen neoklassizistischen Revivals folgten seinem Beispiel und wurden Vorreiter einer neue Stilrichtung der modernen Architektur in der Sowjetunion, dem Konstruktivismus. Velikovsky war nie Mitglied dieser Gruppierung, dennoch wird das Gostorg-Gebäude, das 1927 aus seiner Planung heraus entstand, häufig als klassisches Beispiel des Konstruktivismus betrachtet.

Velikovsky setzte sein produktives Werk in den 1930er Jahren fort. Er entwarf Siedlungen in den Städten Mytischi und Scherbinka, die es heute nicht mehr gibt, und arbeitete am Projekt der Staatlichen Agrarakademie Smolensk. Zwischen 1930 und 1934 entwarf er das Moskauer Haus des Buches in der Orlikov-Gasse 3. Sein Projekt wurde jedoch niemals vollständig umgesetzt und das Gebäude wurde später von Ilya Golosov im Stil des Art Deco fertiggestellt.

Die 1930er Jahre waren eine schwierige Zeit für Architekten in der Sowjetunion, denn sie waren gezwungen, ihren bisherigen Avantgarde-Stil aufzugeben und von der Klassik inspirierte Gebäude zu entwerfen, die das neue Bild der UdSSR als Supermacht mit imperialen Ambitionen widerspiegeln sollten. Schnell begann sich in der sowjetischen Architektur ein totalitärer Stil durchzusetzen.

Diese neue Bewegung zeigte sich in Velikovskys Gestaltung des Smolensk Hotels zwischen 1935 und 1937. Leider war es dem Architekten nicht möglich, sein letztes Projekt zu vollenden, das sich perfekt in das vorgeschriebene Stadtbild eines sowjetischen Stadtzentrums einfügte. 1937 erlag Boris Velikovsky seinen Herzproblemen. Er starb in seinem Haus in Moskau.